Hymns for Living

The Lindsey Press

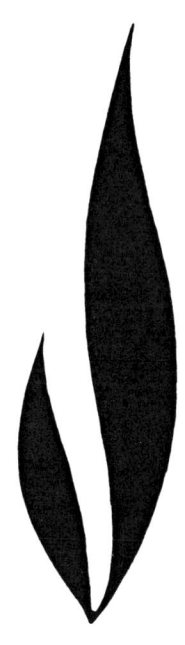

The Lindsey Press, 1-6 Essex Street, London WC2R 3HY
Selection © GENERAL ASSEMBLY OF UNITARIAN AND FREE CHRISTIAN CHURCHES, 1985
Reprinted (with corrections), 1987
Reprinted (with corrections and additions), 1998
Reprinted (with corrections and additions), 2001

Literary Editor: Sydney H. Knight
Music Editor: David Dawson, M.A., G.R.S.M., A.R.M.C.M.

page	xvi	ASPIRATION line 4: for 'undying' read 'widening'
..	xlvi	Taylor, Cyril Vincent (1907-91)
..	xlvii	Clabburn, Frank R. (1947-2000)
..	xlviii	Findlow, Bruce (1922-94)
		After 'Herbert, George' insert 'Hikmet, Nazim . . . . . . 225'
		Johnson-Julian, Joseph (1848-1928)
		Patten, Kenneth L (1911-94)
..	xlix	Storey, John Andrew (1935-97)
..	l	Trapp, Jacob (1899-1993)
		Vallance, Arthur Woolley (1902-90)
		Weston, Robert Terry (1898-1980)
		Wikson, Edwin Henry (1898-1993)
page	48	Cyril Vincent Taylor (1907-1991)
..	69	Music: Noted by . . . *add* 'Meyer Lyon'
..	82	Words and music from *The Children's Bells* (Oxford University Press)
..	87	Words: 'additions by John Andrew Storey (1935-97)'
		Music from *The English Hymnal*
..	96	Music: melody based on a strain of Handel's *Glory to God in Messiah*
..	127	Words: This version by Will Hayes
..	128	Music: First System, last bar, 2nd alto note: D♯
..	152	Music adapt. Walford Davies (1869-1941)
..	157	Words: *Add* 'source, Analects 15:21-24'
..	164	Words: *Add* 'Based on Edward George Bulwer-Lytton (1803-73)'
..	188	Words: traditional American, adapted by Berkley L. Moore (b. 1932)
..	212	Words: *from* Felix Adler
..	220	Words reproduced by permission of Stainer & Bell Ltd. Music by Doreen Potter, Copyright (c) Stainer and Bell, administered by Copycare, P.O. Box 77, Hailsham, BN27 3EF. Used by permission
..	225	Music: Melody by James H. Waters
		Words: translated from Turkish poem of Nazim Hikmet
..	226	Music: arr. David Hugh Jones
..	241	Music: arr. Ralph Vaughan Williams (1872-1958)
..	247	Words: Stanza 1, line 4 to read, 'On each upturned face'
..	266	Words from *The Oxford Book of Carols*
..	267	Words: *Add* from Ralph Waldo Emerson (1803-82)
..	271	Music from *Enlarged Songs of Praise*, 1931
..	279	Words: tr. *Delete* 'and Daniel Niles'
..	286	Cyril Vincent Taylor (1907-1991)
..	289	*Add* (to authors and composers), 'Harry Belafonte'
..	299	Words: 'Recast by Kenneth Patten (1911-94) from . . .'
..	301	Words: *From* Henry Francis Lyte

The corrections and additions given above, though not exhaustive are, we believe, correct. They have been mostly limited to this one page and not repeated on the hymn pages to save the cost of re-setting.   SHK

Contents

PREFACE *page* v

INDEXES
First lines and titles of hymns *page* vii
Topical Index xv
Alphabetical index of tunes xxxiii
Metrical index of tunes xxxvii
Composers, arrangers and sources of tunes xliii
Authors, translators and sources of texts xlvii

ACKNOWLEDGEMENTS *page* li

HYMNS FOR LIVING
Worship and Celebration *numbers* 1-32
The Reflective Spirit 33-63
The Judaeo-Christian Heritage 64-118
World-Wide Heritage 119-132
The Free Spirit 133-149
Personal Commitment 150-170
Love and Community 171-192
A Better World 193-230
The Natural World 231-256
The Seasons 257-278
Morning and Evening 279-288
Seasons of Human Life 289-301
Close of Worship 302-317

Music originated by Halstan & Co. Ltd., Amersham.

Text set in Century Textbook at
Essex Hall, 1-6 Essex Street, London WC2R 3HY

Printed by Halstan & Co. Ltd.,
Plantation Road, Amersham, Bucks. HP6 6HJ

Preface

We have sought to produce a liberal religious hymnbook for use by those who seek in their worship to blend with the traditional, contemporary concerns expressed in a modern idiom.

This book, as its title indicates, is intended as a companion to *Songs for Living* which was published in 1972 for young people. The principles which have guided our selection are generally the same as listed in the preface to that book: hymns and songs varied in form, related to individual experience, rich in contemporary idealism, metrically and poetically attractive, and set to good and singable tunes.

We have not hesitated to edit hymns in terms of theology, imagery and social attitudes to make them as far as possible of contemporary relevance. At the same time we have been guided by the popularity of a hymn, and have occasionally restored original wording. Thus, in blending the new with the old, we have tried to maintain and represent a continuity of tradition.

In response to a growing sensitivity to sexism in the English language, and recognising that language shapes and influences thought, we have taken care over the use of generic pronouns and other words, including those used to describe God. Nevertheless, many familiar hymns have been retained in their traditional form, especially those in the Judaeo-Christian tradition. We have in some cases been restricted by copyright, and thank those copyright holders who have agreed to alterations where requested.

We have included as many familiar tunes as possible and introduced some new ones, many of which (like some of the words) appear here for the first time.

Our research indicates that most people who lead worship select from a range of not more than about one hundred and twenty hymns: therefore the present number of hymns, exceeding three hundred, should be ample. Decisions on selection have not been easy: each member of the committee can list hymns, the omission of which is personally regretted; and similarly each user of the book will inevitably regret some omissions. The range and variety of subjects covered is reflected in the Topical Index.

Although it is some years since we began this task, we have included new hymns almost up to the last minute. In fact, we have progressed collectively and individually as the task has driven us to examine our assumptions, predelictions and theological outlook, as well as to take note of trends among our potential clientele. We hope this book will do the same for its users.

Thanks are due to many people who have made helpful suggestions or contributed material (even if not used); to all six members of our committee who have given spare time out of busy lives, and especially those who have undertaken specific and sometimes onerous tasks, such as compiling indexes, proof-reading, dealing with copyrights and the many other editorial tasks involved; and to Margaret Knight for many hours of personal assistance to the Editor.

David Dawson, *Music Editor* Sydney H. Knight, *Editor and Secretary*
Keith Gilley Celia Midgley
Gabor Kereki John A. Storey

Committee Members

Index of First Lines and Titles of Hymns

Where they differ, the title, as well as the first line, is listed. Titles, then, are in capital letters.

Abide with me! fast falls the eventide 301
A church is a living fellowship 174
A CITY WHICH IS OURS 213
A day like many other days 109
A DREAM OF WIDENING LOVE 42
ADVENT HYMN 81
A fierce unrest seethes at the core 145
A firemist and a planet 233
A GLAD RESPLENDENT DAY 224
A little sun, a little rain 9
All are architects of fate 211
ALL ARE OUR NEIGHBOURS 182
ALL ARE WELCOME HERE 172
All creatures of our God and King 241
ALL EARTH'S CHILDREN 131
ALL FAITHS 130
All heroic lives remind us 166
ALL LOVES EXCELLING 118
All people that on earth do dwell 64
All praise to thee, my God, this night 285
ALL PRAISE TO THEE, THIS NIGHT 285
ALL THESE THINGS BELONG TO ME 245
All things bright and beautiful 243
A MELODY OF LOVE 235
A mighty fortress is our God 73
And did those feet in ancient time 210
A NEW COMMUNITY 192
A noble life, a simple faith 179
Around the crib all peoples throng 97
As each day ends, may I have lived 302
A shelter from the vast we win 178
As tranquil streams that meet and merge 136
As we celebrate the harvest 274
As we come marching, marching 216
AUTUMN FIELDS 276
AUTUMN WAYS 277
Awake my soul, and with the sun 283

A WORLD OF WONDER 247
A WORLD TRANSFIGURED 209

Behold us, God, a little space 47
Bells in the high tower, ringing o'er the white hills 262
Beneath the shadow of the Cross 104
Be thou my vision, O God of my heart 151
BE TRUE, LIVE TRULY 155
BLACK AND WHITE 215
BOLDLY LIVE, MY DAUGHTER 217
BREAD AND ROSES 216
Break not the circle of enabling love 220
Breathe on me, Breath of God 46
BREATH OF GOD 46
Brief our days, but long for singing 2
BRIGHTLY BREAKS THE EASTER MORN 107
By the rutted roads we follow 261

Calm soul of all things, make it mine 53
Can I see another's woe 181
CHILD OF HIROSHIMA 225
CHILDREN OF A BRIGHT TOMORROW 202
Children of the human race 132
CHILDREN OF THE UNIVERSE 132
CHINESE MORNING HYMN 279
Christ cometh not a king to reign 115
City of God, how broad and far 121
CLOSING VERSES 308, 309, 310, 311 312, 313, 314, 315, 316
COME BY HERE 32
Come down, O Love divine 45
Come, my daughter, come with me 217
COME, MY LIFE 44
Come, my way, my truth, my life 44
Come, sing with holy gladness 265
COME TOGETHER IN LOVE 176

vii

INDEX OF FIRST LINES AND TITLES

Come, ye thankful people, come 272
Community, supporting friends... ... 177
COURAGE SHALL CONQUER... 200
Creative Love, our thanks we give 170
CROSSING THE BAR 300

Daisies are our silver... 240
Dare to think, though others frown... 158
DARKNESS PUT TO FLIGHT... 281
Dear Lord and Father of mankind... ...101
DEATH'S DOMINION IS PAST... ... 108
Deck the halls with boughs of holly...278
Die Gedanken sind frei, my thoughts freely flower... 143
Ding dong! merrily on high... 93
Divinity is round us—never gone... ... 52
Down the ages we have trod... 35
Do you hear, O my friend, in the place where you stand... 33

Early in life's morning... 291
EARTH AWAKES AGAIN... 263
EARTH SHALL BE FAIR... 230
Eternal God, whose power upholds...228
Eternal Ruler of the ceaseless round... 13
Every night and every morn... 54

FACING DEATH... 297
Fair is their fame who stand in earth's high places... 296
FAITH... 56
FAITH OF THE FREE... 134
Faith of the larger liberty... 134
FILL MY LIFE WITH PRAISE... 5
Fill thou my life, O God of love... 5
FLAME OF LIVING FIRE... 113
For all that is our life... 15
For all the paths which guide our ways 131
For all the saints, who from their labours rest... 79
For the beauty of the earth... 14
For the glimpses of full knowledge... ...16
For the healing of the nations... 198
For the strength of the hills we bless thee... 242
Forward through the ages... 208

Freedom is the finest gold... 142
FREE FROM THE WORLD'S CARES... 147
From all that dwell below the skies... 310
From all the fret and fever of the day... 48
From out of time's immortal hand... ...205

Gather us in, thou Love that fillest all 127
Give thanks for the corn and the wheat that are reaped... 271
Glad that I live am I... 244
God be in my head... 307
God bless the grass that grows through the crack... 253
God moves in a mysterious way... ...62
God of ages and of nations... 75
God of grace and God of glory... ...193
GOD OF LIFE... 22
God our Father and our Mother... ... 218
GOD'S FARM... 270
God speaks to us in bird and song... ...235
God that madest earth and heaven... 288
God, whose farm is all creation... 270
GOD WITHIN... 29
Golden breaks the dawn... 279
GOODNIGHT HYMN... 284
GO WITH US GOD... 305
Gracious Power, the world pervading...23
Grieve not your heart for want of place 157
GUARD US NIGHT AND DAY... ... 288

Hark! the herald angels sing... 90
HARVEST HOME... 272
HARVEST PRAYER... 270
Hear, O God, the prayer we offer... ... 59
Hear the city noise around us... 51
HERE AND NOW... 293
Here's the time of preparation... 81
HERITAGE... 128
HEROES... 296
High o'er the lonely hills... 282
Holy Spirit, Truth divine... 63
Homage to thee, Perfect Wisdom... ... 11
HONOURABLE SAINTS... 78
Hosanna in the highest!... 102

INDEX OF FIRST LINES AND TITLES

HOW CAN I KEEP FROM SINGING! 133
How happy are they born or taught...147
HUMAN KINDNESS................187
HUSH THE SOUNDS OF WAR......222
HYMN TO PERFECT WISDOM........11
HYMN TO THE SOLE GOD...........12

I bind unto myself today...........152
I cannot find thee! still on restless
  pinion........................41
I CANNOT LOSE THEE!..............41
I come and stand at every door......225
I heard the bells on Christmas Day....94
I held the planets in my hand........256
I learned it in the meadow path.....184
Immortal, invisible, God only wise....76
Immortal Love, for ever full........30
INASMUCH........................165
IN BRAVER MOULD................205
In humble reverence and love........31
In life's complex web of being.....250
IN PRAISE OF WISDOM..............67
In sweet fields of autumn..........276
In the bleak midwinter.............87
In the branches of the forest......207
In their ancient isolation.........126
In the lonely midnight.............86
In the springtime of our year......264
In the spring we ploughed our furrows 273
In this stern hour whene'er the spirit
  falters........................56
INWARD PEACE AND INWARD
  LIVING........................51
I sent my soul some truth to win.....37
It came upon the midnight clear......91
IT IS SOMETHING TO HAVE BEEN 160
It is something to have wept, as we
  have wept.....................160
It sounds along the ages...........129
I walk the unfrequented road.......277
I would be true, for there are those who
  trust me.....................154

JERUSALEM........................210
Jesus died, but Christ has triumphed 110
Joyful, joyful, we adore thee.......117

JOY OF LIVING.....................3
Joy to the world, for peace shall come...96
Judge eternal, throned in splendour...221

King of glory, King of peace........21
Knowledge, they say, drives wonder
  from the world.................38
Kum ba yah, my Lord, kum ba yah.....32

LEISURE..........................49
Let all the world in every corner sing...72
Let freedom span both east and west...125
Let love continue long............188
Let peace encircle all the world....314
Let people living in all lands.....308
LET THERE BE LIGHT...............114
Let us break bread together every day 175
Let us wander where we will.......254
LIBERATION......................218
Life is the greatest gift of all...249
Life of Ages, richly poured......120
LIFE'S GREAT GIFTS...............249
LIFE'S REBIRTH...................109
LIFE'S YEARLY TRIUMPH...........265
LIFE THAT MAKETH ALL THINGS
  NEW...........................8
Lift up your voices, rise and sing!...309
LIVING AND DYING.................298
LONG AGO IN MANGER LOW..........89
Long ago the lilies faded.........100
Long ago they came in conquest....214
Long, long ago, in manger low.....89
Look at the hillside..............275
Lord, as we part and take our
  homeward way..................306
Lord of the wondrous earth..........1
Lo, the earth awakes again........263
Love divine, all loves excelling...118

Make channels for the streams of love 186
MIDNIGHT CLEAR...................91
MIDWINTER.......................278
Mighty Spirit, gracious guide.....111
Mine eyes have seen the glory of a glad,
  resplendent day...............224
MOODS OF SUMMER.................268

INDEX OF FIRST LINES AND TITLES

Morning has broken ... 280
Morning on morning I roam the wild meadow ... 251
Morning, so fair to see ... 246
Mother Spirit, Father Spirit ... 43
MY GOD AND KING ... 72
My God, I thank thee, who hast made ... 20
My life flows on in endless song ... 133
My spirit longs for thee ... 61
Mysterious presence, Source of all ... 238

Nay, do not grieve, though life be full of sadness ... 295
NEW LIFE BEGINNING ... 262
No longer forward nor behind ... 293
NO MORE ALONE ... 294
Not always on the mount may we ... 50
NOT BY BREAD ALONE ... 273
Not on this day, O God, alone ... 303
Now as we part and go our several ways ... 305
Now in the tomb is laid ... 105
Now I recall my childhood when the sun ... 299
Now is the time to live; now is the time ... 248
Now let us sing in loving celebration ... 191
Now once again, to thy dear name we raise ... 304
Now on land and sea descending ... 286
Now open wide your hearts, my friends ... 172
Now praise we great and famous men ... 68
Now sing we of the brave of old ... 106
Now thank we all our God ... 19
Now we gather here to worship ... 202

O come, all ye faithful ... 95
O come together in truth ... 176
O earth, you are surpassing fair ... 206
O'er continent and ocean ... 119
O eternal Life, whose power ... 22
O for that flame of living fire ... 113
O GLAD NEW YEAR OF GOD ... 258
O God of stars and sunlight ... 234

O God, our help in ages past ... 65
O God! the darkness roll away ... 222
O God, where'er thy people meet ... 25
O help the prophet to be bold ... 138
O Life that makest all things new ... 8
O little town of Bethlehem ... 85
O live each day and live it well ... 156
O Living God, that bringest all to birth ... 12
Once the fearless navigator ... 40
Once to every man and nation ... 168
One faith and hope undying ... 223
One holy Church of God appears ... 122
ONE HUMAN COMMONWEALTH ... 125
O never harm the dreaming world ... 312
One world this, for all its sorrow ... 229
"Onward and upward for ever and ever" ... 200
O sacred head, now wounded ... 103
O, Sons and Daughters, lift every voice ... 6
O star of truth, downshining ... 316
OTHERS CALL IT GOD ... 233
O thou that movest all, O Power ... 29
O thou, to whom our parents built ... 124
Our faith is but a single gem ... 130
Our festival is here again ... 83
OUR KINDRED FELLOWSHIPS ... 136
OUR NATION ... 214
Our parents' faith, we'll sing of thee ... 77
OUR PARTING HYMN OF PRAISE ... 304
O what a piece of work are we ... 148
O worship the King, all glorious above ... 70

Past are the cross, the scourge, the thorn ... 107
PAST, PRESENT, FUTURE ... 124
Peace is the mind's old wilderness cut down ... 219
People, look east! The time is near ... 82
People, sing your country's anthem ... 227
PILGRIM'S HYMN ... 150
PRAISE FROM ALL THE HUMAN RACE ... 16
Praise God, the love we all may share ... 313
Praise, my soul, the King of Heaven ... 116
Praise, O my heart, to you, O Source of Life ... 4

INDEX OF FIRST LINES AND TITLES

PRAISE THE GREAT AND FAMOUS 68
Praise to the living God! 69
Praise to the Lord, the Almighty, the King of creation 71
PRAYER FOR STRENGTH 59
Prayer is the soul's sincere desire 58

Rejoice in love we know and share 315
RELEASE FROM BITTER THINGS ... 221
Religion needs to permeate 189
REVERENCE FOR LIFE 250
RING OUT, RING IN 257
Ring out, wild bells, to the wild sky ... 257

Say not the struggle naught availeth ... 197
Scorn not the slightest word or deed ... 55
SEEDS OF GOODNESS 274
Seek not afar for beauty; lo! it glows ... 237
Shalom Havayreem 317
Silent night! peaceful night! 88
Sing in celebration, time to remember 135
Sing of living, sing of dying 298
Sing we of the Golden City 212
SING YOUR COUNTRY'S ANTHEM 227
SONG OF PEACE 226
SONG OF THANKSGIVING 17
SONS AND DAUGHTERS 6
SO SIMPLE IS THE HUMAN HEART ... 9
SOURCE OF ALL 238
Source of all being, throned afar 7
SOURCE OF LIFE 4
Sovereign and transforming Grace 24
Spirit divine! Attend our prayer 26
SPRING BUDS OF HOPE 264
Spring has now unwrapped the flowers 266
STARBORN 36
STRANGER ON THE MOUNTAIN ... 207
SUNRISE IS BORN 282
SUNRISE TO FREEDOM 144
Sunset and evening star 300

Teach me, my God and King 57
The art, the science, and the lore 128
THE AWAKENING SEASON 226

THE BEAUTY OF THE EARTH 14
THE BEST THINGS 184
THE BRAVE OF OLD 106
The ceaseless flow of endless time ... 259
THE CHILD IS PROMISE 80
THE CHOICE IN LIFE 164
THE CHOICE IS OURS 206
The Church is not where altar stands ...173
The day thou gavest, Lord, is ended ... 287
THE DEPTHS OF INNER SPACE 40
THE ETERNAL NOW 259
THE FELLOWSHIP OF THE CHURCH 173
The first Nowell the angel did say 92
THE FLOW OF LIFE 31
The generations as they rise 139
THE GOAL 170
The God of galaxies has more to govern 231
THE GOLDEN CITY 212
THE GOLDEN HERESY OF TRUTH ...139
THE GOLDEN RULE 157
THE HARVEST OF TRUTH 156
THE HEALING OF THE NATIONS ... 198
THE HOLY SPIRIT 112
THE HYMN OF ST. FRANCIS 241
The ink is black, the page is white 215
THE LARGER VIEW 126
THE LAW OF LOVE 186
The lives which touch our own each day 292
THE LIVING GOD 35
The Lord's my Shepherd, I'll not want 66
THE LOVE OF GOD IS BROADER ... 140
The mighty elm tree falls before the storm 196
THE MIRACLE 148
THE MOMENT TO DECIDE 168
The morning hangs a signal 281
THE OLD HUNDREDTH 64
The pen is greater than the sword 164
THE PEOPLE'S PEACE 219
THE POWER OF LOVE 185
THE PRESENCE EVERYWHERE ... 100
There hides within the lily 236

There's a light that was shining when the world began 149
There's a wideness in God's mercy ... 140
THESE FESTIVE DAYS 83
These things shall be! a loftier race ... 203
THE SON OF MAN 98
THE SOUL'S SINCERE DESIRE 58
The spacious firmament on high 232
THE SPIRIT CONQUERS ALL 196
The star of truth but dimly shines 162
The sun at high noon 247
THE SUN OF HOPE WITHIN 161
The sun that shines across the sea 245
THE TIDES OF THE SPIRIT 28
THE UNIVERSAL INCARNATION ... 97
THE UPWARD REACH 239
THE VISION OF A WORLD SET FREE 223
The voice of God is calling 169
The wise one should, with spirit calm 297
The world is full of poverty 165
The world stands out on either side ... 141
This is my song, O God of all the nations 226
This land is your land, this land is my land 255
This old world is full of sorrow 180
This world has been a prison 144
Those who seek wisdom 163
Though it is our boast that we 167
Thou One in all, thou All in one 10
Thou, whose almighty word 114
Thou whose love has given us birth ... 108
THROUGH ALL THE COMING WEEK 303
THROUGH HUMAN MEANS 110
THY KINGDOM COME 37
THY PURPOSE CROWNING ALL ... 236
TILL GREED AND HATE CEASE 228
'Tis the gift to be simple, 'tis the gift to be free 146
'Tis winter now; the fallen snow 260
To cloisters of the spirit 27
To Mercy, Pity, Peace and Love 190
Tomorrow is a highway broad and fair 201
TO WORSHIP RIGHTLY 191

To you each, my friends, tonight 284
TRANQUILLITY 252
TRANSCIENCE 295
TRANSFORMING GRACE 24
TRUE FREEDOM 167
TRUE RELIGION 189
TRUE SIMPLICITY 146
TRUST IN LIFE 60
TURN AROUND 289
Turn back, O Man, forswear thy foolish ways 230

UNDYING ECHOES 292
UNFOLDING LIFE 290
UNIVERSAL SPIRIT 43
UNREST 145

VESPER HYMN 286

WAITING FOR THE PLOUGH 261
WALK IN THE LIGHT 149
WE ARE MET TO WORSHIP THEE ... 23
We are the earth, upright and proud ... 74
We believe in human kindness 187
WE CAN BECOME 177
We celebrate the holy gift of light 80
We come as we are to worship and pray 28
We do not seek a shallow faith 60
We gather together in joyful thanksgiving 18
We know that this life brings its share of sorrow 185
Welcome from God, O glad new year! 258
We lift our hearts in yearning 137
We limit not the truth of God 195
We look no more for tongues of fire ... 112
We move in faith to unseen goals 39
We must be one with all who found ... 182
WE MUST BE TRUE 153
We need a city which is ours 213
We plough the fields, and scatter 269
We rest awhile in quietness 42
WE SHALL BE STRONG AND FREE 137
We shall overcome 204
We sing now together our song of thanksgiving 17

INDEX OF FIRST LINES AND TITLES

We sing of golden mornings 267
We sing the joy of living 3
WE SING THE ROSES WAITING 267
WESTWARD, LOOK 197
We will honour Michael 78
We will speak out, we will be heard! ... 159
We would be one as now we join in
   singing 192
What is this life if, full of care 49
WHAT LOVE CAN DO 171
What purpose burns within our hearts 194
When a deed is done for Freedom 199
When I recall the hopes which almost
   died 161
When I was a child I spoke as a child ... 290
When Jesus walked upon the earth ... 99
When lonely shadows steal the light ... 294
When the summer sun is shining 268
When this day is over 171
When your heart, with joy o'erflowing 183
Where are you going, my little one,
   little one 289

Where cross the crowded ways of life ... 98
WHERE'ER THY PEOPLE MEET 25
Where is our holy church? 123
"Where is your God?" they say 34
While shepherds watched their flocks
   by night 84
Who thou art I know not 239
Who would true valour see 150
Wild waves of storm 252
Winning not, though ever striving ... 153
WISDOM AND COURAGE 193
Wisdom has riches which exceed 67
With joy we claim the growing light ... 311
WITH YOUR NEIGHBOUR SHARE ... 183
WONDER 38
Wonders still the world shall witness ... 209
WORK SHALL BE PRAYER 47

Ye earthborn children of a star 36
You must be true unto yourself 155

Topical Index

Titles are given where these differ from first lines. The titles of subject sections are given in *italics*.

ACCEPTANCE
Trust in Life... 60
Here and Now... 293
Transcience... 295
Facing Death... 297
Through all the Coming Week... 303

ACHIEVEMENT
The Depths of Inner Space... 40
Praise the Great and Famous... 68
Honourable Saints... 78
The Brave of Old... 106
Heritage... 128
Sing in Celebration... 135
The Miracle... 148
All Heroic Lives Remind Us... 166
All are Architects of Fate... 211
The Golden City... 212
God Bless the Grass... 253
Undying Echoes... 292
Heroes... 296

ADVENT
The Child is Promise... 80
Advent Hymn... 81
People, Look East... 82

ADVENTURE
Lord of the Wondrous Earth... 1
Joy of Living... 3
Wonder... 38
The Depths of Inner Space... 40
Prayer for Strength... 59
Our Kindred Fellowships... 136
The Golden Heresy of Truth... 139
Unrest... 145
Pilgrim's Hymn... 150
We Must Be True... 153
It is Something to Have Been... 160
The Star of Truth... 162
Courage Shall Conquer... 200
Tomorrow is a Highway... 201
Boldly Live, My Daughter... 217

AFFIRMATION
Joy of Living... 3
Sons and Daughters... 6
So Simple is the Human Heart... 9
We Gather Together... 18
O God Our Help in Ages Past... 65
The Lord's My Shepherd... 66

We are the Earth... 74
City of God... 121
It Sounds Along the Ages... 129
How Can I Keep From Singing!... 133
Faith of the Free... 134
Walk in the Light... 149
Human Kindness... 187
These Things Shall Be!... 203
We Shall Overcome... 204
Jerusalem... 210
The Spacious Firmament... 232
This Land is Your Land... 255
Now I Recall My Childhood... 299

ALL FAITHS —
    see COMPARATIVE RELIGION

ALL SAINTS
For All the Saints... 79

ANIMALS
Leisure... 49
Stranger on the Mountain... 207
The Hymn of St. Francis... 241
For the Strength of the Hills... 242
All Things Bright and Beautiful... 243
Reverence for Life... 250
Tranquillity... 252
Autumn Fields... 276

ANNIVERSARY (CHURCH)
Song of Thanksgiving... 17
Now Thank We All Our God... 19
Where'er Thy People Meet... 25
To Cloisters of the Spirit... 27
Our Parents' Faith... 77
City of God... 121
One Holy Church... 122
Where is our Holy Church?... 123
Past, Present, Future... 124
Faith of the Free... 134
Sing in Celebration... 135
Our Kindred Fellowships... 136

ARMISTICE
O God Our Help in Ages Past... 65
Hush the Sounds of War... 222
The Vision of a World Set Free... 223

ARTS
Praise the Great and Famous... 68

xv

TOPICAL INDEX

ASPIRATION
Where'er Thy People Meet ... 25
Do You Hear? ... 33
We Move in Faith ... 39
A Dream of Undying Love ... 42
Universal Spirit ... 43
Come, My Life ... 44
Come Down, O Love Divine ... 45
Breath of God ... 46
My Spirit Longs for Thee ... 61
Flame of Living Fire ... 113
Be Thou My Vision ... 151
I Bind unto Myself Today ... 152
Those Who Seek Wisdom ... 163
We Limit Not the Truth of God ... 195
Boldly Live, My Daughter ... 217
The Upward Reach ... 239
Darkness Put to Flight ... 281
Awake, my Soul ... 283
Closing Verses ... 310, 311, 314

AUTUMN
Seasons: Autumn ... 275-277

BABY and BAPTISM
Turn Around ... 289

BEAUTY
The Beauty of the Earth ... 14
Leisure ... 49
A World Transfigured ... 209
Seek Not Afar for Beauty ... 237
The Upward Reach ... 239
Daisies are Our Silver ... 240
The Hymn of St. Francis ... 241
All Things Bright and Beautiful ... 243
Morning, So Fair to See ... 246
Now is the Time ... 248
The Awakening Season ... 266
Look at the Hillside ... 275
Morning Has Broken ... 280

BELLS
Ring Out, Ring In ... 257
New Life Beginning ... 262

BENEDICTIONS —
see CLOSE OF WORSHIP

BEREAVEMENT — *see* DEATH

BETTER WORLD
Sons and Daughters ... 6
Past, Present, Future ... 124
One Human Commonwealth ... 125

Gather Us In ... 127
Sing in Celebration ... 135
Sunrise to Freedom ... 144
True Simplicity ... 146
The Goal ... 170
This Old World ... 180
To Worship Rightly ... 191
A New Community ... 192
A Better World ... *193-230*
Ring Out, Ring In ... 257
Spring Buds of Hope ... 264
Closing Verse ... 314

BLESSING
Now Thank We All Our God ... 19
The Lord's My Shepherd ... 66
Praise to the Lord, the Almighty ... 71
Praise, My Soul ... 116
The Best Things ... 184
The Law of Love ... 186
O God of Stars and Sunlight ... 234
The Hymn of St. Francis ... 241
All These Things Belong to Me ... 245

BROTHERHOOD AND SISTERHOOD —
see FELLOWSHIP

BUDDHISM
Hymn to Perfect Wisdom ... 11
True Religion ... 189
The Spirit Conquers All ... 196
See also COMPARATIVE RELIGION

CARE — *see* COMPASSION

CELEBRATION
Worship and Celebration ... *1-32*
The Old Hundredth ... 64
Praise to the Living God ... 69
We are the Earth ... 74
How Can I Keep From Singing! ... 133
Song of Peace ... 226
The Hymn of St. Francis ... 241
For the Strength of the Hills ... 242
Glad That I Live Am I ... 244
Morning, So Fair to See ... 246
This Land is Your Land ... 255
Midwinter ... 278
Morning Has Broken ... 280

CHANGING WORLD
The Flow of Life ... 31
Inward Peace and Inward Living ... 51
The Larger View ... 126
Unrest ... 145
Our Nation ... 214

TOPICAL INDEX

CHARACTER
Free from the World's Cares... 147
Pilgrim's Hymn... 150
I Would Be True... 154
The Harvest of Truth... 156
The Choice in Life... 164
A Noble Life... 179
Heroes... 296

CHILDREN
Sunrise to Freedom... 144
Can I See Another's Woe?... 181
Black and White... 215
Child of Hiroshima... 225
A Melody of Love... 235
Daisies are Our Silver... 240
Spring Buds of Hope... 264
Turn Around... 289
Unfolding Life... 290
Early in Life's Morning... 291
Now I Recall my Childhood... 299

CHOICE
The Choice in Life... 164
The Moment to Decide... 168
The Choice is Ours... 206

CHRISTIAN HERITAGE
Come, My Life... 44
Come Down, O Love Divine... 45
Not Always on the Mount... 50
The Soul's Sincere Desire... 58
Holy Spirit, Truth Divine... 63
The Judaeo-Christian Heritage... 71-118
Pilgrim's Hymn... 150
Wisdom and Courage... 193
Jerusalem... 210

CHRISTMAS
Judaeo-Christian Heritage: Christmas
83-97
Midwinter... 278

CHURCH
Transforming Grace... 24
Where'er Thy People Meet... 25
To Cloisters of the Spirit... 27
Work Shall be Prayer... 47
City of God... 121
One Holy Church... 122
Where is our Holy Church?... 123
Past, Present, Future... 124
Our Kindred Fellowships... 136
What Love Can Do... 171

All are Welcome Here... 172
The Fellowship of the Church... 173
A Church is a Living Fellowship... 174
Come Together in Love... 176
Wisdom and Courage... 193
What Purpose Burns... 194
Children of a Bright Tomorrow... 202
Goodnight Hymn... 284
The Day Thou Gavest... 287
Our Parting Hymn of Praise... 304

CITIZENSHIP — see COMMUNITY

CITY
Inward Peace and Inward Living... 51
Calm Soul of All Things... 53
City of God... 121
Freedom is the Finest Gold... 142
Jerusalem... 210
The Golden City... 212
A City Which is Ours... 213

CLOSE OF WORSHIP
Dear Lord and Father... 101
Evening... 284-288
Close of Worship... 302-317

COMMEMORATION
Praise the Great and Famous... 68
Our Parents' Faith... 77
Honourable Saints... 78
The Brave of Old... 106
Flame of Living Fire... 113
Sing in Celebration... 135
Heroes... 296

COMMITMENT
We Gather Together... 18
Our Parents' Faith... 77
The Brave of Old... 106
Faith of the Free... 134
Sing in Celebration... 135
Our Kindred Fellowships... 136
Die Gedanken Sind Frei... 143
Sunrise to Freedom... 144
Personal Commitment... 150-170
Tomorrow is a Highway... 201
We Shall Overcome... 204
Forward Through the Ages... 208
Jerusalem... 210
The Golden City... 212
Bread and Roses... 216
Closing Verse... 316
See also DEDICATION

TOPICAL INDEX

COMMUNION WITH GOD
Fill My Life with Praise ... 5
"Where is Your God?" ... 34
I Cannot Lose Thee! ... 41
Come, My Life ... 44
Come Down, O Love Divine ... 45
Breath of God ... 46
Divinity is Round Us ... 52
My Spirit Longs for Thee ... 61
Holy Spirit, Truth Divine ... 63
The Presence Everywhere ... 100
Dear Lord and Father ... 101
The World Stands Out ... 141
Be Thou My Vision ... 151

COMMUNITY
One Human Commonwealth ... 125
Freedom is the Finest Gold ... 142
True Simplicity ... 146
Love and Community ... *171-192*
What Purpose Burns ... 194
Children of a Bright Tomorrow ... 202
A City Which is Ours ... 213
The People's Peace ... 219
Goodnight Hymn ... 284

COMPARATIVE RELIGION
The Living God ... 35
God of Ages and of Nations ... 75
O'er Continent and Ocean ... 119
The Larger View ... 126
Gather Us In ... 127
Heritage ... 128
It Sounds Along the Ages ... 129
All Faiths ... 130
All Earth's Children ... 131
All are Welcome Here ... 172
We Limit Not the Truth of God ... 195

COMPASSION
Do You Hear? ... 33
Scorn Not the Slightest Word ... 55
The Son of Man ... 98
Inasmuch ... 165
True Freedom ... 167
The Voice of God ... 169
Can I See Another's Woe? ... 181
All Are Our Neighbours ... 182
With Your Neighbour Share ... 183
True Religion ... 189
To Worship Rightly ... 191

CONDUCT
Free from the World's Cares ... 147
I Would Be True ... 154
Be True, Live Truly ... 155
The Harvest of Truth ... 156
The Golden Rule ... 157
Dare to Think ... 158
The Choice in Life ... 164
A Noble Life ... 179
True Religion ... 189
Break Not the Circle ... 220
Seeds of Goodness ... 274
As Each Day Ends ... 302
See also LIFE AND LIVING

CONFUCIANISM
The Golden Rule ... 157

CONSERVATION — *see* ECOLOGY

CONTENTMENT
Leisure ... 49
True Simplicity ... 146
A Shelter From the Vast ... 178
The People's Peace ... 219
All These Things Belong to Me ... 245
Moods of Summer ... 268
Autumn Ways ... 277
Here and Now ... 293

CONVICTION — *see* AFFIRMATION

COUNTRYSIDE — *see* NATURE

COURAGE AND ENCOURAGEMENT
Prayer for Strength ... 59
Trust in Life ... 60
For All the Saints ... 79
How Can I Keep from Singing! ... 133
We Shall be Strong and Free ... 137
Die Gedanken Sind Frei ... 143
Pilgrim's Hymn ... 150
Dare to Think ... 158
We Will Speak Out! ... 159
The Star of Truth ... 162
Those Who Seek Wisdom ... 163
True Freedom ... 167
The Moment to Decide ... 168
Wisdom and Courage ... 193
Westward, Look! ... 197
Courage Shall Conquer ... 200
We Sing the Roses Waiting ... 267
Goodnight Hymn ... 284
Transcience ... 295
Facing Death ... 297

CRAFTSMANSHIP —
see WORK AND WORKERS

TOPICAL INDEX

DARING
Unrest 145
Dare to Think 158
The Star of Truth 162

DAUGHTERS AND SONS
Sunrise to Freedom 144
Boldly Live, My Daughter 217
Turn Around 289

DEATH AND BEREAVEMENT
Death's Dominion is Past 108
Child of Hiroshima 225
Undying Echoes 292
No More Alone 294
Transcience 295
Heroes 296
Facing Death 297
Living and Dying 298
Now I Recall my Childhood 299
Abide With Me 301
Lord, as We Part 306

DEDICATION
Lord of the Wondrous Earth 1
Eternal Ruler 13
King of Glory, King of Peace 21
Universal Spirit 43
Breath of God 46
Teach me, my God and King 57
We are the Earth 74
Beneath the Shadow of the Cross 104
Sing in Celebration 135
Pilgrim's Hymn 150
Be Thou My Vision 151
I Bind unto Myself Today 152
The Voice of God 169
A New Community 192
What Purpose Burns 194
Tomorrow is a Highway 201
Others Call it God 233

DEPENDENCE
Source of Life 4
Thou one in All, Thou All in One 10
Hymn to the Sole God 12
Now Thank We All Our God 19
My Spirit Longs for Thee 61
O God Our Help in Ages Past 65
The Lord's My Shepherd 66
Praise to the Lord, the Almighty 71
A Mighty Fortress 73
Immortal, Invisible 76
We Plough the Fields 269

DESIGN — *see* **ORDER**

DIFFICULTY
Divinity is Round Us 52
Faith 56
Prayer for Strength 59
Trust in Life 60
The Lord's My Shepherd 66
The Brave of Old 106
How Can I Keep from Singing! 133
Sunrise to Freedom 144
Unrest 145
Pilgrim's Hymn 150
It is Something to Have Been 160
The Goal 170
Westward Look! 197
The Golden City 212
God Bless the Grass 253
Closing Verse 316

DIVINE LOVE AND CARE
Immortal Love, for Ever Full 30
Come Down, O Love Divine 45
My Spirit Longs for Thee 61
O Worship the King 70
Praise to the Lord, the Almighty 71
The Presence Everywhere 100
Mighty Spirit, Gracious Guide 111
Praise, My Soul 116
Joyful, Joyful, We Adore Thee 117
All Loves Excelling 118
Life of Ages, Richly Poured 120
Gather Us In 127
The Love of God is Broader 140
The Vision of a World Set Free 223
Till Greed and Hate Cease 228
A Melody of Love 235
'Tis Winter Now 260
Vesper Hymn 286
Through all the Coming Week 303

DOUBT
The Tides of the Spirit 28
The Star of Truth 162

DUTY
Not Always on the Mount 50
Our Parents' Faith 77
The Brave of Old 106
Pilgrim's Hymn 150
Dare to Think 158
Inasmuch 165
True Freedom 167
The Moment to Decide 168

TOPICAL INDEX

The Voice of God............................ 169
The Golden City............................. 212

EASTERTIDE
Judaeo-Christian Heritage: Easter 106-110
Earth Awakes Again......................... 263
Life's Yearly Triumph....................... 265

ECOLOGY
The Choice is Ours.......................... 206
Stranger on the Mountain................... 207
Reverence for Life.......................... 250
Waiting for the Plough...................... 261
Closing Verse............................... 312

EDUCATION — see KNOWLEDGE

EMANCIPATION —
see FREEDOM and LIBERATION

ENCOURAGEMENT —
see COURAGE & ENCOURAGEMENT

ENLIGHTENMENT — see REVELATION
and UNDERSTANDING

EPIPHANY
Silent Night.................................. 88
The First Nowell............................. 92
O Come, All ye Faithful..................... 95

EQUALITY
Sons and Daughters........................... 6
Where is our Holy Church?.................. 123
One Human Commonwealth................. 125
Freedom Is the Finest Gold................. 142
True Freedom............................... 167
The Healing of the Nations................. 198
Black and White............................ 215
Bread and Roses............................ 216
Liberation.................................. 218
Break not the Circle........................ 220
See also FREEDOM

ETERNITY — see TIME AND ETERNITY

EVENING
What Love Can Do........................... 171
Evening.................................. 284-288
As Each Day Ends........................... 302
Our Parting Hymn of Praise................ 304

EVOLUTION
God of Life.................................. 22
The Flow of Life............................. 31

Children of the Universe................... 132
Unrest..................................... 145
The Goal................................... 170
The Choice is Ours......................... 206
Others Call it God.......................... 233
Thy Purpose Crowning All................. 236

EXPLORATION
Wonder..................................... 38
Now is the Time............................ 248

FAITH
My God, I Thank Thee...................... 20
Kum ba Yah................................. 32
We Move in Faith........................... 39
Faith....................................... 56
Trust in Life............................... 60
God Moves in a Mysterious Way.......... 62
The Lord's My Shepherd.................... 66
Our Parents' Faith.......................... 77
The Brave of Old........................... 106
Mighty Spirit, Gracious Guide............. 111
Faith of the Free........................... 134
Pilgrim's Hymn............................. 150
I Bind unto Myself Today.................. 152
The Spirit Conquers All.................... 196
We Shall Overcome......................... 204
Forward Through the Ages................. 208
Abide With Me............................. 301
See also TRUST

FAMILY
A Shelter from the Vast.................... 178
The People's Peace......................... 219

FATHERS AND MOTHERS —
see PARENTS

FEELINGS — see SENSES

FELLOWSHIP
Love and Community................... 171-192
See also COMMUNITY and FRIENDS AND FRIENDSHIP and LOVE AND KINDNESS and TOGETHERNESS

FOOD
The Choice is Ours......................... 206
Seasons: Harvest...................... 269-274

FREEDOM
Life that Maketh All Things New............ 8
Joy to the World............................ 96
Life of Ages, Richly Poured................ 120
Where is Our Holy Church?................ 123

TOPICAL INDEX

One Human Commonwealth............ 125
The Free Spirit..................*133-149*
True Freedom.......................... 167
The Healing of the Nations......... 198
When a Deed is Done for Freedom... 199
In Braver Mould........................205
Black and White........................215
Bread and Roses........................216
Liberation...............................218
Break Not the Circle...................220
A Glad, Resplendent Day..............224
This Land is Your Land................ 255
Unfolding Life.......................... 290
Closing Verse...........................311

FREE SPIRIT
Sons and Daughters..................... 6
Honourable Saints...................... 78
Life of Ages, Richly Poured...........120
The Free Spirit..................*133-149*
We Will Speak Out.....................159
The Spirit Conquers All...............196
We Shall Overcome.....................204
A World Transfigured..................209
Boldly Live, My Daughter............. 217

FRIENDS AND FRIENDSHIP
True Simplicity........................146
Let us Break Bread Together......... 175
Come Together in Love................. 176
We Can Become..........................177
A Melody of Love...................... 235
Life's Great Gifts.................... 249
Goodnight Hymn........................ 284
Shalom Havayreem......................317

FULFILMENT
Come, My Life.......................... 44
Breath of God...........................46
In Praise of Wisdom.................... 67
All Loves Excelling...................118
It Is Something to Have Been.........160
A Shelter from the Vast...............178

FUTURE TIME
Heritage.............................. 128
Children of the Universe.............132
Sing in Celebration...................135
The Sun of Hope Within...............161
The Goal.............................. 170
We Can Become.........................177
We Limit Not the Truth of God........195
Tomorrow is a Highway.................201
Children of a Bright Tomorrow........202

These Things Shall Be!................ 203
We Shall Overcome.....................204
In Braver Mould....................... 205
A World Transfigured..................209
Bread and Roses........................216
The Vision of a World Set Free.......223
Earth Shall be Fair...................230
Ring Out, Ring In.....................257

GIFTS AND GIVING
Thou One in All, Thou All in One...... 10
For All that is Our Life.............. 15
Advent Hymn............................ 81
True Simplicity.......................146
The Law of Love.......................186
All Things Bright and Beautiful...... 243
All These Things Belong to Me........245
Life's Great Gifts.................... 249
We Plough the Fields..................269
See also BLESSING

GOD
Source of Life.......................... 4
Fill My Life with Praise................5
Source of All Being.....................7
Hymn to the Sole God................... 12
God of Life............................ 22
God Within.............................29
Immortal Love, for Ever Full.......... 30
"Where is Your God?".................. 34
The Living God........................ 35
Divinity is Round Us................... 52
God Moves in a Mysterious Way........ 62
O God Our Help in Ages Past.......... 65
Praise to the Living God.............. 69
O Worship the King.....................70
Praise to the Lord, the Almighty..... 71
My God and King........................ 72
A Mighty Fortress...................... 73
Immortal, Invisible................... 76
Past, Present, Future.................124
The Love of God is Broader............140
The God of Galaxies................... 231
Others Call it God....................233
O God of Stars and Sunlight...........234
A Melody of Love...................... 235
Seek Not Afar for Beauty..............237
Source of All.........................238
The Upward Reach......................239
God Be in My Head.....................307
Closing Verse.........................313

GOLDEN RULE
The Golden Rule.......................157

TOPICAL INDEX

GOVERNMENT
A City Which is Ours ...213

GRACE
Transforming Grace ...24

GRASS
God Bless the Grass ...253

GROWTH AND MATURITY
Boldly Live, My Daughter ...217
Glad That I Live Am I ...244
God Bless the Grass ...253
Spring Buds of Hope ...264
Turn Around ...289
Unfolding Life ...290
Living and Dying ...298

GUIDANCE
Eternal Ruler ...13
Prayer for Strength ...59
The Lord's My Shepherd ...66
Praise, My Soul ...116
Be Thou My Vision ...151
I Bind unto Myself Today ...152
Guard us Night and Day ...288
Closing Verse ...316

HANUKKAH
These Festive Days ...83

HAPPINESS — see JOY IN LIFE

HARVEST
The Harvest of Truth ...156
With Your Neighbour Share ...183
The Choice is Ours ...206
The Seasons: Harvest ... *269-274*
Autumn Ways ...277

HELPING — see LOVE AND KINDNESS

HERE AND NOW
Brief our Days ...2
So Simple is the Human Heart ...9
Leisure ...49
The Harvest of Truth ...156
Seek Not Afar for Beauty ...237
Now is the Time ...248
The Eternal Now ...259
Here and Now ...293

HERESY
Honourable Saints ...78
The Golden Heresy of Truth ...139
Dare to Think ...158

HERITAGE
Song of Thanksgiving ...17
The Judaeo-Christian Heritage ... *64-118*
World-Wide Heritage ...*119-132*
Faith of the Free ...134
Sing in Celebration ...135
Our Kindred Fellowships ...136
Our Nation ...214
For the Strength of the Hills ...242

HINDUISM —
see COMPARATIVE RELIGION

HOLIDAYS
These Festive Days ...83
Midwinter ...278

HOME AND HOMELAND
A Shelter From the Vast ...178
Our Nation ...214
The People's Peace ...219
Song of Peace ...226
A Melody of Love ...235
Let us Wander where we Will ...254
This Land is Your Land ...255
Give Thanks ...271

HONOUR
Honourable Saints ...78
Freedom is the Finest Gold ...142
True Freedom ...167
A Noble Life ...179
Heroes ...296

HOPE
We Gather Together ...18
The Sun of Hope Within ...161
Spring Buds of Hope ...264
We Sing the Roses Waiting ...267

HUMAN CONDITION, THE
Seasons of Human Life ... *289-301*
See also LIFE AND LIVING

HUMANISM (RELIGIOUS)
So Simple is the Human Heart ...9
Praise From All the Human Race ...16
We are the Earth ...74
The Holy Spirit ...112
Where is Our Holy Church? ...123
Children of the Universe ...132
The Miracle ...148

TOPICAL INDEX

True Religion............................189
To Mercy, Pity, Peace and Love......190
Children of a Bright Tomorrow........202
A World Transfigured..................209
I Held the Planets in My Hand........256

HUMAN RIGHTS
Die Gedanken Sind Frei................143
True Freedom..........................167
The Moment to Decide..................168
The Voice of God......................169
The Healing of the Nations............198
Bread and Roses.......................216
See also JUSTICE

HUMILITY
Hymn to Perfect Wisdom................11
King of Glory, King of Peace..........21
The Tides of the Spirit...............28
The Flow of Life......................31
Come Down, O Love Divine..............45
My Spirit Longs for Thee..............61
Dear Lord and Father..................101

IDEALS
Our Parents' Faith....................77
O Help the Prophet to be Bold.........138
Freedom is the Finest Gold............142
I Would Be True.......................154
The Harvest of Truth..................156
The Golden Rule.......................157
Dare to Think.........................158
The Moment to Decide..................168
A New Community.......................192
The Spirit Conquers All...............196
A World Transfigured..................209
Closing Verses........310, 311, 313, 315

INDEPENDENCE — *see* FREEDOM

INDIVIDUAL, THE
Walk in the Light.....................149
Pilgrim's Hymn........................150
The Sun of Hope Within................161
All These Things Belong to Me.........245
This Land is Your Land................255
I Held the Planets in My Hand........256
Look at the Hillside..................275
Autumn Ways...........................277
Here and Now..........................293
No More Alone.........................294
Crossing the Bar......................300

INDUCTION
Personal Commitment.............150-170

INDUSTRY —
see WORK AND WORKERS

INEFFABLE, THE
Hymn to Perfect Wisdom................11
God Within............................29
I Cannot Lose Thee!...................41
Faith.................................56
The God of Galaxies...................231

INFLUENCE
Undying Echoes........................292

INNER LIGHT
Walk in the Light.....................149
Goodnight Hymn........................284

INSPIRATION
Transforming Grace....................24
Seek Not Afar for Beauty..............237
Source of All.........................238
Darkness Put to Flight................281

INTEGRITY
The Brave of Old......................106
Free from the World's Cares...........147
Walk in the Light.....................149
Personal Commitment.............150-170
A Noble Life..........................179
True Religion.........................189

INTERNATIONAL —
see NATION AND NATIONS

INSIGHT
My God, I Thank Thee..................20
God Within............................29
The Flow of Life......................31
The Depths of Inner Space.............40
From all the Fret and Fever...........48
Calm Soul of All Things...............53
Every Night and Every Morn............54
It is Something to Have Been..........160

ISLAM —
see COMPARATIVE RELIGION

JESUS
Come, My Life.........................44
The Soul's Sincere Desire.............58
The Judaeo-Christian Heritage...78-118
The Spirit Conquers All...............196
Jerusalem.............................210
Thy Purpose Crowning All..............236

TOPICAL INDEX

JOURNEY OF LIFE
Pilgrim's Hymn...150
We Must Be True...153
All Heroic Lives Remind Us...166
Tomorrow is a Highway...201
Boldly Live, My Daughter...217
Morning, So Fair to See...246
This Land is Your Land...255
I Held the Planets in My Hand...256
Closing Verse...316

JOY IN LIFE
Lord of the Wondrous Earth...1
Brief our Days...2
Joy of Living...3
Sons and Daughters...6
The Beauty of the Earth...14
We Gather Together...18
Joy to the World...96
Flame of Living Fire...113
Joyful, Joyful, We Adore Thee...117
Boldly Live, My Daughter...217
Glad That I Live Am I...244
All These Things Belong to Me...245
Midwinter...278
Morning, So Fair to See...246
Now is the Time...248
This Land is Your Land...255
We Sing the Roses Waiting...267
Morning Has Broken...280

JUDAEO-CHRISTIAN HERITAGE
The Judaeo-Christian Heritage...64-118

JUDAISM
Source of Life...4
The Judaeo-Christian Heritage...64-69
God of Ages and of Nations...75
Flame of Living Fire...113
Release from Bitter Things...221
Source of All...238
For the Strength of the Hills...242

JUSTICE
True Freedom...167
The Moment to Decide...168
The Healing of the Nations...198
When a Deed is Done for Freedom...199
We Shall Overcome...204
Black and White...215
Bread and Roses...216
See also HUMAN RIGHTS

KINDNESS —
see LOVE AND KINDNESS

KINGDOM (COMMONWEALTH) OF GOD
Thy Kingdom Come...37
Christ Cometh not a King...115
All Loves Excelling...118
These Things Shall Be!...203
Forward Through the Ages...208
The Golden City...212
Release from Bitter Things...221
The Vision of a World Set Free...223
Till Greed and Hate Cease...228
The Day Thou Gavest...287

KNOWLEDGE
Joy of Living...3
Wonder...38
The Depths of Inner Space...40
The Larger View...126
Not By Bread Alone...273

LEARNING — *see* KNOWLEDGE

LEISURE
Leisure...49
The People's Peace...219
Moods of Summer...268
Autumn Ways...277

LIBERATION
Our Kindred Fellowships...136
We Shall be Strong and Free...137
True Simplicity...146
Black and White...215
Bread and Roses...216
Boldly Live, My Daughter...217
Liberation...218
Unfolding Life...290

LIBERTY — *see* FREEDOM

LIFE AND LIVING
Brief Our Days...2
Joy of Living...3
Fill My Life with Praise...5
Life that Maketh All Things New...8
For All that is Our Life...15
The Tides of the Spirit...28
The Flow of Life...31
Leisure...49
Inward Peace and Inward Living...51
Every Night and Every Morn...54
We Must Be True...153
The Harvest of Truth...156
All Heroic Lives Remind Us...166
We Can Become...177

TOPICAL INDEX

Boldly Live, My Daughter ... 217
Glad That I Live Am I ... 244
Now is the Time ... 248
Life's Great Gifts ... 249
Seasons of Human Life ... 289-301

LONELINESS
Inasmuch ... 165
What Love Can Do ... 171
No More Alone ... 294

LOVE AND COMMUNITY
Love and Community ... 171-192
Life's Great Gifts ... 249

LOVE AND KINDNESS
When Jesus Walked ... 99
Beneath the Shadow of the Cross ... 104
Mighty Spirit, Gracious Guide ... 111
The Holy Spirit ... 112
O Help the Prophet to be Bold ... 138
I Would Be True ... 154
Break not the Circle ... 220
The Vision of a World Set Free ... 223
See also LOVE AND COMMUNITY

MATURITY —
see GROWTH AND MATURITY

MEDITATION
The Reflective Spirit ... 33-63

MIRACLE
The Miracle ... 148
The Power of Love ... 185
See also WONDER and WONDERFUL WORLD.

MORNING
Morning on Morning ... 251
We Sing the Roses Waiting ... 267
Morning and Evening: Morning 279-283

MOTHERS AND FATHERS —
see PARENTS

MOUNTAIN
Stranger on the Mountain ... 207
For the Strength of the Hills ... 242

MUSIC
A Melody of Love ... 235

NATION AND NATIONS
God of Ages and of Nations ... 75
Jerusalem ... 210
Our Nation ... 214
Song of Peace ... 226
Sing Your Country's Anthem ... 227
See also ONE WORLD

NATURAL WORLD
The Natural World ... 231-256

NATURE
So Simple is the Human Heart ... 9
The Beauty of the Earth ... 14
Wonder ... 38
Leisure ... 49
The Presence Everywhere ... 100
Joyful, Joyful, We Adore Thee ... 117
I Bind unto Myself Today ... 152
The Best Things ... 184
Stranger on the Mountain ... 207
Song of Peace ... 226
The Natural World ... 231-256
The Seasons ... 257-278
Chinese Morning Hymn ... 279
Morning Has Broken ... 280
Early in Life's Morning ... 291
Now I Recall my Childhood ... 299
Closing Verse ... 312

NEED
Kum ba Yah ... 32
Inasmuch ... 165
Can I See Another's Woe? ... 181
All Are Our Neighbours ... 182
The Power of Love ... 185
The Choice is Ours ... 206

NEIGHBOURS
Kum ba Yah ... 32
Freedom is the Finest Gold ... 142
This Old World ... 180
All Are Our Neighbours ... 182
With Your Neighbour Share ... 183
See also FRIENDS AND FRIENDSHIP

NEW AND OLD YEAR
In Braver Mould ... 205
The Seasons: Old and New Year 257-259

NOW AND HERE —
see HERE AND NOW

NUCLEAR WAR
Child of Hiroshima ... 225

OLD AGE
Seasons of Human Life ... 289-301

TOPICAL INDEX

OLD YEAR — see NEW AND OLD YEAR

ONE WORLD AND ONE PEOPLE
O'er Continent and Ocean ... 119
One Human Commonwealth ... 125
The Larger View ... 126
Gather Us In ... 127
Children of the Universe ... 132
All Are Our Neighbours ... 182
A New Community ... 192
A Better World ... 193-230
Tranquillity ... 252
Let us Wander Where we Will ... 254
The Day Thou Gavest ... 287
Closing Verse ... 310

OPENING OF WORSHIP
Worship and Celebration ... *1-32*
The Old Hundredth ... 64
Praise to the Living God ... 69
O Worship the King ... 70
Praise to the Lord, the Almighty ... 71
Praise, My Soul ... 116
How Can I Keep from Singing! ... 133
Those Who Seek Wisdom ... 163
What Love Can Do ... 171
Come Together in Love ... 176
To Worship Rightly ... 191
What Purpose Burns ... 194
Children of a Bright Tomorrow ... 202
In Braver Mould ... 205
Morning, So Fair to See ... 246
Morning and Evening: Morning *279-283*

OPENNESS
The Tides of the Spirit ... 28
Do You Hear? ... 33
The Love of God is Broader ... 140
True Simplicity ... 146
All are Welcome Here ... 172
We Can Become ... 177
A Noble Life ... 179
Break not the Circle ... 220
The Vision of a World Set Free ... 223
Now is the Time ... 248
Here and Now ... 293
Living and Dying ... 298

ORDER
Wonder ... 38
God Moves in a Mysterious Way ... 62
All are Architects of Fate ... 211
The Spacious Firmament ... 232
O God of Stars and Sunlight ... 234

The Upward Reach ... 239
Reverence for Life ... 250
Morning on Morning ... 251
Let us Wander Where we Will ... 254
Seeds of Goodness ... 274

PALM SUNDAY
Hosanna in the Highest ... 102

PARENTS
Sunrise to Freedom ... 144
Can I See Another's Woe? ... 181
Boldly Live, My Daughter ... 217
Turn Around ... 289

PASSIONTIDE
O Sacred Head, Now Wounded ... 103
Beneath the Shadow of the Cross ... 104
Now in the Tomb is Laid ... 105

PATIENCE
The Tides of the Spirit ... 28
We Move in Faith ... 39
The Brave of Old ... 106
God Bless the Grass ... 253

PEACE BETWEEN NATIONS
Joy to the World ... 96
O'er Continent and Ocean ... 119
To Worship Rightly ... 191
The Healing of the Nations ... 198
A World Transfigured ... 209
Hush the Sounds of War ... 222
The Vision of a World Set Free ... 223
A Glad, Resplendent Day ... 224
Child of Hiroshima ... 225
Song of Peace ... 226
Sing Your Country's Anthem ... 227
Till Greed and Hate Cease ... 228
Closing Verses ... 308, 314
Shalom Havayreem ... 317

PEACE WITHIN
Calm Soul of All Things ... 53
Dear Lord and Father ... 101
The People's Peace ... 219
Tranquillity ... 252
Autumn Ways ... 277
All Praise to Thee this Night ... 285
Vesper Hymn ... 286
Our Parting Hymn of Praise ... 304
Shalom Havayreem ... 317

PERSONAL COMMITMENT
Personal Commitment ... *150-170*

TOPICAL INDEX

PIONEERS —
see PROPHETS AND PIONEERS

PLAY
Midwinter 278

PLOUGHING
Waiting for the Plough 261
Harvest Prayer 270

PRAISE
Worship and Celebration 1-32
The Old Hundredth 64
Praise the Great and Famous 68
Praise to the Living God 69
O Worship the King 70
Praise to the Lord, the Almighty 71
My God and King 72
Praise, My Soul 116
The God of Galaxies 231
The Hymn of St. Francis 241
All Things Bright and Beautiful 243
Morning has Broken 280
Awake, My Soul 283
Closing Verses 309, 313

PRAYER
Transforming Grace 24
Where'er Thy People Meet 25
Spirit Divine! Attend our Prayer 26
To Cloisters of the Spirit 27
Kum ba Yah 32
Work Shall Be Prayer 47
The Reflective Spirit 33-63
To Mercy, Pity, Peace and Love 190

PROGRESS
Song of Thanksgiving 17
Inward Peace and Inward Living 51
We are the Earth 74
The Larger View 126
Our Kindred Fellowships 136
Unrest 145
The Goal 170
A Better World 193-230
Closing Verse 311
See also EVOLUTION

PROPHETS AND PIONEERS
Song of Thanksgiving 17
The Depths of Inner Space 40
God of Ages and of Nations 75
Honourable Saints 78
Hosanna in the Highest 102
The Brave of Old 106

Flame of Living Fire 113
O'er Continent and Ocean 119
Life of Ages, Richly Poured 120
All Earth's Children 131
Sing in Celebration 135
O Help the Prophet to be Bold 138
Walk in the Light 149
Forward Through the Ages 208
Darkness Put to Flight 281
Heroes 296

PROVIDENCE
My God, I Thank Thee 20
God Moves in a Mysterious Way 62
The Lord's My Shepherd 66
O Worship the King 70
The Presence Everywhere 100
We Plough the Fields 269
Harvest Prayer 270
Harvest Home 272

PURIFICATION
Release from Bitter Things 221

QUAKERS
Walk in the Light 149

QUIET
To Cloisters of the Spirit 27
The Reflective Spirit 33-63
Dear Lord and Father 101
Tranquillity 252
Autumn Ways 277
All Praise to Thee this Night 285
Vesper Hymn 286

RACIAL EQUALITY
Where is our Holy Church? 123
One Human Commonwealth 125
Black and White 215

REASON — *see* THOUGHT

REFLECTIVE SPIRIT
The Reflective Spirit 33-63

RELIGION
True Religion 189
See also COMPARATIVE RELIGION

REMEMBRANCE DAY —
see ARMISTICE

RENEWAL
Life that Maketh All Things New 8
So Simple is the Human Heart 9

We are Met to Worship Thee... 23
Spirit Divine! Attend Our Prayer... 26
The Flow of Life... 31
Come, My Life... 44
Breath of God... 46
From All the Fret and Fever... 48
Not Always on the Mount... 50
Life's Rebirth... 109
The Holy Spirit... 112
Joyful, Joyful, We Adore Thee... 117
How Can I Keep from Singing!... 133
True Simplicity... 146
Those Who Seek Wisdom... 163
Human Kindness... 187
Now is the Time... 248
Earth Awakes Again... 263
Life's Yearly Triumph... 265
The Awakening Season... 266
Morning Has Broken... 280
Sunrise is Born... 282
Awake, My Soul... 283
Transcience... 295

REPENTANCE —
see WRONG AND REPENTANCE

RESTORATION
Stranger on the Mountain... 207
Reverence for Life... 250

REVELATION
"Where is Your God?"... 34
God Moves in a Mysterious Way... 62
Praise to the Living God!... 69
God of Ages and of Nations... 75
Let There be Light... 114
It Sounds Along the Ages... 129
The World Stands Out... 141
We Limit Not the Truth of God... 195
The Spacious Firmament... 232
Others Call it God... 233
A Melody of Love... 235
Thy Purpose Crowning All... 236
Seek Not Afar for Beauty... 237
Source of All... 238
Chinese Morning Hymn... 279
Sunrise is Born... 282

REVERENCE FOR LIFE
The Miracle... 148
Stranger on the Mountain... 207
A World of Wonder... 247
Life's Great Gifts... 249
Reverence for Life... 250
God Bless the Grass... 253
Closing Verse... 312

RIGHTS — see HUMAN RIGHTS and
WOMEN'S RIGHTS AND AWARENESS

SCHOOL
Black and White... 215

SCIENCE — see KNOWLEDGE

SEARCH FOR TRUTH
The Living God... 35
Star Born... 36
Thy Kingdom Come... 37
We Move in Faith... 39
The Depths of Inner Space... 40
I Cannot Lose Thee!... 41
A Dream of Widening Love... 42
Divinity is Round Us... 52
Where is Our Holy Church?... 123
The Larger View... 126
Our Kindred Fellowships... 136
The Star of Truth... 162
What Purpose Burns... 194

SEASONS
O God of Stars and Sunlight... 234
Morning on Morning... 251
The Seasons... 257-278

SEASONS OF HUMAN LIFE
Seasons of Human Life... 289-301

SELF CONTROL
Free from the World's Cares... 147
The Golden Rule... 157

SELF KNOWLEDGE —
see UNDERSTANDING

SENSES AND FEELINGS
Joy of Living... 3
The Beauty of the Earth... 14
Leisure... 49
It is Something to Have Been... 160
Boldly Live, My Daughter... 217
Others Call it God... 233
O God of Stars and Sunlight... 234
All Things Bright and Beautiful... 243
A World of Wonder... 247
Now is the Time... 248
Let us Wander Where we Will... 254
This Land is Your Land... 255
Moods of Summer... 268
Not by Bread Alone... 273
Autumn Ways... 277

SERENITY —
see PEACE WITHIN and QUIET

TOPICAL INDEX

SERVICE OF OTHERS
Lord of the Wondrous Earth ... 1
For All that is Our Life ... 15
Scorn Not the Slightest Word ... 55
Praise the Great and Famous ... 68
When Jesus Walked ... 99
The Brave of Old ... 106
I Would Be True ... 154
Inasmuch ... 165
True Freedom ... 167
The Voice of God ... 169
Can I See Another's Woe? ... 181
With Your Neighbour Share ... 183
The Power of Love ... 185
To Worship Rightly ... 191
See also SOCIAL IDEALISM

SEX EQUALITY
Bread and Roses ... 216
Liberation ... 218
A Glad Resplendent Day ... 224

SHARING
True Freedom ... 167
Let Us Break Bread Together ... 175
Come Together in Love ... 176
We Can Become ... 177
With Your Neighbour Share ... 183
The Best Things ... 184
The Law of Love ... 186
Bread and Roses ... 216
Goodnight Hymn ... 284
No More Alone ... 294

SIMPLICITY
So Simple is the Human Heart ... 9
Leisure ... 49
When Jesus Walked ... 99
True Simplicity ... 146
Free from the World's Cares ... 147
A Shelter From the Vast ... 178
A Noble Life ... 179
The People's Peace ... 219
Seek Not Afar for Beauty ... 237
Glad That I Live Am I ... 244
All These Things Belong to Me ... 245
Here and Now ... 293
Now I Recall my Childhood ... 299

SIN
Human Kindness ... 187
Stranger on the Mountain ... 207
Release from Bitter Things ... 221

SISTERHOOD AND BROTHERHOOD —
see FELLOWSHIP

SOCIAL CONSCIENCE
We Will Speak Out! ... 159
Inasmuch ... 165
True Freedom ... 167
The Moment to Decide ... 168
All Are Our Neighbours ... 182
The Power of Love ... 185
Jerusalem ... 210
Child of Hiroshima ... 225

SOCIAL IDEALISM
Sons and Daughters ... 6
To Cloisters of the Spirit ... 27
City of God ... 121
Where is our Holy Church? ... 123
One Human Commonwealth ... 125
Freedom is the Finest Gold ... 142
We Must Be True ... 153
The Moment to Decide ... 168
The Fellowship of the Church ... 173
A Church is a Living Fellowship ... 174
Let Us Break Bread Together ... 175
True Religion ... 189
The Healing of the Nations ... 198
Tomorrow is a Highway ... 201
Bread and Roses ... 216
Liberation ... 218
Ring Out, Ring In ... 257
See also SERVICE OF OTHERS

SONS AND DAUGHTERS —
See DAUGHTERS AND SONS

SORROW —
see SUFFERING AND SORROW

SOUL
Not By Bread Alone ... 273
See also SPIRIT WITHIN

SPACE (OUTER AND INNER)
Brief Our Days ... 2
Star Born ... 36
The Depths of Inner Space ... 40
Children of the Universe ... 132
The God of Galaxies ... 231
A World of Wonder ... 247
I Held the Planets in My Hand ... 256

SPIRITUAL GROWTH
We Move in Faith ... 39
Come Down, O Love Divine ... 45
Breath of God ... 46
Divinity is Round Us ... 52
Holy Spirit, Truth Divine ... 63
The Miracle ... 148

TOPICAL INDEX

We Limit Not the Truth of God ... 195
The Golden City ... 212
Living and Dying ... 298
Closing Verse ... 311

SPIRIT WITHIN, THE
Source of Life ... 4
God Within ... 29
Do You Hear? ... 33
"Where is Your God?" ... 34
Thy Kingdom Come ... 37
The Depths of Inner Space ... 40
I Cannot Lose Thee! ... 41
A Dream of Widening Love ... 42
Come Down, O Love Divine ... 45
From All the Fret and Fever ... 48
Divinity is Round Us ... 52
My Spirit Longs for Thee ... 61
Holy Spirit, Truth Divine ... 63
Through Human Means ... 110
Tranquillity ... 252

SPRING
Now is the Time ... 248
Morning on Morning ... 251
God Bless the Grass ... 253
The Seasons: Spring ... 262-267
Early in Life's Morning ... 291

STRUGGLE — see DIFFICULTY

SUFFERING AND SORROW
Kum ba Yah ... 32
Every Night and Every Morn ... 54
Trust in Life ... 60
The Son of Man ... 98
The Brave of Old ... 106
It is Something to Have Been ... 160
Inasmuch ... 165
True Freedom ... 167
The Voice of God ... 169
Can I See Another's Woe? ... 181
All Are Our Neighbours ... 182
The Power of Love ... 185
To Mercy, Pity, Peace and Love ... 190
Child of Hiroshima ... 225
No More Alone ... 294
Transcience ... 295
Living and Dying ... 298
Abide With Me ... 301

SUMMER
Moods of Summer ... 268

TAOISM —
    see COMPARATIVE RELIGION

THANKSGIVING
Worship and Celebration ... *1-32*
For the Strength of the Hills ... 242
All These Things Belong to Me ... 245
We Plough the Fields ... 269
Harvest Prayer ... 270
Give Thanks ... 271
Harvest Home ... 272
    See also PRAISE

THOUGHT
Praise From All the Human Race ... 16
A Dream of Widening Love ... 42
God of Ages and of Nations ... 75
Die Gedanken Sind Frei ... 143
The Spacious Firmament ... 232

TIME AND ETERNITY
So Simple is the Human Heart ... 9
O God Our Help in Ages Past ... 65
Praise to the Living God ... 69
Life of Ages, Richly Poured ... 120
In Braver Mould ... 205
All are Architects of Fate ... 211
Now is the Time ... 248
The Eternal Now ... 259
Abide With Me ... 301

TOGETHERNESS
We Gather Together ... 18
We Must Be True ... 153
What Love Can Do ... 171
Let Us Break Bread Together ... 175
Come Together in Love ... 176
We Can Become ... 177
We Shall Overcome ... 204
Black and White ... 215
Morning, So Fair to See ... 246

TOLERANCE
The Living God ... 35
The Love of God is Broader ... 140
Freedom is the Finest Gold ... 142
Let Love Continue Long ... 188
Our Nation ... 214
Black and White ... 215
    See also COMPARATIVE RELIGION

TRANSCIENCE
Brief Our Days ... 2
O God Our Help in Ages Past ... 65
Morning on Morning ... 251
Transcience ... 295
Abide With Me ... 301

TOPICAL INDEX

TRINITY
Let There be Light 114

TRUST
Kum ba Yah 32
Trust in Life 60
God Moves in a Mysterious Way ... 62
O God Our Help in Ages Past 65
The Lord's My Shepherd 66
Be Thou My Vision 151
Guard us Night and Day 288
See also FAITH

TRUTH
The Golden Heresy of Truth 139
Be True, Live Truly 155
The Harvest of Truth 156
We Will Speak Out! 159
The Moment to Decide 168
A City Which is Ours 213
God Bless the Grass 253
Closing Verse 316

UNDERSTANDING
A Dream of Widening Love 42
Every Night and Every Morn 54
The Golden Rule 157
What Love Can Do 171
Come Together in Love 176
A New Community 192
Our Nation 214

UNITARIANISM
Our Parents' Faith 77
Honourable Saints 78

UNIVERSALISM
World-Wide Heritage 119-132
We Limit Not the Truth of God ... 195
When a Deed is Done for Freedom ... 199
Children of a Bright Tomorrow 202
These Things Shall Be! 203
A World Transfigured 209
The Vision of a World Set Free ... 223
Till Greed and Hate Cease 228
One World This 229
Earth Shall Be Fair 230

UNIVERSAL SPIRIT
Source of Life 4
Source of All Being 7
God of Life 22
We Are Met to Worship Thee 23
Immortal Love, for Ever Full 30
Universal Spirit 43

Divinity is Round Us 52
Praise to the Living God! 69
Immortal, Invisible 76
Life of Ages, Richly Poured 120
Till Greed and Hate Cease 228
The Spacious Firmament 232

UNREST
Inward Peace and Inward Living ... 51
My Spirit Longs for Thee 61
Dear Lord and Father 101
Unrest 145
It is Something to Have Been 160

VISION
Lord of the Wondrous Earth 1
Not Always on the Mount 50
Sing in Celebration 135
The Golden Heresy of Truth 139
The World Stands Out 141
Sunrise to Freedom 144
Be Thou My Vision 151
Those Who Seek Wisdom 163
The Goal 170
What Purpose Burns 194
Jerusalem 210
Earth Shall be Fair 230

WHITSUN
Spirit Divine! Attend Our Prayer ... 26
Come, My Life 44
Come Down, O Love Divine 45
Breath of God 46
My Spirit Longs for Thee 61
Holy Spirit, Truth Divine 63
The Judaeo-Christian Heritage:
        Whitsuntide 111-114
Past, Present, Future 124

WINTER
'Tis Winter Now 260
Midwinter 278

WISDOM
Hymn to Perfect Wisdom 11
From All the Fret and Fever 48
In Praise of Wisdom 67
Wisdom and Courage 193
Facing Death 297

WOMEN'S RIGHTS AND AWARENESS
Bread and Roses 216
Boldly Live, My Daughter 217
Liberation 218
A Glad, Resplendent Day 224

TOPICAL INDEX

WONDER
Source of Life.................................. 4
So Simple is the Human Heart............9
The Beauty of the Earth.................. 14
Star Born.. 36
Those Who Seek Wisdom............. 163
A World of Wonder........................247
Now is the Time............................248
Tranquillity................................... 252
Now I Recall my Childhood...........299

WONDERFUL WORLD
Brief Our Days..................................2
So Simple is the Human Heart............9
The Beauty of the Earth.................. 14
Wonder... 38
Song of Peace................................226
The Natural World..................231-256
Look at the Hillside........................275

WORK AND WORKERS
For All that is Our Life..................... 15
Song of Thanksgiving...................... 17
Work Shall be Prayer...................... 47
Teach me, My God and King............57
Praise the Great and Famous........... 68
The Brave of Old............................106
Let us Break Bread Together......... 175
Courage Shall Conquer.................. 200
All are Architects of Fate................211
The Golden City.............................212

Bread and Roses............................216
Waiting for the Plough................... 261
Harvest Prayer...............................270
Give Thanks..................................271

WORLD-WIDE HERITAGE
World-Wide Heritage..............119-132

WORSHIP
Worship and Celebration.............. 1-32
The Old Hundredth.......................... 64
We Are the Earth.............................74
How Can I Keep from Singing!.......133
To Worship Rightly........................191
The Hymn of St. Francis.................241

WRONG AND REPENTANCE
Inasmuch.......................................165
The Voice of God........................... 169
The Power of Love.........................185
Human Kindness............................ 187
Wisdom and Courage.....................193
The Choice is Ours........................206
Release from Bitter Things............221
Child of Hiroshima........................225
Earth Shall be Fair........................230

YOUTH
Lord of the Wondrous Earth............. 1
Sons and Daughters.......................... 6
Boldly Live, My Daughter.............. 217
Early in Life's Morning..................291

Alphabetical Index of Tunes

Abbot's Leigh	286	Caithness	58
Aberystwyth	167	Calon Lân	268
Abridge	36	Campian II	105
Adam's Song	4	Capel	259
Addison's London	131	Carlisle	46
Adeste fideles	95	Carol	83
Agincourt (Deo gracias)	162	Charity	111
Alcuin	178	Childhood	235
All for Jesus	11	Christus der ist mein Leben	27
Alstone	141	Church Triumphant	94
Amazing Grace	177	Come labour on	252
An die Freude	199	Come together	176
Angel's Song (Song 34)	194	Consolation	277
Angelus	170	Coolinge	48
Antioch	96	Corinth (Tantum ergo)	298
Ar hyd y nos	288	Cranham	87
Aurelia	233	Crimond	66
Austria	75	Cromer	184
		Cross of Christ	165
Barnfield	245	Cross of Jesus	202
Battle Hymn	224	Crüger	42, 102
Beatitudo	60	Cuttle Mills	183
Beethoven	117	Cwm Rhondda	198
Belmont	179		
Besançon Carol	82		
Bethany	166	Danby	130
Birmingham	196	Daniel	53
Bishopthorpe	30	Darmstadt	34
Bythinia—see Corinth		Dawn (Watchman)	282
Black and White	215	Deerhurst	250
Blaenwern	209	Deo gracias (Agincourt)	162
Branle de l'Official	93	Deus tuorum militum	257
Bread and Roses	216	Die Gedanken sind frei	143
Break bread together	175	Dix	284
Bremen	234	Dominica	123
Breslau	128	Dominus regit me	77
Bristol	138	Donne secours	41
Brother James's Air	249	Down Ampney	45
Buckden	29	Drake's Boughton	100
Buckland	63	Duke Street	37
Bunessan	275, 280	Dundee	213

xxxiii

ALPHABETICAL INDEX OF TUNES

Easter Alleluia (Lasst uns Erfreuen)	241
Easter Hymn	108
Ebenezer	168
Ein' feste Burg	73, 74
Eintracht	239
Ellacombe	195
Ellers	304, 305, 306
England's Lane	14
Engelberg	80
Epiphany Hymn	200
Epsom	190
Erfyniad	38
Evelyns	78
Eventide	301
Ewing	267
Far off Lands	129
Finlandia	226
Firmament	232
Forest Green	85
Foundation	33
Freshwater	300
Galilee	124
Gauntlett	28
Gerontius	125
Glenfinlas	240
God be in my head	307
God bless the grass	253
Golden Wheat	9
Gonfalon Royal	98
Gosterwood	236
Gott will's machen	273
Gragareth	164
Greenside	217
Guter Hirte	110
Gwalchmai	21
Hanover	70
Heaton	218
Herongate	155, 225
Holywell	227
Horsley	55
Hyfrydol	212
Innocents	254
Intercessor	185
Irish	222
Jerusalem	210
Keith	160
Kesteven	157
Kingsfold	99
Kremser	17, 18
Kum ba yah	32
Kremser	17, 18
Krisztus Urunk	262
Kum ba yah	32
Lancaster	174
Lasst uns erfreuen (Easter Alleluia)	241
Laudate Dominum (Parry)	247
Laus Deo (Redhead No. 46)	214
Lawnswood	86
Leoni	69
Le P'ing	279
Les Commandemens de Dieu	197
Leytonen	220
Limpsfield	237, 299
Little Cornard	1
Llanfair	263
Llangloffan	119
Llef	67
Lobe den Herren	71
London (Addison's)	131
Londonderry Air	191
London New	62
Loth to depart	31
Love Divine	118
Love Unknown	188
Lowbury	276
Lübeck	211
Lucerna Laudoniae	264
Luckington	72
Lux Eoi	187
Mainzer	25
Manchester College	52
Marching	59
Martyrdom	294
Maryton	136

ALPHABETICAL INDEX OF TUNES

xxxv

Máti Sveta	43
Meirionydd	223
Melcombe	50
Melita	109
Mendelssohn	90
Mendip	293
Merthyr Tydfil	206
Missionary	169
Mit Freuden zart	134
Monkland	24
Monks Gate	150
Morning Hymn	283
Morning Light	265
Moscow	114
Mossdale	39
Mountain Alone	207
Mountain Christian	242
Nativity	89
Niagara	182
Nicaea	135
Noel	91
Norber	248
Northbrook	56
Nos Galan	278
Nun danket	19
Nun danket all	148
O filii et filiae	6
Old 100th	64, 308, 309
Old 120th	15
Old 124th	230
Ombersley	7
O Perfect Love	192, 295, 296
Orientis partibus	158
Orkney	225
O Waly, Waly	189
Passion Chorale	103
Pen-lan	137, 316
Petersham	173
Posen	44
Praise, my soul	116
Princethorpe	171
Puer nobis nascitur	260

Redhead No. 46 (Laus Deo)	214
Repton	101
Restoration	180
Rhuddlan	221
Richmond	121
Riddings	231
Rimington	156
Rockingham	292
Rodmell	5
Royal Oak	243
Russia	163
Ruth	291
St. Agnes	219
St. Agnes, Durham	26
St. Anne	65
St. Bavon	16
St. Bees	181
St. Catherine	205
St. Cecilia	61
St. Clement	287
St. Columba	68
St. Denio	76
St. Fulbert	186
St. George, Windsor	272
St. Gertrude	208
St. Magnus	112
St. Matthew	302, 303
St. Oswald	140
St. Patrick	152
St. Peter	122
St. Philip	142
St. Saviour	104
St. Stephen	115
St. Theodulph	3
Saltzburg	22
Salvation	145
Sandys	57
Sarie Marais	290
Schmücke dich	229
Schönster Herr Jesu	246
Seabeck	256
Shaker Song	146
Shalom havayreem	317
Sharon	40

ALPHABETICAL INDEX OF TUNES

Sheringham	274
Shipston	270
Simeon	203
Sine Nomine	79
Singing	133
Slane	151
Solothurn	97
Song 1	13
Song 24	12
Song 34 (Angel's Song)	194
Spanish Hymn	132
Stabat Mater	23
Star of the County Down	228
Stenka Razin	126
Stille Nacht	88
Stowey	271
Stracathro	47
Stransgill	49
Streets of Laredo	251
Strength and Stay	154
Stuttgart	51
Surrey	297
Sursum Corda	161
Sussex	261
Tallis' Canon	285, 313, 314, 315
Tallis' Ordinal	159
Tantum ergo (Corinth)	298
Tempus adest floridum	266
The Call	54
The First Nowell	92
The truth from above	10
This land is your land	255
Thornbury	281
Tomorrow is a highway	201
Triumph	193
Truro	113
Turn around	289
University	258
University College	120
Victory	106
Vienna	35
Vom Himmel hoch	139
Vulpius	107
Wachet auf	81
Walk in the light	149
Wareham	147
Warrington	238
Watchman (Dawn)	282
Water End	244
Wentworth	20
Werde Munter, mein Gemüte	2
We shall overcome	204
Westminster	172
Winchester New	8, 310, 311, 312
Winchester Old	84
Wir pflügen	269
Wolvercote	144
Woodlands	127
Wynnstay	153

Metrical Index of Tunes

S.M.

Carlisle	46
Dominica	123
Sandys	57

C.M.

Abridge	36
Amazing Grace	177
Beatitudo	60
Belmont	179
Bishopthorpe	30
Bristol	138
Caithness	58
Capel	259
Consolation	277
Crimond	66
Dundee	213
Epsom	190
Gerontius	125
Horsley	55
Irish	222
Kesteven	157
London New	62
Martyrdom	294
Mendip	293
Nativity	89
Nun danket all	148
Richmond	121
Rodmell	5
St. Agnes, Durham	26
St. Anne	65
St. Fulbert	186
St. Magnus	112
St. Peter	122
St. Saviour	104
St. Stephen	115
Stracathro	47
Tallis' Ordinal	159
University	258
Westminster	172
Winchester Old	84

C.M. with repeats

Antioch	96

C.M.D.

Carol	83
Cross of Christ	165
Ellacombe	195
Forest Green	85
Kingsfold	99
Noel	91
Petersham	173
St. Matthew	302, 303
Salvation	145
Sarie Marais	290
Star of the County Down	228

L.M.

Alstone	141
Agincourt (Deo gracias)	162
Angel's Song (Song 34)	194
Angelus	170
Breslau	128
Church Triumphant	94
Cromer	184
Danby	130
Daniel	53
Deo Gracias (Agincourt)	162
Deus tuorum militum	257
Duke Street	37
Galilee	124
Gonfalon Royal	98
Herongate	155, 225
Llef	67
Loth to depart	31
Mainzer	25
Maryton	136
Melcombe	50
Morning Hymn	283
Niagara	182
Old 100th	64, 308, 309
Ombersley	7

xxxviii METRICAL INDEX OF TUNES

Orkney.................................225
O Waly, Waly.......................189
Puer nobis nascitur................260
Rimington............................156
Rockingham.........................292
Seabeck...............................256
Simeon.................................203
Solothurn............................. 97
Song 34 (Angel's Song)..........194
Stransgill............................. 49
Tallis' Canon............ 285, 313, 314, 315
The truth from above............. 10
Truro................................... 113
Vom Himmel hoch................ 139
Wareham.............................. 147
Warrington........................... 238
Winchester New......... 8, 310, 311, 312

L.M. with Alleluias

Lasst uns Erfreuen (Easter Alleluia)...241

L.M.D.

Alcuin.................................178
Firmament............................232
Golden Wheat...................... 9
Jerusalem.............................210
London (Addison's)...............131
Merthyr Tydfil......................206
Mossdale.............................. 39
St. Patrick............................152

4 4. 3. T.

Máti Sveta............................ 43

4. 10 10 10. 4

Come labour on....................252

5 5. 5 4. D.

Bunessan.....................275, 280

5 5. 5 5. D.

Le P'ing...............................279

5 5. 5 5. 6 5. 6 5.

Laudate Dominum (Parry).........247

5 5 7. 9 7.

We shall overcome................204

6 4. 6 4. 6 6. 6 4.

Watchman (Dawn).................282

6 5. 6 5.

Glenfinlas............................240

6 5. 6 5. Irregular.

Water End...........................244

6 5. 6 5. D.

Cranham.............................. 87
Evelyns............................... 78
Lawnswood......................... 86
Princethorpe........................171
Ruth...................................291

6 5. 6 5. T.

St. Gertrude........................208

6 5. 6 5. 6 6 6. 5.

Monks Gate.........................150

6 6 4. 6 6 6 4.

Moscow..............................114

6 6. 6 6.

Campian II..........................105
St. Cecilia........................... 61

6 6. 6 6. 6 6.

Old 120th............................ 15

6 6. 6 6. D. Anapaestic

Lowbury............................. 276

METRICAL INDEX OF TUNES

xxxix

6 6. 6 6. 8 8.
Love Unknown 188

6 6. 6 6. 8 8. Dactylic
Little Cornard 1

6 6. 7 7 5.
Stille Nacht 88

6 6. 8 4. D.
Leoni 69

6 6 9. 6 6 8.
Schönster Herr Jesu 246

6 6 11. D.
Down Ampney 45

6 7. 6 7. 6 6. 6 6.
Darmstadt 34
Nun danket 19

7 4. 7 4. D.
Gwalchmai 21

7 5. 7 5. D.
Eintracht 239

7 6. 7 6.
Christus der ist mein Leben 27

7 6. 7 6. with Refrain
Royal Oak 243

7 6. 7 6. D. Iambic
Aurelia 233
Bremen 234
Crüger 42, 102
Ewing 267
Far off Lands 129
Gosterwood 236
Missionary 169
Morning Light 265
Pen-lan 137, 316
Passion Chorale 103
St. Theodulph 3
Thornbury 281
Wolvercote 144

7 6. 7 6. D. Trochaic.
Tempus adest floridum 266

7 6. 7 6. D. Irregular.
Mountain Christian 242

7 6. 7 6. D. 6 6. 8 4.
Wir pflügen 269

7 6. 7 6. 7 7. 7 8. Irregular
Bread and Roses 216

7 6. 8 6. D.
Llangloffan 119
Meirionydd 223

7 7 6.
St. Philip 142

7 7 7. 5.
Charity 111

7 7. 7 7.
Buckland 63
Innocents 254
Lübeck 211
Monkland 24
Orientis partibus 158
Posen 44
St. Bees 181
The Call 54
University College 120
Vienna 35

METRICAL INDEX OF TUNES

7 7. 7 7. with Alleluias
Easter Hymn ... 108
Llanfair ... 263

7 7. 7 7. 7 7.
Dix ... 284
England's Lane ... 14
Lucerna Laudoniae ... 264

7 7. 7 7. D.
Aberystwyth ... 167
St. George, Windsor ... 272
Salzburg ... 22
Spanish Hymn ... 132

7 7. 7 7. D. with Refrain.
Mendelssohn ... 90

7 7. 7 7. 10 10.
Branle de l'Official ... 93

7 10. 11 7.
Greenside ... 217

8 4. 8 4. 8 4.
Wentworth ... 20

8 4. 8 4. 8 8 8 4.
Ar hyd y nos ... 288
Wynnstay ... 153

8 5. 8 3.
Cuttle Mills ... 183

8 6. 8 6. 8 6.
Brother James's Air ... 249

8 6. 8 8 6.
Repton ... 101

8 7. 8 7. Iambic
Dominus regit me ... 77
St. Columba ... 68

8 7. 8 7. Trochaic.
All for Jesus ... 11
Cross of Jesus ... 202
Drake's Boughton ... 100
Gott will's machen ... 273
Guter Hirte ... 110
Laus Deo (Redhead No. 46) ... 214
Love Divine ... 118
Marching ... 59
Redhead No. 46 (Laus Deo) ... 214
Restoration ... 180
St. Bavon ... 16
St. Oswald ... 140
Sharon ... 40
Sheringham ... 274
Shipston ... 270
Stuttgart ... 51
Sussex ... 261

8 7. 8 7. 6 6. 6 6 7.
Ein' feste Burg ... 73

8 7. 8 7. 8 7.
Cwm Rhondda ... 198
Praise, my soul ... 116
Rhuddlan ... 221
Triumph ... 193

8 7. 8 7. D. Iambic
Singing ... 133

8 7. 8 7. D. Trochaic.
Abbot's Leigh ... 286
An die Freude ... 199
Austria ... 75
Beethoven ... 117
Bethany ... 166
Blaenwern ... 209
Calon Lân ... 268

METRICAL INDEX OF TUNES

Corinth (Tantum ergo) ...298
Deerhurst ...250
Ebenezer ...168
Holywell ...227
Hyfrydol ...212
Lux Eoi ...187
Stenka Razin ...126
Tantum ergo (Corinth) ...298

8 7. 8 7. 8 8 7.
Mit Freuden zart ...134

8 7. 8 7. 8 8. 7 7.
Werde munter mein Gemüte ...2

8 7. 9 8. 8 7.
Besançon Carol ...82

8 8. 7.
Stabat Mater ...23

8 8 8.
Gragareth ...164
Heaton ...218

8 8 8. 4.
Victory ...106
Vulpius (with Alleluias) ...107

8 8 8. 5.
Kum ba yah ...32

8 8 8. 6.
Childhood ...235

8 8. 8 8. 8 8.
Barnfield ...245
Melita ...109
St. Catherine ...205
Surrey ...297

8 8. 8 8. D. Trochaic
Schmücke dich ...229

8 9. 8 7. D.
Mountain Alone ...207

8 9 8. D. 6 6 4. 8 8.
Wachet auf ...81

8 9. 8 9. D.
Nos Galan ...278

9 4. 10 10 10. 4.
O filii et filiae ...6

9 6. 9 6.
Lancaster ...174

9 8. 9 8.
Buckden ...29
Les commandemens de Dieu ...197
St. Clement ...287

10 4. 6 6. 6 6. 10 4.
Luckington ...72

10 4. 10 4.
Manchester College ...52

10 10. 7 8. 9.
Break bread together ...175

10 10 10. 4.
Engelberg ...80
Sine nomine ...79

10 10 10. 8. Irregular
This is your land ...255

10 10. 10 9. 6. Irregular
Tomorrow is a highway ...201

10 10. 10 10. Iambic
Birmingham ...196
Coolinge ...48
Ellers ...304, 305, 306
Erfyniad ...38
Eventide ...301
Limpsfield ...237, 299

METRICAL INDEX OF TUNES

St. Agnes 219
Song 24 12
Sursum Corda 161
Woodlands 127

10 10. 10 10. Dactylic
Slane 151

10 10. 10 10. 10.
Adam's Song 4
Old 124th 230

10 10. 10 10. 10 10.
Norber 248
Song 1 13

10 10. 11 10.
Russia 163

10 10. 11 11.
Gauntlett 28
Hanover 70

10 11. 10 11.
Leytonen 220

11 10. 11 10. Iambic
Donne secours 41
Intercessor 185
Keith 160
Northbrook 56
O Perfect Love 192, 295
Riddings 231
Strength and Stay 154

11 10. 11 10. Dactylic
Epiphany Hymn 200
Streets of Laredo 251

11 10. 11 10. 11 10.
Finlandia 226

11 10. 11 10. D.
Londonderry Air 191

11 11 11. 5.
Krisztus Urunk 262

11 11. 11 11.
Foundation 33
St. Denio 76

11 11. 12 12. Anapaestic
Stowey 271

11 12. 12 10.
Nicaea 135

12 11. 13 12.
Kremser 17, 18

12 12. 12 11.
Die Gedanken sind frei 143

14 14. 4. 7. 8.
Lobe den Herren 71

14 15 15. 7. with Refrain.
Battle Hymn 224

Irregular or P.M.
Adeste fideles 95
Black and White 215
Come together 176
Freshwater 300
God be in my head 307
God bless the grass 253
Shaker Song 146
Shalom Havayreem 317
The First Nowell 92
Turn around 289
Walk in the light 149

Index of Composers, Arrangers and Sources of Tunes

Agincourt Tune (1415) 162
American Gospel Tune 133
American Traditional 180, 224, 251
Angelus, Silesius (Johann Scheffler)
    (1624-77): *Heilige Seelenlust* (1657) 170
Antes, John (1740-1811) 24
Antiphons (Webbe) (1792) 298
Arbeau, Thoinot:
    Orchésographie (1588) 93
Arfon, Gutyn
    (Griffith H. Jones) (1849-1919) 67
Armes, Philip (1836-1908) 124
A Selection of Psalm Tunes,
    (F. Cunningham) (1834) 196
As Hymnodus Sacer,Leipzig (1625) ... 128

Bach, Johann Sebastian (1685-1750)
    2, 3, 22, 27, 34, 81, 103
Bachelder, Evangeline Morris (1920-) 256
Bain, James Leith Macbeth (d. 1925)...249
Baker, Frederick George (1821-77)... 104
Barnby, Joseph (1838-96) 192, 295
Barthélemon, François Hippolyte
    (1741-1808) 283
Beauvais Liturgical Play (13th Cent.)...158
Beethoven, Ludwig van (1770-1827)... 117
Belafonte, Harry 289
Bohemian Bretheren,
    Hemlandssanger (1892) 129
    Kirchengeseng (1566) 134
Bourgeois, Louis (c. 1523-1600)
    64, 197, 308, 309
Boyce, William (1710-79) 40
Breedlove, Leonard P. (d.c. 1879) 165
Broadwood, Evelyn Henry Tschudi
    (1889-1975) 259
Broadwood, Lucy (1858-1929) 99, 259, 270
Buck, Percy Carter (1871-1947) 98
Butler, Douglas L. 176

Caldwell, William (1837) 33
Campian, Thomas (c. 1567-1620) 105
Caniadau y Cyssegr (1839) 76
Capek, Norbert F. (1870-1942) 43

Carawan, Guy 204
Carey, Henry (1692?-1743) 297
Carr, Benjamin (1768-1831) 132
Carter, Sydney 149
Clarke, Henry Leland (1907—) 277
Clarke, Jeremiah (c. 1670-1707)... 30, 112
Croft, William (1678-1727) 65, 70, 302, 303
Crüger, Johann (1598-1662)
    19, 42, 102, 229
Cummings, William H. (1831-1915)... 90
Cunningham, F.,
    A Selection of Psalm Tunes (1834)... 196

Davies, Henry Walford (1869-1941)
    232, 235, 307
Davisson, Ananias:
    Kentucky Harmony (c. 1815) 145
Dawson, David...... 10, 29, 31, 39, 43, 49
    86, 97, 126, 145, 146, 149, 157, 164, 174
    177, 178, 180, 189, 191, 215, 217, 218
    224, 228, 231, 239, 245, 248, 249, 251
    257, 274, 276, 279
Duckworth, Francis (b. 1862) 156
Dykes, John Bacchus (1823-76)
    26, 60, 77, 109, 125, 135, 140, 154, 181

Elgar, Edward (1857-1934) 100
Elliott, James William (1833-1915)...... 94
Elvey, George Job (1816-93) 272
English Traditional...... 5, 10, 14, 31, 57
    85, 92, 99, 130, 155, 157, 189, 225, 236
    243, 259, 261, 270, 271, 293
Este's *Psalter* (1592) 15, 84
Evans, Daniel:
    Hymnau a Thônau (1865) 119
Evans, David (1874-1948)...... 38, 151, 264
Ewing, Alexander (1830-95) 267

Fallersleben, A. H. Hoffmann von:
    Schlesische Volkslieder (1842) 246
Ferguson, William Harold (1874-1950) 144
Finlay, Kenneth George (1882-1974) 240
Freeman, Andrew 237, 299

xliii

INDEX OF COMPOSERS, etc.

French Carol............................ 82
French Melody........................ 6, 23
Freylinghausen, Johann August
  (1670-1739): *Geistreiches Gesangbuch*
  (1704) ... 44, 211.   (1705)..... 110
Fritsch, Ahasuerus (1629-1701)...........34

Gaelic Melody...................... 275, 280
Gardiner's *Sacred Melodies* (1812)... 179
Gauntlett, Henry John (1805-76)
  28, 120, 186, 193
Geistreiches Gesangbuch(1704)... 44, 211
Geistreiches Gesangbuch (1705)...... 110
Genevan Psalter (1543).................. 197
Genevan Psalter (1551)............... 41, 230
German Traditional................ 143, 199
Gesangbuch (Schumann) (1539)...... 139
Giardini, Felice (1716-96)..............114
Gibbons, Orlando (1583-1625) 12, 13, 194
Gladstone, William Henry (1840-91)......7
Glandŵr (John Hughes) (1872-1914)... 268
Goss, John (1800-80).................... 116
Grant, David............................. 66
Greatorex, Walter (1877-1949)......... 127
Greene, Alan............................ 289
Grenoble Church Melody (1868)...... 257
Griffith, William (1867-1929).......... 183
Grover, Dorothy........................176
Grüber, Franz (1787-1863)..............88
Guthrie, Woody........................ 255
Gwyllt, Ieuan (1859).................... 38

Harrison, Ralph (1748-1810)............238
Harwood, Basil (1859-1949)...... 72, 281
Hassler, Hans Leo (1564-1612)........ 103
Hatton, John (d. 1793).................. 37
Haweis, Thomas (1734-1820)........... 121
Haydn, Franz Josef (1732-1809)......... 75
Hayne, Leighton George (1836-83) 61, 63
Hebrew Melody.................... 69, 317
Heilige Seelenlust (Scheffler) (1657)...170
Hémy, Henri F. (1818-88)............. 205
Henllan (John Roberts) (1839)......... 76
Hille, Waldemar (1908—)............6, 207
Hintze, Jacob (1622-1702).............. 22

Holst, Gustav Theodore (1874-1934)... 87
Hopkins, Edward John (1818-1901)
  304, 305, 306
Horsley, William (1774-1858)............55
Hughes, John (1873-1932)............. 198
Hughes, John (Glandŵr) (1872-1914) 268
Hungarian Carol........................262
Hutcheson, Charles (1792-1860).........47
Hu Te-Ai (b. ca. 1900)................. 279
Hymnau a Thônau (1865)..............119
Hymns and Sacred Poems,
  Dublin (1749)........................ 222

Ingham, Thomas Herbert (1878-1948) 282
Ireland, John (1879-1962).............. 188
Irish Melody ... 53, 68, 151, 152, 191, 228
Irvine, Jessie Seymour (1836-87)....... 66

Jackson, Robert (1842-1914)............182
Jagger, A.T.I. (b. 1911)..................16
Jenkins, David (1848-1915)...... 137, 316
Jewish Traditional................. 69, 317
Jones, Griffith H.
  (Gutyn Arfon) (1849-1919)........... 67
Jones, Joseph David (1827-70)......... 21
Jones, Trevor Howarth (1932—)...... 175
Jones, William (1726-1800)............ 115

Kentucky Harmony
  (Davisson) (c. 1815)................. 145
Knapp, William (1698-1768)............147
Knecht, Justin Heinrich (1752-1817)   35
Knight, Sydney Henry (1923—)...... 276
Kocher, Conrad (1786-1872)............284
Kohlsaat, Caroline..................... 216
Kölner Gesangbuch(1623)............ 241
Kremser, Edward (1838-1914)...... 17, 18

Lahee, Henry (1826-1912).............. 89
Langran, James (1835-1909)...... 219, 250
Latin Carol (15th Cent.)............... 260
Ley, Henry George (1887-1962)...... 107
Lloyd, John Ambrose (1815-74)... 153, 184
Lloyd, William (1786-1852)............ 223
Llyfr Tonau Cynulleidfaol (1859).........38

INDEX OF COMPOSERS, etc.

Lockhart, Charles (1745-1815) 46
Luther, Martin (1483-1546) 73, 74
Lvov, Alexis Feodorovitch (1799-1871) 163
Lyra Davidica (1708) 108

Mainzer, Joseph (1801-51) 25
Mainz Gesangbuch (1833) 195
Maker, Frederick Charles (1844-1927)...20
Mannin, J. 242
Mason, Lowell (1792-1872) 96, 169
Mathias, Franz Xavier (1871-1939) ... 239
Mendelssohn-Bartholdy, Felix (1809-47)
90, 128
Miller, Edward (1731-1807) 292
Monk, William Henry (1823-89)
42, 78, 102, 106, 142, 301
Morgannwg, Iolo (Edward Williams)
(1747-1826) 9
Musikalisches Handbuch,
Hamburg (1690) 8, 310, 311, 312
Nederlandtsch Gedenckclanck (1626)
17, 18
Negro Spiritual 32
Newtoun, — 62
Nicolai, Philipp (1556-1608) 81

Oakeley, Herbert Stanley (1830-1903) 123
Olivers, Thomas (1725-99) 69

Palestrina, Giovanni Pierluigi da (1525-94)
106
Parish Choir, The (1850) 254
Parry, Charles Hubert Hastings
(1848-1918)... 101, 185, 210, 247, 300
Parry, Joseph (1841-1903) 167, 206
Piae Cantiones (1582) 266
Pitts, William (1829-1903) 171
Playford's *Psalms* (1671) 62
Poole, Clement William (1828-1924)... 173
Potter, Doreen (1925-80) 220
Praetorius, Michael (1571-1621) 260
Praxis Pietatis Melica (1653) 148
Prichard, Rowland Hugh (1811-87)... 212
Psalmodia Evangelica (1789) 113
Psalter (Ravenscroft) (1621) 138

Randall, John (1715-99) 258
Ravenscroft, Thomas (1592-ca.1640):
Psalter (1621) 138
Redhead, Richard (1820-1901) 214
Reinagle, Alexander Robert (1799-1877)
122
Repository of Sacred Music,
Part II (1813) 277
Reynolds, Malvina 253, 289
Roberts, John (Henllan):
Caniadau y Cyssegr (1839) 76
Robinson, Earl (1910—) 215
Rowlands, William Penfro (1860-1937) 209
Russian Traditional 126

Sacred Melodies (Gardiner) (1812)... 179
Sanders, Robert L. (1906-74)...4, 160, 165
Scheffler, Johann (Silesius Angelus)
(1624-77): *Heilige Seelenlust* (1657) 170
Schlesische Volkslieder (Fallersleben)
(1842) 246
Scholefield, Clement Cotterill (1839-1904)
287
Schop, Johann (d.ca. 1665) 2
Schulz, Johann Abraham Peter
(1747-1800) 269
Schumann, Valentin: *Gesangbuch* (1539)
139
Scottish Psalter (1615) 213
Scottish Psalter (1635) 58, 62
Seeger, Pete 201, 204
Shaker Traditional 146
Sharp, Cecil James (1859-1924) 271
Shaw, Geoffrey (1879-1943) 14, 244
Shaw, Martin Fallas (1875-1958)
1, 53, 59, 243, 275, 280
Sheeles, John (ca. 1720) 131
Sibelius, Jean (1865-1957) 226
Smart, Henry (1813-79) 166
Smith, Alfred Morton (b. 1879) 161
Smith, Henry Percy (1825-98) 136
Smith, Isaac (1725-1800) 36
Smith, Robert Archibald (1780-1829) 294
Smith, Samuel (1821-1917) 291
Somerset Folk Song 189

INDEX OF COMPOSERS, etc.

South African Traditional................290
Spicer, Harold William (1888-1977)
    52, 227
Stainer, John (1840-1901)
    11, 82, 92, 111, 118, 202
Stanford, Charles Villiers (1852-1924)...80
Stanley, Samuel (1767-1822)..........203
Steiner, J. L. (1688-1761)..............273
Storey, John Andrew (1935—)..........274
Störl, Johann Georg Christian:
    Würtemberg Gesangbuch (1710)... 234
Stralsund Gesangbuch (1665)............71
Strattner, Georg Christopher (1650-1705)
    44
Sullivan, Arthur Seymour (1842-1900)
    91, 187, 208
Swiss Traditional........................97

Tallis, Thomas (c.1505-85)
    159, 285, 313, 314, 315
Tans'ur, William (1706-83)..............190
Taylor, Cyril Vincent (1907—)......48, 286
Teschner, Melchior (ca.1613)..............3
Thatcher, Reginald Sparshatt
    (1888-1957)..........................56
The Parish Choir (1850)................254
Thrupp, Joseph Francis (1827-67)......200
Traditional...............91, 162, 175, 177
Traditional American   133, 180, 224, 251
Traditional English... 5, 10, 14, 31, 57, 85,
    92, 99, 130, 155, 157, 189, 225, 236, 243,
    259, 261, 270, 271, 293
Traditional French..................23, 82
Traditional Gaelic..................275, 280
Traditional German..............143, 199
Traditional Hebrew..................69, 317
Traditional Irish   53, 68, 151, 152, 191, 228
Traditional Jewish..................69, 317

Traditional Negro Spiritual..............32
Traditional Russian......................126
Traditional Shaker.......................146
Traditional South African................290
Traditional Swiss.........................97
Traditional Welsh......76, 221, 278, 288
Turle, James (1802-82)..................172

Valerius, Adrian (1626)..............17, 18
Vulpius, Melchior (1560-1616)......27, 107

Wade, John Francis (1711-86)..........95
Waters, James............................225
Webb, George James (1803-87)........265
Webbe, Samuel (the elder) (1740-1816) 50
    Antiphons (1792)..................298
Welsh Traditional......76, 221, 278, 288
Wesley, Samuel Sebastian (1810-76)...233
Wilkes, John Bernard (1785-1869)......24
Williams, Edward
    (Iolo Morgannwg) (1747-1826).........9
Williams, Ralph Vaughan (1872-1958)
    5, 45, 54, 79, 85, 99, 130, 150, 155, 225,
    236, 261, 270, 271
Williams, Robert (ca. 1781-1821)......263
Williams, Thomas:
    Psalmodia Evangelica (1789)........113
Williams, Thomas John (1869-1944)... 168
Willing, Christopher Edwin (1830-1904)
    141
Willis, Richard Storrs (1819-1900)......83
Wilson, Hugh (1766-1824)..............294
Witt, Christian Friedrich (1660-1716)... 51
Wood, Charles (1866-1926)..............93
Wrigley, Charles H.......................252
Würtemberg Gesangbuch (Störl) (1710)
    234

Wyeth, John (1770-1858):
    Repository of Sacred Music (1813)...277

Index of Authors, Translators and Sources of Texts

Adams, James Luther ... 16
Addison, Joseph (1672-1719) ... 232
Adler, Felix (1851-1933) ... 212
Akhenaton (ca.1400 B.C.) ... 12
Alexander (née Humphreys), Cecil Frances (1823-95) ... 152, 243
Alexander, James Waddell (1804-59) 103
Alford, Henry (1810-71) ... 272
American Traditional ... 180, 188
Andrews, Jane ... 89
Arkin, David (1934—) ... 207, 215
Arlott, John (1914—) ... 261, 270
Arnold, Matthew (1822-88) ... 53
Author unknown ... 158, 187, 225, 245, 271, 314

Bacon, Josephine Daskam ... 227
Bathurst, William Hiley Bragge (1796-1877) ... 113
Bax, Clifford (1886-1962) ... 230
Beach, Seth Curtis (1837-1932) ... 10, 238
Beardsley, Monroe (1915—) ... 48
Bernard of Clairvaux (1091-1153) ... 103
Bianco da Siena (d. 1434) ... 45
Blake, James Vila (1842-1925) ... 22
Blake, William (1757-1827) 54, 181, 190, 210
Boeke, Richard Frederick (1931—) 43, 163
Bonar, Horatius (1808-89) ... 5, 155, 156
Book of Hours (1514) ... 307
Bortnianski, Dimitri Stepanovitch (1752-1825) ... 245
Box, Howard (1926—) ... 262
Bragge-Bathurst, William Hiley (1796-1877) ... 113
Brooke, Stopford Augustus (1832-1916) 9
Brooks, Phillips (1835-93) ... 85
Browne, Felicia Dorothea (Mrs. Hemans) (1793-1835) ... 242
Buddhist ... 11
Buehrer, Edwin Theophil (1894-1969) ... 17
Bunyan, John (1628-88) ... 150
Byrom, John (1691-1763) ... 61

Campbell, Jane Montgomery (1817-78) 269
Capek, Norbert F. (1870-1942) ... 43
Carruth, William Herbert (1859-1924) 233
Carter, Sydney ... 149
Chadwick, John White (1840-1904) 13, 77, 258
Chao, T. C. (b. 1888) ... 279
Chesterton, Gilbert Keith (1874-1936) 160
Clabburn, Frank R. (1947—) 42, 109, 171, 174
Claudius, Matthias (1740-1815) ... 269
Clough, Arthur Hugh (1819-61) ... 197
Colum, Padraic (1881-1972) ... 105
Confucius (551-479 B.C.) ... 157
Cowper, William (1731-1800) ... 25, 62

Dalai Lama ... 189
Daniel ben Judah (14th Century) ... 69
Daniel, John Irving (1903—) ... 83
Daniell, John J. (1819-98) ... 265
Davies, William Henry (1871-1940) ... 49
Dawson, Albert M. P. (1880-1963) ... 106
Dearmer, Percy (1867-1936) ... 266
Dodgshun, Ernest ... 223
Doren, Mark van ... 231
Draper, William Henry (1855-1933) ... 241
Duclaux, Agnes Mary Frances A. (A. Mary Robinson) (1857-1944) ... 29
Dyke, Henry van (1852-1933) ... 117

Egyptian *Book of the Dead* (ca. 4500 B.C.) ... 302
Eliot, Frederick May (1889-1958) ... 124
Ellerton, John (1826-93) ... 47, 287, 304
Emerson, Ralph Waldo (1803-82) ... 267
Etkin, Anne (1923—) ... 251

Faber, Frederick William (1814-63) ... 140
Fahs, Sophia Lyon (1876-1978) ... 52
Farjeon, Eleanor (1881-1965) ... 82, 280

xlvii

INDEX OF AUTHORS

Findlow, Bruce (1922—)
   15, 28, 31, 51, 185, 213
Foote, Henry Wilder (1875-1964) ... 108
Fosdick, Harry Emerson (1878-1969)...193
Fox, William Johnson (1786-1864) ... 23
Francis of Assisi (1182-1226) ... 241

Galbraith, Peter ... 172, 284
Gannett, William Channing (1840-1923)
   27, 69, 89, 129, 236, 281
Gaskell, William (1805-84) ... 222, 303
Gerhardt, Paulus (1607-76) ... 103
German Folk Song ... 143
Gordon, Elias ... 142
Grant, Robert (1779-1838) ... 70
Grover, Dorothy ... 176
Guggenberger, Louise ... 138
Guthrie, Woody ... 255

Ham, Marion Franklin (1867-1956) ... 136
Hamilton, Frank ... 204
Hatch, Edwin (1835-89) ... 46
Hays, Lee ... 201
Heber, Reginald (1783-1826) ... 288
Hedge, Frederic Henry (1805-90) ... 24, 73
Hemans (née Browne), Felicia Dorothea
 (1793-1835) ... 242
Herbert, George (1593-1632)
   21, 44, 57, 72
Hill, Andrew McKean (1942—) ... 16, 78
Hille, John H. ... 6
Hille, Waldemar (1908—) ... 224, 249
Hincks, Thomas (1818-99) ... 55
Holland, Henry Scott (1847-1918) ... 221
Holmes, John (1904-1962) ... 219, 234
Holmes, John Haynes (1879-1964) 119, 169
Holmes, Oliver Wendell (1809-94) ... 7
Horton, Zilphia ... 204
Hosmer, Frederick Lucian (1840-1929)
   50, 208, 277
Housman, Laurence (1865-1959) ... 296
How, William Walsham (1823-97) ... 79
Hull, Eleanor Henrietta (1860-1935) ... 151
Hyde, William De Witt (1858-1917) ... 170

Ide, Beth (1921—) ... 124, 170
Isaacs, A. S. ... 179

Jenkins, Willaim Vaughan (1868-1920) 305
Jewish Traditional ... 317
Jewitt, Alfred Charles (1845-1925) ... 107
Johnson, Eleanor Shipp (1863-1947) ... 56
Johnson, Joseph (1849-1926) ... 235
Johnson, Samuel (1822-82) ... 120, 121
Jones, Trevor Howarth (1932—) ... 175
Jones, Walter Royal (1920—) ... 309

Kaan, Fred (1929—) ... 198, 220
Kemp, Harry (1883-1960) ... 239
Ken, Thomas (1637-1711) ... 283, 285
Kethe, William (d. 1593) ... 64
Kevess, Arthur ... 143
Khayyam, Omar (d. 1123) ... 37
Knight, Sydney Henry (1923—)
   60, 196, 247, 252, 268, 294
Kramer, Aaron (1921—) ... 144

Larcom, Lucy (1826-93) ... 184
Lathrop, John Howland (1880-1967) ... 102
Latin (18th Century) ... 95
Littledale, Richard Frederick (1833-90) 45
Longfellow, Henry Wadsworth (1807-82)
   94, 166, 211
Longfellow, Samuel (1819-92) ... 8, 26, 63,
   75, 104, 122, 260, 263, 286, 311
Lowell, James Russell (1819-91)
   159, 167, 168, 199
Luther, Martin (1483-1546) ... 73
Lysaght, Sidney Royse (1856-1941) ... 178
Lyte, Henry Francis (1793-1847) 116, 301
Lyttle, Charles H. (1884-1980) ... 313, 315

McDade, Carolyn ... 217
MacKinnon, John G. (1903-1985) ... 36
Madison, Elizabeth ... 276
Mann, Newton (19th Century) ... 69
Marquis, Don (1878-1937) ... 145
Marriott, John (1780-1825) ... 114
Martineau, James (1805-1900) ... 34

INDEX OF AUTHORS

Matheson, George (1842-1906) ... 127
Midgley, John Andrew (1939—) ... 81
Mikelson, Thomas Jarl (1936—) ... 298
Millay, Edna St.Vincent (1892-1950) ... 141
Mohr, Joseph (1792-1848) ... 88
Montgomery, James (1771-1854) ... 58
Morrison, Linda Carol (1947—) ... 161
Munk, Anita ... 43
Munk, Paul ... 43

Naidu, Sarojini (1879-1949) ... 295
Neander, Joachim (1650-80) ... 71
Negro Spiritual ... 32, 175
Niles, Daniel ... 279
North, Frank Mason (1850-1935) ... 98
Noyes, Alfred (1880-1958) ... 38

Oakeley, Frederick (1802-80) ... 95
Ogden, Althea A. ... 153
Oliver, William E. ... 6, 249
Oppenheim, James (1882-1932) ... 216

Palmer, Robert C. (1911—) ... 137
Patrick, St. (ca.385-ca.461) ... 152
Patton, Kenneth L. (1911—)
   2, 74, 256, 308
Piae Cantiones (1582) ... 266
Pickles, Herbert (1903—) ... 306
Pierpoint, Folliott Sandford (1835-1917) 14
Placzek, Joyce Anstruther
   (Jan Struther) (1901-53) ... 240, 282
Price, Frank W. ... 279
Procter, Adelaide Anne (1825-64) ... 20

Quaker Song ... 133
Quin, Malcolm (1854-1944) ... 39

Rahulabhadra (Mahayana Buddhist) ... 11
Raine, Kathleen (b. 1908) ... 312
Rawson, George (1807-89) ... 195
Reed, Andrew (1787-1862) ... 26
Reed, Clifford Martin (1947—) ... 110
Reese, Lizette Woodworth (1856-1935) 244
Reeve, Wilfrid Edward (1909—) ... 182
Reynolds, Malvina ... 148, 253, 289
Rinckart, Martin (1586-1649) ... 19

Robinson, Agnes Mary Frances
   (Madame Duclaux) (1857-1944) ... 29
Rossetti, Christina Georgina (1830-94) 87
Russell, George William (1867-1935) ... 139

Sandys, W. (fl. 1833) ... 92
Savage, Minot Judson (1841-1918)
   194, 237, 316
Scottish Psalter ... 66
Scudder, Eliza (1821-96) ... 41
Sears, Edmund Hamilton (1810-76) ... 91
Senghas, Dorothy C. (1930—) ... 18
Senghas, Robert E. (1928—) ... 18
Sèverance, Caroline M. (1820-1914) ... 224
Shaker Song ... 146
Shelton, Marion Brown ... 99
Silliman, Vincent Brown (1894-1979)
   134, 229, 246
Simonsson, Thomas,
   (of Strangnas, Sweden) (d. 1443) ... 142
Smith, Walter Chalmers (1824-1908) ... 76
Socrates (before 469-399 B.C.) ... 297
Starr, Deane (1923—) ... 3
Stevens, Doris Jeanine ... 177
Stevenson, Robert Louis (1850-94) ... 254
Stone, Lloyd (1913—) ... 226
Storey, John Andrew (1935—) ... 11, 12,
   35, 37, 40, 67, 97, 112, 126, 130, 131,
   132, 135, 157, 162, 164, 165, 173, 189,
   200, 206, 214, 218, 245, 250, 259, 273,
   274, 279, 292, 297, 302
Struther, Jan (Mrs. Joyce Anstruther
   Placzek) (1901-53) ... 240, 282
Summers, Helen (b. 1857) ... 291
Symonds, John Addington (1840-93) ... 203

Tagore, Rabindranath (1861-1941) ... 299
Tarrant, William George (1853-1928)
   68, 100
Tate, Nahum (1652-1715) ... 84
Tennyson, Alfred (1809-92) ... 257, 300
Thorn, Emily Lenore Luch (1915—) ... 33
Torrence, Ridgely (1875-1951) ... 4
Traditional American ... 180, 188
Traditional English Carol ... 92
Traditional Jewish ... 317

INDEX OF AUTHORS

Traditional Negro Spiritual ... 32, 175
Traditional Quaker ... 133
Traditional Shaker Song ... 146
Traditional Welsh ... 278
Trapp, Jacob (1899–) ... 125, 128, 209
Trench, Richard Chenevix (1825-97) ... 186
Tweedy, Henry Hallam (1868-1953) ... 228

Vallance, Arthur Woolley (1902–) ... 1
Van Doren, Mark ... 231
Van Dyke, Henry (1852-1933) ... 117
Vaughn, Don Wayne ... 80

Walke, Roger Taylor (1924–) ... 202
Walter, Howard Arnold (1883-1918) ... 154
Watts, Isaac (1647-1748) ... 65, 96, 310
Welsh Traditional ... 278

Wesley, Charles (1707-88) ... 90, 118
Weston, Robert Terry (1898–) ... 248
Whitcomb, Marion Sheahan (1924–) ... 275, 290
Whittier, John Greenleaf (1807-92) ... 30, 101, 115, 191, 205, 293
Williams, Theodore Chickering (1855-1915) ... 86, 183
Willis, Love Maria (1824-1908) ... 59
Wilson, Edwin Henry (1898–) ... 123
Winkworth, Catherine (1827-78) ... 19, 71
Wolff, William ... 96, 205, 264
Woodward, George Ratcliffe (1848-1934) ... 93
Wordsworth, Christopher (1807-85) ... 111
Wotton, Henry (1568-1639) ... 147
Wright, Samuel Anthony (1919–) ... 192

Acknowledgements

Every effort has been made to trace copyright holders, but in a few cases we have been unsuccessful, and in some others it is not clear whether copyright has remained with the author or composer, or has been transferred to a publisher. If any copyright has been inadvertently infringed, we apologise and ask to be informed so that amends may be made in any future edition.

Acknowledgement of permission to reproduce copyright material is given alongside the texts and music as appropriate.

We record thanks to the following, who have generously granted copyright permission without fee:

To the authors of all texts by Dr M. Beardsley, Revd R.F. Boeke, Revd H. Box, Revd F.R. Clabburn, Revd J.I. Daniel, Mrs Anne Etkin, Revd B. Findlow, Mr P. Galbraith, Revd A.M. Hill, Revd T.H. Jones, Revd W.R. Jones (jr.), Revd S.H. Knight, Mr A. Kramer, Revd J.G. MacKinnon, Revd T.J. Mikelson, Revd J.A. Midgley, Revd R.C. Palmer, Revd K.L. Patton, Mr H. Pickles, Revd C.M. Reed, Mr W.E. Reeve, Revd R.E. and Mrs D.C. Senghas, Revd D. Starr, Revd J.A. Storey, Mrs Emily L. Thorn, Revd J. Trapp, Revd A.W. Vallance, Revd D.W. Vaughn, Revd R.T. Weston, Ms Marion S. Whitcomb, Revd E.H. Wilson and Revd S.A. Wright.

To the following holders or administrators of copyright of texts: The American Ethical Union (52, 229); Arlington Street Church, Boston, Mass. (217); The Beacon Press, Boston, Mass. (106, 108, 134, 136, 219, 227, 234, 246); Mrs B. Buehrer (17); Miss D.E. Collins (per A.P. Watt, Ltd.) (160); Mr J.L. Davis (56); The Devin-Adair Co., Connecticut (105); Mr E.J. Dietrich (244); Doubleday & Co., Inc., N.Y. (145); Mrs Norma Millay Ellis (141); Harper & Row, Inc., N.Y. (228); Mr Bradford Lyttle (313, 315); Messrs Charles Scribner's Sons, N.Y. (117); The United Church Press (99); The Hodgin Press, Los Angeles, Cal., and their associated authors: David Arkin (207), John Hille (6), Waldemar Hille (224, 249), Arthur Kevess (143), Elizabeth Madison (276), Althea A. Ogden (153), William E. Oliver (6, 249), James Oppenheim (216), Doris Jeannine Stevens (177) and William Wolff (per Mrs Janet Wolff) (96, 205, 264); The Religious Arts Guild, Boston, Mass., and their associated authors, Dorothy Grover (176), Beth Ide (124, 170), Linda C. Morrison (161) and Roger T. Walke (202); and River Road Church, New York (193).

To the following for their musical compositions or arrangements: Ms Evangeline M. Bachelder, Mr David Dawson, Revd T.H. Jones, Revd S.H. Knight and Revd J.A. Storey.

To the following holders or administrators of music copyrights: The Beacon Press, Boston, Mass. (4, 110, 129, 160, 165, 246, 262, 277); Mrs D. Evans (168); Mrs B. Capek Haspl (43); Mrs M. Spicer (52, 227); The Hodgin Press, Los Angeles, Cal., and their associated composers and arrangers, Waldemar Hille (6, 207) and Caroline Kohlsaat (216); and the Religious Arts Guild, Boston, Mass., in association with Douglas L. Butler and Dorothy Grover (176).

Worship and Celebration

1 Lord of the Wondrous Earth

LITTLE CORNARD 66. 66. 88 (Dactylic) Martin Fallas Shaw, 1875-1958
By permission of J. Curwen & Sons, Ltd.

Lord of the wondrous earth,
  Into thy courts we throng,
Seeking to serve with mirth,
  Stirring our hearts with song.
Creator-Spirit, touch with power
Our youthful wills, this worship-hour.

Lift from our laden lives
  All we have wrought with shame;
Stir every heart that strives,
  Tense with unswerving aim,
To consecrate our talent-skill
And with delight our days to fill.

WORSHIP AND CELEBRATION

Grant us the vision keen
   Heroes of old time knew;
Faith in the things not seen;
   Faith in our strength to do;
That through our seeming-tedious days
Our feet may find the brightest ways.

Daring the truth to speak,
   E'en to the worldly-wise;
Swift to defend the weak,
   Eager for enterprise,
We steel our wills for sacrifice,
And banish faithless cowardice.

So may our tongues unite
   Strong in their glad accord,
Cleaving the zenith-height,
   Splendid with song outpoured,
To rouse the nations with our call,
That Youth may serve the Lord of all.

                             Arthur Woolley Vallance, 1902 —
                                       Used by permission.

2 Brief Our Days

WERDE MUNTER, MEIN GEMÜTE   87. 87. 88. 77   Johann Schop, d. ca. 1665
Adapted and har. Johann Sebastian Bach, 1685-1750

Brief our days, but long for singing,
  When to sing is made our call,
For a million stars now flinging
  Light upon this earthly ball.
In a setting of what splendour
Are we given chance to render
  Tribute for the whirling sky
  Where we live and where we die.

Planet earth for us a dwelling,
  Cool in wind and warm in light,
In its praise our song is swelling,
  Grateful for this day and night,
We, the citizens of heaven,
Riding earth as it is driven
  Down the spangled course of space,
  Know the glory of this place.

Kenneth L. Patton, 1911—
Used by permission

WORSHIP AND CELEBRATION

3 Joy of Living

ST. THEODULPH   76. 76. D.
Melchior Teschner, c. 1613
har. Johann Sebastian Bach, 1685-1750

We sing the joy of living,
  We sing the mystery,
Of knowledge, lore and science,
  Of truth that is to be;
Of searching, doubting, testing,
  Of deeper insights gained,
Of freedom claimed and honoured,
  Of minds that are unchained.

We sing the joy of living,
  We sing of harmony,
Of textures, sounds and colours,
  To touch, to hear, to see;
Of order, rhythm, meaning,
  Of chaos and of strife,
Of richness of sensation,
  Of the creating life.

We sing the joy of living,
  We sing of ecstasy,
Of warmth, of love, of passion,
  Of flights of fantasy.
We sing of joy of living,
  The dear, the known, the strange,
The moving, pulsing, throbbing—
  A universe of change.

Deane Starr, 1923 —
Used by permission.

WORSHIP AND CELEBRATION

4 Source of Life

ADAM'S SONG   10 10. 10 10 10   Robert L. Sanders, 1906-74

By permission of Beacon Press, Boston, Mass

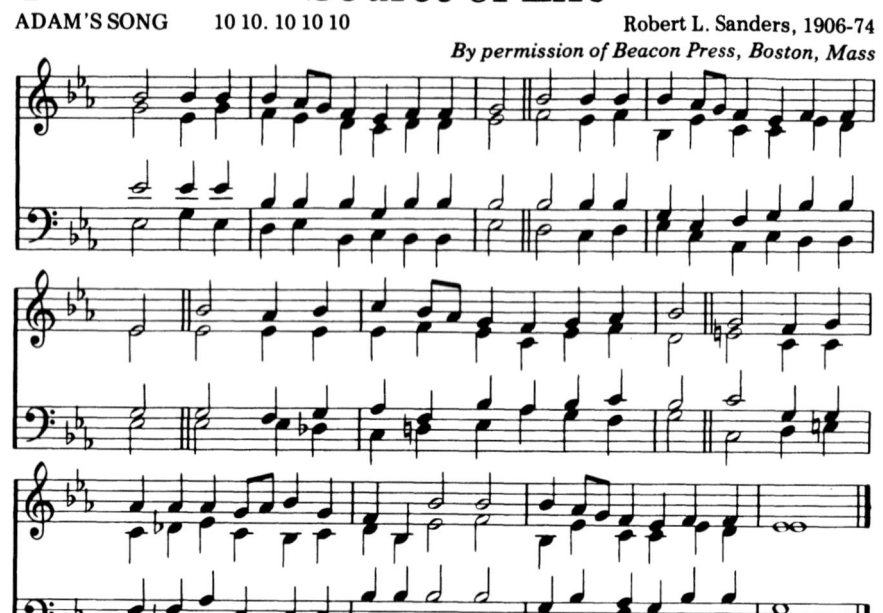

Praise, O my heart, to you, O Source of Life,
You are my tide of joy, my sea, my shore,
My field of sky with stars that never set;
Now I will learn your wonders all my days,
And my blind ways in darkness be no more.

Your glory is for ever, and with dance
You move among your works and they to you.
You look upon the earth, and at your glance
It sways with trembling, and above the hills
A smoke ascends where you have touched their rest.

They wait for you alone, all forms of life,
To have their food from you, and they are fed.
When your hand opens they are satisfied;
You give; they gather. When they think you far
A trouble comes upon them and a dread.

They go again to be the dust they tread.
You breathe upon the dust, they rise and are.
I will sing praises to you while life fills
My flesh with breath; as long as life shall stream
From you within me, I will sing your light.

Ridgely Torrence, 1875-1951

WORSHIP AND CELEBRATION

5 Fill My Life with Praise

RODMELL   C.M.

English Traditional Melody
Coll. and arr. Ralph Vaughan Williams, 1872-1958
From the English Hymnal by permission of Oxford University Press

Fill thou my life, O God of love,
In every part with praise,
That my whole being may proclaim
Thy being and thy ways.

Not for the lip of praise alone,
Nor e'en the praising heart,
I ask, but for a life made up
Of praise in every part.

Praise in the common words I speak,
Life's common looks and tones;
In family life and fellowship
With my belovèd ones.

Praise in the common things of life,
The common daily scene;
Praise in each duty and each deed,
However small and mean;

Not in the temple crowd alone
Where holy voices chime;
But in the silent paths of earth,
The quiet rooms of time.

So shall no part of day or night
From sacredness be free:
But all my life, in every step,
Be fellowship with thee.

from Horatius Bonar, 1808-89

WORSHIP AND CELEBRATION

6 Sons and Daughters

O FILII ET FILIAE 9 4. 10 10 10. 4.

15th Century French Melody
arr. Waldemar Hille, 1908—
Used by permission

O, Sons and Daughters, lift every voice!
Sing and rejoice!

Take joy in freedom of conscience and mind;
Take joy in living each truth that you find;
Scorn superstition and errors that blind;
Sing and rejoice!

O, Sons and Daughters, lift every voice!
Sing and rejoice!

WORSHIP AND CELEBRATION

Take joy in each golden hour of your span;
Take joy in striving to build while you can;
Glowing in vision and boundless in plan;
    Sing and rejoice!

O, Sons and Daughters, lift every voice!
Sing and rejoice!

Take joy in righting the wrongful decree;
Take joy in working for all to be free;
Challenge oppression, wherever it be;
    Sing and rejoice!

O, Sons and Daughters, lift every voice!
Sing and rejoice!

Take joy in living the truth that you feel;
Take joy in working for our common weal;
Build peaceful morrows with courage and zeal;
    Sing and rejoice!

O, Sons and Daughters, lift every voice!
Sing and rejoice!

from William E. Oliver
and John H. Hille

The Hodgin Press, Los Angeles.
Used by permission.

7 Source of All Being

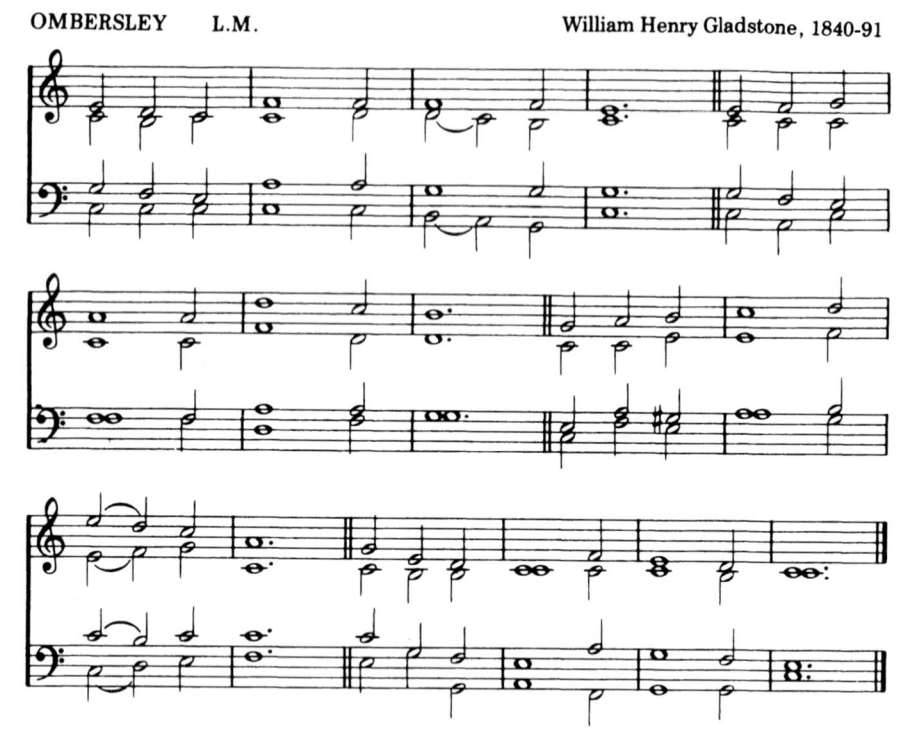

OMBERSLEY L.M.
William Henry Gladstone, 1840-91

Source of all being! throned afar,
Thy glory flames from sun and star;
Centre and soul of every sphere,
Yet to each loving heart how near!

Sun of our life! Thy quickening ray
Sheds on our path the glow of day:
Star of our hope! Thy softened light
Cheers the long watches of the night.

God of all life, below, above,
Whose light is truth, whose warmth is love,
Before thy ever-blazing throne
We ask no lustre of our own.

Grant us thy truth to make us free,
And kindling hearts that burn for thee,
Till all thy living altars claim
One holy light, one heavenly flame.

WORSHIP AND CELEBRATION from Oliver Wendell Holmes, 1809-94

8 Life that Maketh All Things New

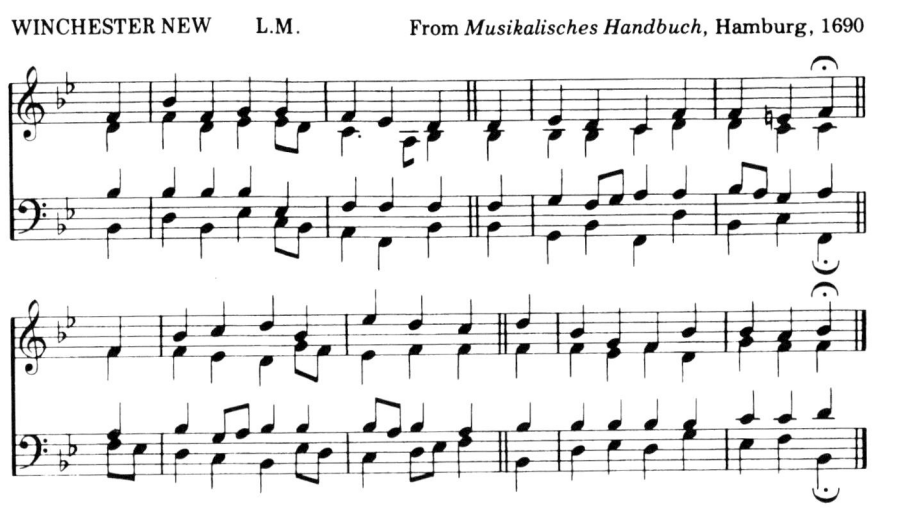

WINCHESTER NEW   L.M.   From *Musikalisches Handbuch*, Hamburg, 1690

O Life that makest all things new,
The flowers of earth, the thoughts within;
Our pilgrim feet, wet with thy dew,
In gladness hither turn again.

From hand to hand the greeting flows,
From eye to eye the signals run,
From heart to heart the bright hope glows;
The seekers of the light are one:

One in the freedom of the truth,
One in the joy of paths untrod,
One in the soul's perennial youth,
One in the larger thought of God;

The freer step, the fuller breath,
The wide horizon's grander view;
The sense of life that knows no death,
The Life that maketh all things new.

from Samuel Longfellow, 1819-92

WORSHIP AND CELEBRATION

GOLDEN WHEAT   L.M.D.   from Edward Williams (Iolo Morgannwg), 1747-1826

WORSHIP AND CELEBRATION

9 So Simple is the Human Heart

A little sun, a little rain,
   A soft wind blowing from the west —
And woods and fields are sweet again,
   And warmth within the mountain's breast.
So simple is the earth we tread,
   So quick with love and life her frame,
Ten thousand years have dawned and fled,
   And still her magic is the same.

A little love, a little trust,
   A soft impulse, a sudden dream,
And life as dry as desert dust
   Is fresher than a mountain stream.
So simple is the human heart,
   So ready for new hope and joy;
Ten thousand years have played their part,
   But left it young as girl or boy.

from Stopford Augustus Brooke, 1832-1916

10 Thou One in All, Thou All in One

THE TRUTH FROM ABOVE   L.M.

English Traditional Melody
arr. David Dawson
Used by permission

Thou One in all, thou All in one,
Source of the grace that crowns our days,
For all thy gifts 'neath cloud or sun,
We lift to thee our grateful praise.

We bless thee for the life that flows,
A pulse in every grain of sand,
A beauty in the blushing rose,
A thought and deed in brain and hand.

For life that thou hast made a joy,
For strength to make our lives like thine,
For duties that our hands employ,
We bring our offerings to thy shrine.

Be thine to give and ours to own
The truth that sets thy children free,
The law that binds us to thy throne,
The love that makes us one with thee.

Seth Curtis Beach, 1837-1932

WORSHIP AND CELEBRATION

11   Hymn to Perfect Wisdom

ALL FOR JESUS   87. 87   John Stainer, 1840-1901

Homage to thee, Perfect Wisdom,
   Boundless and transcending thought!
Thou who art devoid of blemish
   By the wise art daily sought.

All perfections thee encircle
   As the stars the crescent moon,
And to those who bow before thee
   Thou dost grant thy richest boon.

Who is able here to praise thee,
   Thou beyond the range of speech?
Yet we laud and magnify thee,
   Thou above our highest reach.

By our praise of Perfect Wisdom
   Others may be led to thee,
Till the world shall be enlightened
   By the Truth that makes us free.

Mahayana Buddhist, re-cast from the *Rahulabhadra*
by John Andrew Storey, 1935 —
Used by permission.

WORSHIP AND CELEBRATION

12   Hymn to the Sole God

O Living God, that bringest all to birth,
Thy power sheds its brightness on the earth;
All living things alike thy glory praise,
And trees and plants adorn the golden days.

The winter's cool and summer's heat fulfil
The purposes of thy almighty will;
The sun in splendour shines upon our land,
And all is nourished by thy loving hand.

The breath of life, to creatures high and low,
Thy everlasting bounty doth bestow;
To all thou givest freely of thy grace,
And makest one the members of our race.

And when the sun sets in the western skies,
In peaceful sleep thy children close their eyes;
The world is in thy hand as day departs,
Yet is thy habitation in our hearts.

O thou sole God, no other can possess
Thy power to uphold our lives and bless:
Majestic as the sun above us shines,
So excellent, O God, are thy designs.

John Andrew Storey, 1935 —
after Akhenaton, c. 1400 B.C.
Used by permission.

WORSHIP AND CELEBRATION

SONG 24   10 10. 10 10   Orlando Gibbons, 1583-1625

WORSHIP AND CELEBRATION

13   Eternal Ruler

SONG 1   10 10. 10 10. 10 10   Orlando Gibbons, 1583-1625

Eternal Ruler of the ceaseless round
Of circling planets singing on their way;
Guide of the nations from the night profound
Into the glory of the perfect day;
Rule in our hearts that we may ever be
Guided and strengthened and upheld by thee.

We would be one in hatred of all wrong,
One in our love of all things sweet and fair;
One with the joy that breaketh into song,
One with the grief that trembles into prayer;
One in the power that makes thy children free
To follow truth, and thus to follow thee.

John White Chadwick, 1814-1904

WORSHIP AND CELEBRATION

14 The Beauty of the Earth

ENGLAND'S LANE 77. 77. 77

English Melody
Adapt. and har. Geoffrey Shaw, 1879-1943
By permission of Oxford University Press

For the beauty of the earth,
For the splendour of the skies,
For the love which from our birth
Over and around us lies:
For all these with joy we raise
This, our song of grateful praise.

For the wonder of each hour
Of the day and of the night,
Hill and vale and tree and flower,
Sun and moon and stars of light:
For all these with joy we raise
This, our song of grateful praise.

For the joy of ear and eye,
For the heart and mind's delight,
For the mystic harmony
Linking sense to sound and sight:
For all these with joy we raise
This, our song of grateful praise.

For the joy of human care,
Brother, sister, parent, child,
For the fellowship we share,
For all gentle thoughts and mild:
For all these with joy we raise
This, our song of grateful praise.

from Folliott Sandford Pierpoint, 1835-1917

WORSHIP AND CELEBRATION

15   For All that is Our Life

OLD 120TH   66. 66. 66

Melody from *Este's Psalter*, 1592

For all that is our life
We sing our thanks and praise;
For all life is a gift
Which we are called to use
To build the common good
And make our own days glad.

For needs which others serve,
For services we give,
For work and its rewards,
For hours of rest and love:
We come with praise and thanks
For all that is our life.

For sorrow we must bear,
For failures, pain and loss,
For each new thing we learn,
For fearful hours that pass:
We come with praise and thanks
For all that is our life.

For all that is our life
We sing our thanks and praise;
For all life is a gift
Which we are called to use
To build the common good
And make our own days glad.

Bruce Findlow, 1922 —
Used by permission.

WORSHIP AND CELEBRATION

16 Praise From All the Human Race

ST. BAVON   87. 87.   A. T. I. Jagger, 1911—

For the glimpses of full knowledge
   To the human race disclosed,
And the portion, it's acknowledged,
   Which from human effort rose;

For sufficient space for freedom
   Without which the human mind
Never could apply the reason
   With which insights are refined;

For the values earth embraces,
   Searching for community,
Building just, sustaining places
   For a rich humanity;

For the comradeship of others
   With whose help so bountiful
We turn strangers into neighbours
   And do tasks impossible;

For the deep-felt reassurance
   That, despite earth's stricken plight,
There's a confident reliance
   Past the darkness there is light:

Praise to you, sustaining Power,
   Praise from all the human race:
Praise to you, commanding Splendour,
   Praise to you, transforming Grace!

Andrew McKean Hill, 1942 —
based on *Five Smooth Stones of Liberalism* by James Luther Adams
Used by permission.

WORSHIP AND CELEBRATION

KREMSER 12 11.13 12. Adrian Valerius' *Nederlandtsch Gedenckclanck*, 1626
arr. Edward Kremser, 1838-1914

WORSHIP AND CELEBRATION

17   Song of Thanksgiving

We sing now together our song of thanksgiving,
   Rejoicing in goods which the ages have wrought,
For Life that enfolds us, and helps and heals and holds us,
   And leads beyond the goals which our ancestors sought.

We sing of the freedoms which martyrs and heroes
   Have won by their labour, their sorrow, their pain;
The oppressed befriending, our ampler hopes defending,
   Their death becomes our triumph, their loss is our gain.

We sing of the prophets, the teachers, the dreamers,
   Designers, creators, and workers, and seers;
Our own lives expanding, our gratitude commanding,
   Their deeds have made immortal their days and their years.

We sing of earth's comradeship now in the making
   In every far continent, region and land;
With folk of all races, all times and names and places,
   We pledge ourselves in fellowship firmly to stand.

From Edwin Theophil Buehrer, 1894-1969
By permission of Mrs Bernadine Buehrer

18   We Gather Together

We gather together in joyful thanksgiving,
   Acclaiming creation, whose bounty we share;
Both sorrow and gladness we find now in our living,
   We sing a hymn of praise to the life that we bear.

We gather together to join in the journey,
   Confirming, committing our passage to be
A true affirmation, in joy and tribulation,
   When bound to human care and hope—then we are free!

Dorothy C. Senghas, 1930 —
and Robert E. Senghas, 1928 —
By permission of the authors
and The Religious Arts Guild, Boston, Mass.

WORSHIP AND CELEBRATION

NUN DANKET   67. 67. 66. 66

Present form of Melody by
Johann Crüger, 1598-1662

WORSHIP AND CELEBRATION

19 Now Thank We All Our God

Now thank we all our God,
With heart, and hands, and voices,
Who wondrous things hath done,
In whom the world rejoices;
Who from our mothers' arms
Hath blessed us on our way
With countless gifts of love,
And still is ours today.

O may this bounteous God
Through all our life be near us,
With ever-joyful hearts
And blessed peace to cheer us;
And keep us rich in grace,
And guide us when perplexed,
And free us from all ills
In this world and the next.

All praise and thanks to God
In joyfulness be given,
To whom we lift our hearts,
Who reigns in highest heaven;
The One Eternal God,
Whom earth and heaven adore,
Who was of old, is now,
And shall be evermore.

Martin Rinckart, 1586-1649
from tr. Catherine Winkworth, 1827-78

20 My God, I Thank Thee

WENTWORTH 84. 84. 84   Frederick Charles Maker, 1844-1927

My God, I thank thee, who hast made
The earth so bright,
So full of splendour and of joy,
Beauty and light;
So many glorious things are here,
Noble and right!

WORSHIP AND CELEBRATION

I thank thee, too, that thou hast made
    Joy to abound;
So many gentle thoughts and deeds
    Circling us round,
That in the darkest spot on earth
    Some love is found.

I thank thee more, that all our joy
    Is touched with pain;
That shadows fall on brightest hours;
    That thorns remain;
So that earth's bliss may be our guide,
    And not our chain.

For thou, who knowest just how soon
    Our weak heart clings,
Hast given us joys tender and true,
    Yet all with wings;
So that we see, gleaming on high,
    Diviner things.

I thank thee, then, that thou hast kept
    The best in store:
We have enough, yet not too much
    To long for more,
A yearning for a deeper peace
    Not known before.

from Adelaide Anne Procter, 1825-64

21

GWALCHMAI 74. 74. D   Joseph David Jones, 1827-70

WORSHIP AND CELEBRATION

King of Glory, King of Peace

King of glory, King of peace,
    I will love thee;
And that love may never cease,
    I will move thee.
Thou hast granted my request,
    Thou hast heard me;
Thou didst note my working breast,
    Thou hast spared me.

Wherefore with my utmost art
    I will sing thee,
And the cream of all my heart
    I will bring thee.
Though my sins against me cried,
    Thou didst clear me;
And alone, when they replied,
    Thou didst hear me.

Seven whole days, not one in seven,
    I will praise thee;
In my heart, though not in heaven,
    I can raise thee.
Small it is, in this poor sort
    To enrol thee:
E'en eternity's too short
    To extol thee.

George Herbert, 1593-1632

22 God of Life

SALZBURG 77. 77. D.

Melody by Jacob Hintze, 1622-1702
har. Johann Sebastian Bach, 1685-1750

O Eternal Life, whose power
Causes time and space to flow;
From whose being breaks the flower,
From whose glory people grow;
By the whisper of whose breath
Atoms wake that seem but death;
With whose silent-working will
The eternal ages thrill!

Lord of life, to heaven tower
Spires of being high and grand,
Till on us thou lay the power
That we serve with heart and hand;
Till thou flood us with thy light,
That we see thee with our sight,
Who art Reason, who art Right,
Majesty of Love and Might!

from James Vila Blake, 1842-1925

WORSHIP AND CELEBRATION

23 We are Met to Worship Thee

STABAT MATER 88. 7 French Church Melody

Gracious Power, the world pervading,
Blessing all, and none upbraiding,
   We are met to worship thee.

By thy wisdom mind is lighted,
By thy love the heart excited,
   Light and love all flow from thee;

And the soul of thought and feeling
In the voice thy praises pealing,
   Must thy noblest homage be.

Not alone in our devotion;
In all being, life and motion,
   We the present Godhead see.

Gracious Power, the world pervading,
Blessing all, and none upbraiding,
   We are met to worship thee.

William Johnson Fox, 1786-1864

WORSHIP AND CELEBRATION

24 Transforming Grace

MONKLAND 77.77

Melody by (?) John Antes, 1740-1811
arr. John Bernard Wilkes, 1785-1869

Sovereign and transforming Grace,
We invoke thy quickening power;
Reign the spirit of this place,
Bless the purpose of this hour.

This thy house, the house of prayer;
This the day we hallow thine.
O let now thy grace appear,
Hallowing every place and time.

Holy and creative Light,
We invoke thy kindling ray;
Dawn upon our spirits' night,
Turn our darkness into day.

To the anxious soul impart
Hope all other hopes above;
Stir the dull and hardened heart
With a longing and a love.

Work in all; in all renew
Day by day the life divine;
All our wills to thee subdue,
All our hearts to thee incline.

Frederic Henry Hedge, 1805-90

WORSHIP AND CELEBRATION

25 Where'er Thy People Meet

MAINZER L.M. Joseph Mainzer, 1801-51

O God, where'er thy people meet,
There they behold thy mercy-seat;
Where'er they seek thee, thou art found,
And every place is hallowed ground.

For thou, within no walls confined,
Inhabitest the humble mind;
Such ever bring thee where they come,
And going, take thee to their home.

Here may we prove the power of prayer
To strengthen faith, and sweeten care; .
To teach our faint desires to rise,
And bring all heaven before our eyes.

from William Cowper, 1731-1800

WORSHIP AND CELEBRATION

26 Spirit Divine! Attend our Prayer

ST. AGNES, DURHAM   C.M.   John Bacchus Dykes, 1823-76

Spirit divine! attend our prayer,
  And make our hearts thy home;
Descend with all thy gracious power:
  Come, Holy Spirit, come!

Come as the light: to waiting minds,
  That long the truth to know,
Reveal the narrow path of right,
  The way of duty show.

Come as the dew: on hearts that pine
  Descend in this still hour,
Till every barren place shall own
  With joy thy quickening power.

Come as the wind: sweep clean away
  What dead within us lies,
And search and freshen all our souls
  With living energies.

Andrew Reed, 1787-1862
alt. Samuel Longfellow, 1819-92

WORSHIP AND CELEBRATION

27   To Cloisters of the Spirit

CHRISTUS DER IST MEIN LEBEN   76. 76   Melody by Melchior Vulpius, 1560-1616
har. Johann Sebastian Bach, 1685-1750

To cloisters of the Spirit
  These aisles of quiet lead:
Here shall the vision gladden,
  The voice within us plead.

The song these walls shall echo
  Be song the heart within,
The prayer in consecration's
  Sweet privacies begin.

Here be no-one a stranger,
  No holy cause be banned;
No good for one be counted
  Not good for all the land.

Work on, creative Spirit,
  Perfect thy inner shrine,
Till song pass into service,
  Prayer into life divine.

from William Channing Gannett, 1840-1923

WORSHIP AND CELEBRATION

28 The Tides of the Spirit

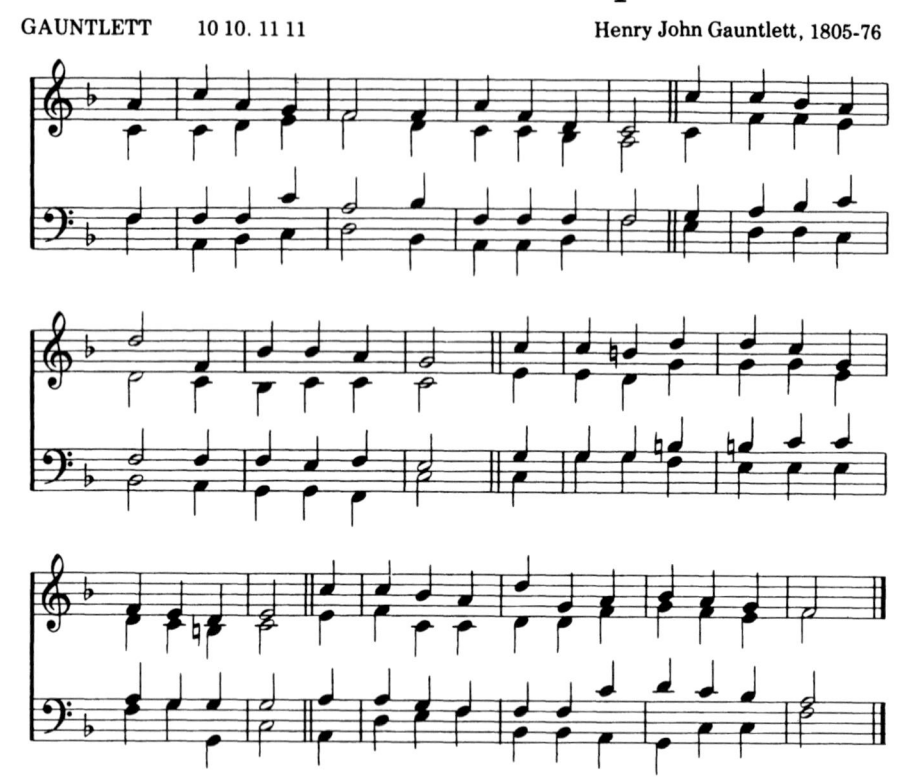

GAUNTLETT   10 10. 11 11   Henry John Gauntlett, 1805-76

We come as we are to worship and pray,
Unsure of ourselves, unsure what to say:
O may we be patient and willing to be
Receptive and open to hear and to see.

The God of our life is ever at hand
But not to be called by our proud command;
The tides of the spirit have their ebb and flow
And we must be patient and move as they go.

O let us be glad and hungry of heart
To wait upon God and learn our own part,
To give life the best of the powers we have
As servants of life and clear channels of love.

Bruce Findlow, 1922 —
Used by permission

WORSHIP AND CELEBRATION

29 God Within

BUCKDEN 98.98

David Dawson
Used by permission

O thou that movest all, O Power
   That bringest life where'er thou art,
O breath of God in star and flower,
   Mysterious aim of soul and heart.

Within the thought that cannot grasp thee
   In its unfathomable hold,
We worship thee who may not clasp thee,
   O God, unreckoned and untold!

Yet, though the worlds maintain unbroken
   The silence of their awesome round,
A voice within our souls has spoken
   And we who seek have more than found.

Agnes Mary Frances Duclaux, 1857-1944
(A. Mary Robinson)

WORSHIP AND CELEBRATION

30 Immortal Love, for Ever Full

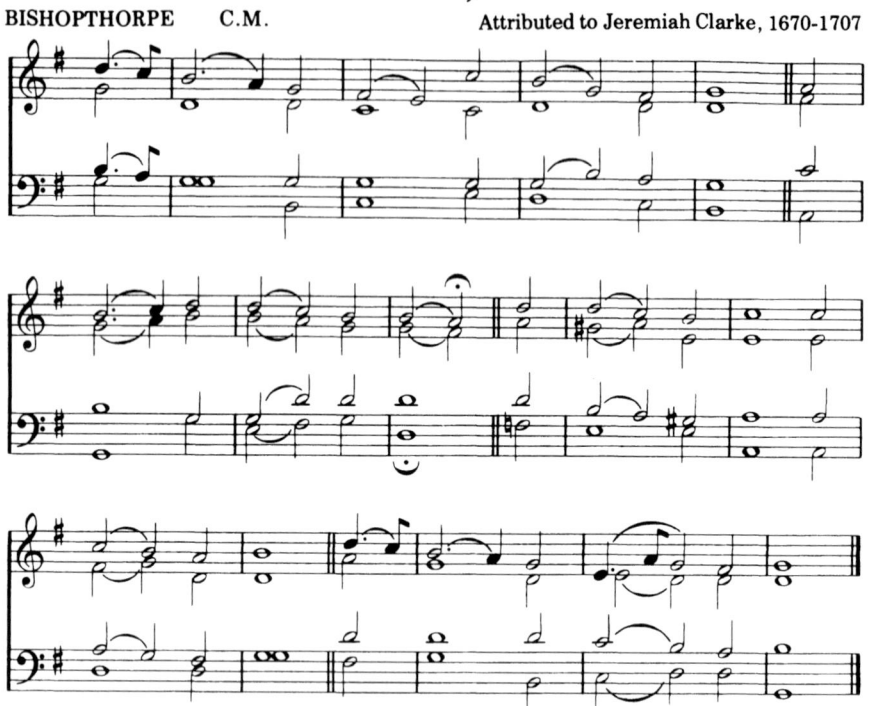

BISHOPTHORPE C.M. Attributed to Jeremiah Clarke, 1670-1707

Immortal Love, for ever full,
   For ever flowing free,
For ever shared, for ever whole,
   A never-ebbing sea!

Our outward lips confess the Name
   All other names above;
Love only knoweth whence it came,
   And comprehendeth love.

Blow, winds of God, awake and blow
   The mists of earth away;
Shine out, O Light divine, and show
   How wide and far we stray.

The letter fails, the systems fall,
   And every symbol wanes:
The Spirit over-brooding all,
   Eternal Love, remains.

John Greenleaf Whittier, 1807-92

WORSHIP AND CELEBRATION

31 The Flow of Life

LOTH TO DEPART L.M.

Traditional English Melody
arr. David Dawson

In humble reverence and love
We celebrate the changing world;
Thankful and glad to live and move
As part of all that's new and old.

Humble before so much unknown
And for the failures of our kind;
Resolved to turn again and learn
Our place and task and destined end.

Reverent before the mighty works
And daily wonders of this life,
The endless unseen power which makes
Unceasing changes sure and safe.

In love with life, before its truth
Of hurt and healing, ebb and flow;
We move with all things on the path
Of living, loving, learning now.

Bruce Findlow, 1922 —
Used by permission.

WORSHIP AND CELEBRATION

32 Kum ba Yah (Come by Here)

KUM BA YAH   8 8 8. 5   Traditional Negro Spiritual, arranged

Kum ba yah, my *Lord, kum ba yah,
Kum ba yah, my Lord, kum ba yah,
Kum ba yah. my Lord, kum ba yah,
O Lord, kum ba yah.

Someone's crying, Lord, kum ba yah,
Someone's crying, Lord, kum ba yah
Someone's crying, Lord, kum ba yah,
O Lord, kum ba yah.

Someone's starving, Lord, kum ba yah,
Someone's starving, Lord, kum ba yah,
Someone's starving, Lord, kum ba yah,
O Lord, kum ba yah.

Someone's praying, Lord, kum ba yah,
Someone's praying, Lord, kum ba yah,
Someone's praying, Lord, kum ba yah,
O Lord, kum ba yah.

Someone's singing, Lord, kum ba yah,
Someone's singing, Lord, kum ba yah,
Someone's singing, Lord, kum ba yah,
O Lord, kum ba yah.

Come by here, my Lord, kum ba yah,
Come by here, my Lord, kum ba yah,
Come by here, my Lord, kum ba yah,
O Lord, kum ba yah.

* or Love or God.

from a Traditional Negro Spiritual

The Reflective Spirit

33 Do You Hear?

FOUNDATION 12 12. 12 12. Anapaestic William Caldwell's *Union Harmony*, 1837

Do you hear, O my friend, in the place where you stand,
Through the sky, through the land, do you hear, do you hear,
In the heights, on the plain, in the vale, on the main,
In the sun, in the rain, do you hear, do you hear?

Through the roar, through the rush, through the throng, through the
Do you hear in the hush of your soul, of your soul, [crush,
Hear the cry fear won't still, hear the heart's call to will,
Hear a sigh's startling trill, in your soul, in your soul?

From the place where you stand, to the outermost strand,
Do you hear, O my friend, do you hear, do you hear,
All the dreams, all the dares, all the sighs, all the prayers—
They are yours, mine, and theirs: do you hear, do you hear?

THE REFLECTIVE SPIRIT

Emily Lenore Luch Thorn, 1915 —
Used by permission

34 Where is Your God?

DARMSTADT 67. 67. 66. 66

Ahasuerus Fritsch, 1629-1701
har. Johann Sebastian Bach, 1685-1750

"Where is your God?" they say:
Answer them, God most holy!
Reveal thy secret way
Of visiting the lowly:
  Not wrapped in moving cloud,
  Or nightly-resting fire;
  But veiled within the shroud
  Of silent high desire.

Come not in flashing storm,
Or bursting frown of thunder:
Come in the viewless form
Of wakening love and wonder;
  To every waiting soul
  Speak in thy still small voice,
  Till broken love's made whole,
  And saddened hearts rejoice.

from James Martineau, 1805-1900

THE REFLECTIVE SPIRIT

35 The Living God

VIENNA 77. 77

Melody by Justin Heinrich Knecht, 1752-1817

Down the ages we have trod
Many paths in search of God,
Seeking ever to define
The Eternal and Divine.

Some have seen eternal good
Pictured best in Parenthood,
And a Being throned above
Ruling over us in love.

There are others who proclaim
God and Nature are the same,
And the present Godhead own
Where Creation's laws are known.

There are eyes which best can see
God within humanity,
And God's countenance there trace
Written in the human face.

Where compassion is most found
Is for some the hallowed ground,
And these paths they upward plod
Teaching us that love is God.

Though the truth we can't perceive,
This at least we must believe,
What we take most earnestly
Is our living Deity.

Our true God we there shall find
In what claims our heart and mind,
And our hidden thoughts enshrine
That which for us is Divine.

John Andrew Storey, 1935—
Used by permission

THE REFLECTIVE SPIRIT

36 Star Born

ABRIDGE C.M. Isaac Smith, c.1725 - c.1800

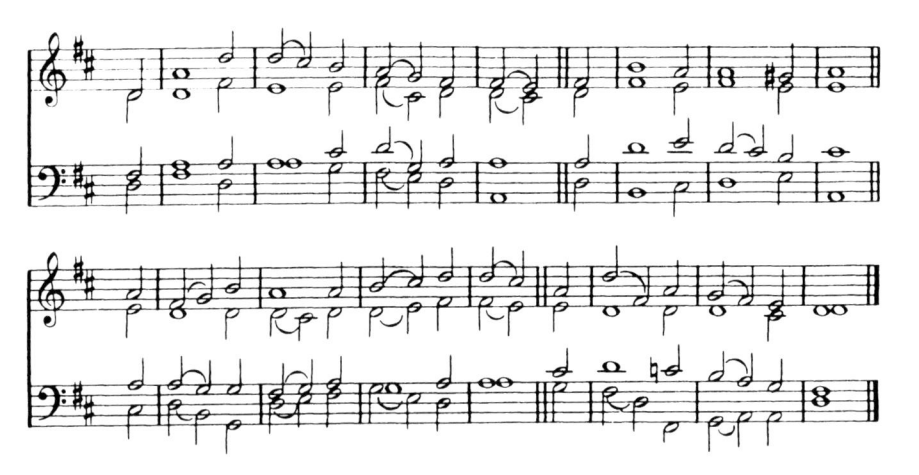

Ye earthborn children of a star
  Amid the depths of space,
The cosmic wonder from afar
  Within your minds embrace.

Look out, with awe, upon the art
  Of countless living things;
The counterpoint of part with part,
  As nature's chorus sings.

Beyond the wonder you have wrought
  Within your little time;
The knowledge won, the wisdom sought,
  The ornaments of rhyme;

Seek deeper still within your souls
  And sense the wonder there;
The ceaseless thrust to noble goals
  Of life, more free and fair.

Ye earthborn children of a star
  Who seek and long and strive,
Take humble pride in what you are:
  Be glad to be alive!

John G. MacKinnon, 1903-85
Used by permission

THE REFLECTIVE SPIRIT

37 Thy Kingdom Come

DUKE STREET L.M. John Hatton, d. 1793

I sent my soul some truth to win;
My soul returned these words to tell:
"Look not beyond, but turn within,
For I myself am heaven and hell."

And as my thoughts were gently led,
Half-held beliefs were seen as true;
I heard, as new, words Jesus said:
"My friend, God's kingdom lies in you."

Now though I labour, as I must,
To build the kingdom yet to be,
I know my hopes will turn to dust
If first it is not built in me.

John Andrew Storey, 1935 —
developed from a verse by
Omar Khayyam, d. 1123
Used by permission

THE REFLECTIVE SPIRIT

38 Wonder

ERFYNIAD   10 10. 10 10   Ieuan Gwyllt's *Llyfr Tonau Cynulleidfaol*, 1859
har. David Evans, 1874-1948
By permission of Oxford University Press and the Exors. of David Evans

Knowledge, they say, drives wonder from the world:
They'll say it still, though all the dust's ablaze
With marvels at their feet — while Newton's laws
Foretell that knowledge one day shall be song.

We seem like children wandering by the shore,
Gathering pebbles coloured by the wave;
While the great sea of truth, from sky to sky
Stretches before us, boundless, unexplored.

from Alfred Noyes, 1880-1958
Used by permission of Hugh Noyes

THE REFLECTIVE SPIRIT

MOSSDALE   L.M.D.

David Dawson
Used by permission

THE REFLECTIVE SPIRIT

39 We Move in Faith

We move in faith to unseen goals;
We strive in patience through the night
Which weighs upon our doubting souls,
To some great realm of love and light.
For still the ignorance that kills,
And still the hatreds that divide,
And still the strife of warring wills
Subdue our strength and check our pride.

But even as we fail, our aim
Grows larger from our high attempt;
And while we suffer love's large blame,
And reason's most august contempt,
We grow in greatness of design,
In higher powers of patient toil,
In hopes that seize the secret sign
Of far-off joys which naught may foil.

Malcolm Quin, 1854-1944

40 The Depths of Inner Space

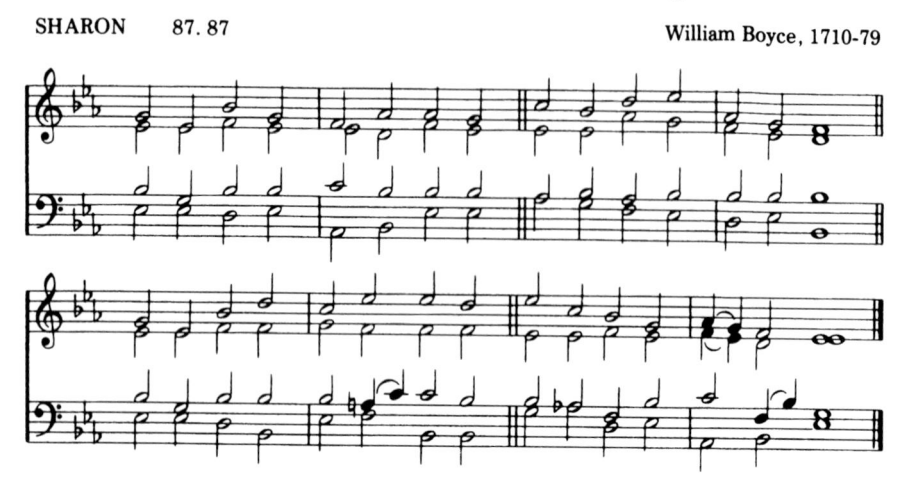

SHARON   87. 87   William Boyce, 1710-79

Once the fearless navigator
   Sailing from some native shore,
Bravely crossed uncharted waters,
   Finding new lands to explore.

Now we look beyond our planet,
   Reaching upward to the stars:
We have walked the lunar deserts —
   Soon we'll tread the soil of Mars.

All that science may discover,
   As the Universe it delves,
Will be only scraps of knowledge
   If we fail to know ourselves.

So the journey of the spirit,
   Which each human soul must face,
Takes us on a greater voyage
   To the depths of inner space.

John Andrew Storey, 1935 —
Used by permission

THE REFLECTIVE SPIRIT

41   I Cannot Lose Thee!

DONNE SECOURS   11 10. 11 10   Psalm 12 in the *Genevan Psalter*, 1551
Unison

I cannot find thee! Still on restless pinion
  My spirit beats the void where thou dost dwell:
I wander lost through all thy vast dominion,
  And shrink beneath thy light ineffable.

I cannot find thee! E'en when most adoring
  Before thy shrine I bend in lowliest prayer:
Beyond these bounds of thought my thought upsoaring
  From farthest quest comes back: thou art not there!

Yet high above the limits of my seeing,
  And folded far within my inmost heart,
And deep below the deeps of conscious being,
  Thy splendour shineth: there, O God, thou art!

I cannot lose thee! Still in thee abiding,
  The end is clear, how wide soe'er I roam:
The law that holds the worlds my steps is guiding,
  And I must rest at last in thee, my home.

                              Eliza Scudder, 1821-96

THE REFLECTIVE SPIRIT

42   A Dream of Widening Love

CRÜGER   76. 76. D.

William Henry Monk, 1823-89
from a Chorale by Johann Crüger, 1598-1662

We rest awhile in quietness,
   The world not to forget,
But rather shape the silence
   And words and thoughts we've met
To nobler ways of living,
   To hope-filled truth, above
Our narrow selves, to seek one
   Great dream of widening love.

THE REFLECTIVE SPIRIT

We share a world where sorrow
　　And poverty and greed
Live side by side with privilege
　　Of wealth beyond true need;
Yet though we cannot alter
　　All ways of humankind,
We ask a strength within us
　　To right the wrongs we find.

We know that strength is weakened
　　By narrow truths and fears,
That still we claim true knowledge,
　　Deny the changing years:
Yet here, within the silence,
　　We question what we know,
That through more honest persons
　　All humankind may grow.

To find Eternal Meaning
　　Deep in each passing hour,
To seek beyond the confines
　　Of our small powers, one Power.
Strength deep within our being,
　　Arise as hope and will:
Come, silent living Spirit,
　　With peace our spirits fill.

　　　　　　　　　Frank R. Clabburn, 1947 —
　　　　　　　　　　　Used by permission

43 Universal Spirit

MÁTI SVETA   4 4. 3. T.

Norbert F. Capek, 1870-1942
har. David Dawson
by permission of Mrs. B. Capek Haspl

Mother Spirit,
Father Spirit,
  Where are you?
In the skysong,
In the forest,
  Sounds your cry.
What to give you,
What to call you,
  What am I?

Many drops are
In the ocean,
  Deep and wide.
Sunlight bounces
Off the ripples
  To the sky.
What to give you,
What to call you,
  Who am I?

I am empty,
Time flies from me;
  What is time?
Dreams eternal,
Fears infernal
  Haunt my heart.
What to give you,
What to call you,
  O, my God?

Mother Spirit,
Father Spirit,
  Take our hearts.
Take our breath and
Let our voices
  Sing our parts.
Take our hands and
Let us work to
  Shape our art.

English version by Richard Frederick Boeke, 1931—
of tr. by Paul and Anita Munk
of Czech Hymn by Norbert F. Capek, 1870-1942
Used by permission

THE REFLECTIVE SPIRIT

44 Come, My Life

POSEN 7 7. 7 7.

Georg Christoph Strattner, 1650-1705
Version in *Geistreiches Gesangbuch* (1704)
of Johann August Freylinghausen, 1670-1739

Come, my way, my truth, my life:
Such a way as gives us breath,
Such a truth as ends all strife,
Such a life as killeth death.

Come, my light, my feast, my strength:
Such a light as shows a feast,
Such a feast as mends in length,
Such a strength as makes a guest.

Come, my joy, my love, my heart:
Such a joy as none can move,
Such a love as none can part,
Such a heart as joys in love.

from George Herbert, 1593-1632

THE REFLECTIVE SPIRIT

DOWN AMPNEY 6 6. 11. D. Ralph Vaughan Williams, 1872-1958
From the English Hymnal, by permission of Oxford University Press

THE REFLECTIVE SPIRIT

45 Come Down, O Love Divine

Come down, O Love divine,
Seek thou this soul of mine,
And visit it with thine own ardour glowing;
O Comforter, draw near,
Within my heart appear,
And kindle it, thy holy flame bestowing.

O let it freely burn,
Till earthly passions turn
To dust and ashes in its heat consuming;
And let its glorious light
Shine ever on my sight,
And clothe me round, the while my path illuming.

Let holy charity
Mine outward vesture be,
And lowliness become my inner clothing;
True lowliness of heart,
Which takes the humbler part,
And o'er its own shortcomings weeps with loathing.

And so the yearning strong,
With which the soul will long,
Shall far outpass the power of human telling;
For none can guess its grace,
Till we become the place
Wherein the Holy Spirit makes a dwelling.

Bianco da Siena, d. 1434
tr. Richard Frederick Littledale, 1833-90

46 Breath of God

CARLISLE S. M. Charles Lockhart, 1745-1815

Breathe on me, Breath of God,
Fill me with life anew,
That I may love what thou dost love,
And do what thou wouldst do.

Breathe on me, Breath of God,
Until my heart is pure,
Until with thee I will one will,
To do or to endure.

Breathe on me, Breath of God,
Till I am wholly thine,
Till all this earthly part of me
Glows with thy fire divine.

Breathe on me, Breath of God,
So shall I never die,
But live with thee the perfect life
Of thine eternity.

Edwin Hatch, 1835-89

THE REFLECTIVE SPIRIT

47 Work Shall Be Prayer

STRACATHRO C. M. Melody by Charles Hutcheson, 1792-1860

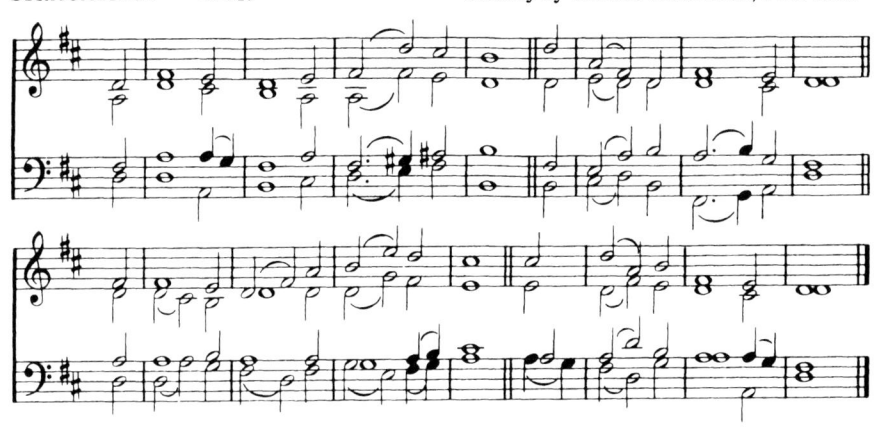

Behold us, God, a little space
From daily tasks set free,
And met within thy holy place
To rest awhile with thee.

Around us rolls the ceaseless tide
Of business, toil and care,
And scarcely can we turn aside
For one brief hour of prayer.

Yet these are not the only walls
Wherein thou may'st be sought:
On homeliest work thy blessing falls,
In truth and patience wrought.

Thine are the loom, the forge, the mart,
The wealth of land and sea,
The worlds of science and of art
Revealed and ruled by thee.

Work shall be prayer, if all be wrought
As thou would'st have it done;
And prayer, by thee inspired and taught,
Itself with work be one.

from John Ellerton, 1826-93

THE REFLECTIVE SPIRIT

48 From All the Fret and Fever

COOLINGE   10 10. 10 10.   Cyril Vincent Taylor, 1907—
From the B.B.C. Hymnbook by permission of Oxford University Press

From all the fret and fever of the day,
Let there be moments when we turn away,
And, deaf to all confusing outer din,
Intently listen for the voice within.

In quietness and solitude we find
The soundless wisdom of the deeper mind;
With clear, harmonious purpose we impart
A richer meaning to the human heart.

from Monroe Beardsley, 1915 —
Used by permission

THE REFLECTIVE SPIRIT

49 Leisure

STRANSGILL L.M.
David Dawson
Used by permission

What is this life if, full of care,
We have no time to stand and stare —
No time to stand beneath the boughs
And stare as long as sheep or cows;

No time to see, when woods we pass,
Where squirrels hide their nuts in grass —
No time to see in broad daylight,
Streams full of stars, like stars at night;

No time to turn at Beauty's glance,
And watch her feet, how they can dance.
A poor life this if, full of care,
We have no time to stand and stare.

William Henry Davies, 1871-1940
From The Complete Poems of W.H.Davies
by permission of Jonathan Cape Ltd.
and the Executors of The W.H.Davies Estate

THE REFLECTIVE SPIRIT

50 Not Always on the Mount

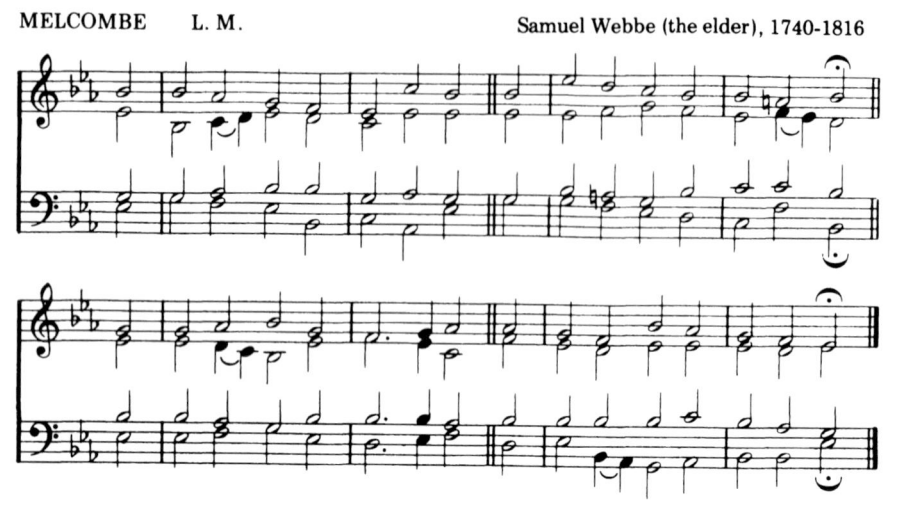

MELCOMBE L. M. Samuel Webbe (the elder), 1740-1816

Not always on the mount may we
Rapt in the heavenly vision be:
The shores of thought and feeling know
The spirit's tidal ebb and flow.

Yet shall one such exalted hour
Bring to the soul redeeming power,
And in new strength through after days
We travel our appointed ways.

Now all the lowly vale grows bright,
Transfigured in remembered light,
And in untiring souls we bear
The freshness of the upper air.

The mount for vision: but below
The paths of daily duty go,
And nobler life therein shall own
The pattern on the mountain shown.

Frederick Lucian Hosmer, 1840-1929

THE REFLECTIVE SPIRIT

51 Inward Peace and Inward Living

STUTTGART 87. 87.   Christian Friedrich Witt, 1660-1716

Hear the city noise around us,
  Feel its escalating pace,
Touch its nerve and note its tension;
  Set ourselves to run its race.

Swiftly, strongly we must function,
  Later we may know some peace;
All our days are meant for action,
  Progress rules and must not cease.

Who dares stop to tell another
  When it's wrong to fall behind?
Who can halt the rush of progress
  When the blind drive on the blind?

Inward peace and inward living
  Must be given rightful place,
Even though we live in cities,
  Even as we run the race.

Care for weakness, ours and others',
  May restore us to the way,
Teaching us to live as neighbours,
  Using well each numbered day.

Bruce Findlow, 1922 —
Used by permission

THE REFLECTIVE SPIRIT

52 Divinity is Round Us

MANCHESTER COLLEGE   10 4. 10 4.   Harold William Spicer, 1888-1977
By permission of Mrs. Muriel Spicer

Divinity is round us — never gone
    From earth or star,
From life or death, from good or even wrong —
    In all we are.

Seek not for God in only noblest deeds —
    Those seldom done;
For God's life throbs in all our anguished needs
    Beneath the sun.

We yearn for God in a perfected one
    By signs foretold —
While in mistakes and virtues just begun
    God's ways unfold.

Wait not at last in truth and love made whole
    Your God to see;
In every timid, false, or angered soul
    There's love to free.

Then wake, O Soul, respect yourself today;
    Create your part;
And look to find your life and truth and way
    With honest art.

from Sophia Lyon Fahs, 1876-1978
by permission of the American Ethical Union

THE REFLECTIVE SPIRIT

53 Calm Soul of All Things

DANIEL L.M.

In moderate time. Unison.

Irish Traditional Melody
Har. Martin Fallas Shaw, 1875-1958
from Songs of Praise for Boys & Girls,
by permission of Oxford University Press

Calm soul of all things, make it mine
To feel, amid the city's jar,
That there abides a peace of thine
We did not make, and cannot mar.

The will to neither strive nor cry,
The power to feel with others, give.
Calm, calm me more; nor let me die
Before I have begun to live.

from Matthew Arnold, 1822-88

THE REFLECTIVE SPIRIT

54 Every Night and Every Morn

THE CALL   77. 77.

Ralph Vaughan Williams, 1872-1958
By permission of Stainer & Bell, Ltd.

Every night and every morn
Some to misery are born;
Every morn and every night
Some are born to sweet delight.

Joy and woe are woven fine,
Clothing for the soul divine:
Under every grief and pine
Runs a joy with silken twine.

It is right and should be so:
We are made for joy and woe;
And when this we rightly know,
Safely through the world we go.

William Blake, 1757-1827

THE REFLECTIVE SPIRIT

55. Scorn Not the Slightest Word

HORSLEY C.M.   William Horsley, 1774-1858

Scorn not the slightest word or deed,
  Nor deem it void of power;
There's fruit in each wind-wafted seed
  That waits its natal hour.

A whispered word may touch the heart,
  And call it back to life;
A look of love bid sin depart
  And still all human strife.

No act falls fruitless; none can tell
  How vast its power may be,
Nor what results infolded dwell
  Within it silently.

Work on, despair not; bring thy mite,
  Nor care how small it be.
God is with all who serve the right,
  The holy, true, and free.

Thomas Hincks, 1818-99

THE REFLECTIVE SPIRIT

56 Faith

NORTHBROOK 11 10. 11 10. Reginald Sparshatt Thatcher, 1888-1957
From the Clarendon Hymn Book, by permission of Oxford University Press

In this stern hour, whene'er the spirit falters
  Before the weight of fear, the nameless dread;
When lights burn low upon accustomed altars,
  And meaningless are half the prayers we've said —

THE REFLECTIVE SPIRIT

Faith seeks a rock, immovable, unchanging,
   On which to build the fortress of its strength,
Some pole-star, fixed, beyond the planets' ranging,
   Steadfast and true throughout the journey's length.

Older than any creed of our evolving,
   Wiser than any prophet of the day —
The human heart, the brown sweet earth revolving!
   Take these, O faith! although they both be clay.

Yet through them both there runs a fire supernal —
   Part of the very stars' bright diagram:
They spell that Word, primordial and eternal,
   Which said, "Before Jehovah was, I AM!"

Eleanor Shipp Johnson, 1863-1947
By permission of John Lamar Davis

57 Teach me, my God and King

SANDYS S.M.
English Traditional Carol

Teach me, my God and King,
In all things thee to see,
And what I do in anything
To do it as for thee.

Whoever looks on glass
On it may stay the eye;
Or if it pleaseth, through it pass,
And then the heaven espy.

All may of thee partake:
Nothing can be so mean,
Which, with this tincture, "For thy sake,"
Will not grow bright and clean.

A servant with this clause
Makes drudgery divine:
Who sweeps a room, as for thy laws,
Makes that and the action fine.

This is the famous stone
That turneth all to gold:
For that which God doth touch and own
Cannot for less be told.

from George Herbert, 1593-1632

THE REFLECTIVE SPIRIT

58 The Soul's Sincere Desire

CAITHNESS C.M. Melody in *Scottish Psalter*, 1635

Prayer is the soul's sincere desire,
　　Uttered or unexpressed,
The motion of a hidden fire
　　That trembles in the breast.

Prayer is the burden of a sigh,
　　The falling of a tear,
The upward glancing of an eye
　　When none but God is near.

Prayer is the simplest form of speech
　　That infant lips can try;
Prayer the sublimest strains that reach
　　The Majesty on high.

O thou by whom we come to God,
　　The life, the truth, the way,
The path of prayer thyself has trod;
　　Lord, teach us how to pray.

James Montgomery, 1771-1854

THE REFLECTIVE SPIRIT

59 Prayer for Strength

MARCHING 87. 87.

Martin Fallas Shaw, 1875-1958
By permission of J. Curwen & Sons, Ltd.

Hear, O God, the prayer we offer:
   Not for ease that prayer shall be,
But for strength that we may ever
   Live our lives courageously.

Not for ever in green pastures
   Do we ask our way to be;
But by steep and rugged pathways
   Would we strive to climb to thee.

Not for ever by still waters
   Would we idly quiet stay;
But would win the living fountains
   From the rocks along our way.

Be our strength in hours of weakness,
   In our wanderings be our guide;
Through endeavour, failure, danger,
   Be thou ever at our side.

from Love Maria Willis, 1824-1908

THE REFLECTIVE SPIRIT

60 Trust in Life

BEATITUDO C. M. John Bacchus Dykes, 1823-76

We do not seek a shallow faith,
   A God to keep us free
From trial and error, harm and death,
   Wherever we may be.

For none can live and not grow old,
   Nor love and not risk loss:
Though life bring raptures manifold,
   Each one must bear some cross.

When future days seem but a mass
   Of menace more than hope,
We pray not for the cup to pass,
   But strength that we may cope.

God grant us faith that when some ill
   Unwonted comes our way,
Deep in our hearts, thy Spirit will
   Give power to win the day.

And if from fear of pain or strife,
   Calm peace we cannot win,
Then give us faith to trust thy Life
   Invincible within.

Sydney Henry Knight, 1923 —

THE REFLECTIVE SPIRIT

61 My Spirit Longs for Thee

ST. CECILIA 66. 66. Leighton George Hayne, 1836-83

My spirit longs for thee
Within my troubled breast,
Though I unworthy be
Of so divine a guest:

Of so divine a guest
Unworthy though I be,
Yet has my heart no rest,
Unless it come from thee:

Unless it come from thee,
In vain I look around:
In all that I can see
No rest is to be found:

No rest is to be found,
But in thy blessèd love:
O let my wish be crowned,
And send it from above!

John Byrom, 1691-1763

THE REFLECTIVE SPIRIT

62 God Moves in a Mysterious Way

LONDON NEW   C. M.   *Playford's Psalms*, 1671
                                         Adapted from Newtoun in *Scottish Psalter*, 1635

God moves in a mysterious way
   His wonders to perform;
He plants his footsteps in the sea,
   And rides upon the storm.

Deep in unfathomable mines
   Of never-failing skill
He treasures up his bright designs,
   And works his sovereign will.

Ye fearful saints, fresh courage take;
   The clouds ye so much dread
Are big with mercy, and shall break
   In blessings on your head.

Judge not the Lord by feeble sense,   His purposes will ripen fast,
   But trust him for his grace;   Unfolding every hour;
Behind a frowning providence   The bud may have a bitter taste,
   He hides a smiling face.   But sweet will be the flower.

Blind unbelief is sure to err,
   And scan his work in vain;
God is his own interpreter,
   And he will make it plain.

William Cowper, 1731-1800

THE REFLECTIVE SPIRIT

63 Holy Spirit, Truth Divine

BUCKLAND 77. 77. Leighton George Hayne, 1836-83

Holy Spirit, Truth divine,
Dawn upon this soul of mine!
Word of God and inward Light,
Wake my spirit, clear my sight.

Holy Spirit, Love divine,
Glow within this heart of mine!
Kindle every high desire,
Perish self in thy pure fire!

Holy Spirit, Power divine,
Fill and nerve this will of mine!
By thee may I strongly live,
Bravely bear and nobly strive.

Holy Spirit, Right divine,
Now within my conscience reign!
Be my law, and I shall be
Firmly bound, for ever free.

Holy Spirit, Peace divine,
Still this restless heart of mine!
Speak to calm this tossing sea,
Stayed in thy tranquillity.

Holy Spirit, Joy divine,
Gladden thou this heart of mine!
In the desert ways I sing—
"Spring, O Well, for ever spring!"

Samuel Longfellow, 1819-92

THE REFLECTIVE SPIRIT

The Judaeo-Christian Heritage

64 The Old Hundredth

OLD HUNDREDTH   L.M.   Louis Bourgeois, c.1523-1600

All people that on earth do dwell,
Sing to the Lord with cheerful voice;
Him serve with mirth, his praise forth tell;
Come ye before him and rejoice.

O enter, then, his gates with praise,
Approach with joy his courts unto;
Praise, laud, and bless his name always,
For it is seemly so to do.

For why, the Lord our God is good,
His mercy is for ever sure;
His truth at all times firmly stood,
And shall from age to age endure.

William Kethe, d.1593

THE JUDAEO-CHRISTIAN HERITAGE

65   O God Our Help in Ages Past

ST. ANNE   C.M.   Probably by William Croft, 1678-1727

O God, our help in ages past,
   Our hope for years to come,
Our shelter from the stormy blast,
   And our eternal home!

Before the hills in order stood,
   Or earth received her frame,
From everlasting thou art God,
   To endless years the same.

A thousand ages in thy sight
   Are like an evening gone,
Short as the watch that ends the night
   Before the rising sun.

Time, like an ever-rolling stream,
   Bears all of us away;
We fly forgotten, as a dream
   Dies at the opening day.

O God, our help in ages past,
   Our hope for years to come,
Be thou our guard while troubles last,
   And our eternal home.

from Isaac Watts, 1674-1748

THE JUDAEO-CHRISTIAN HERITAGE

66 The Lord's My Shepherd

CRIMOND   C.M.

Jessie Seymour Irvine, 1836-87
adapted by David Grant

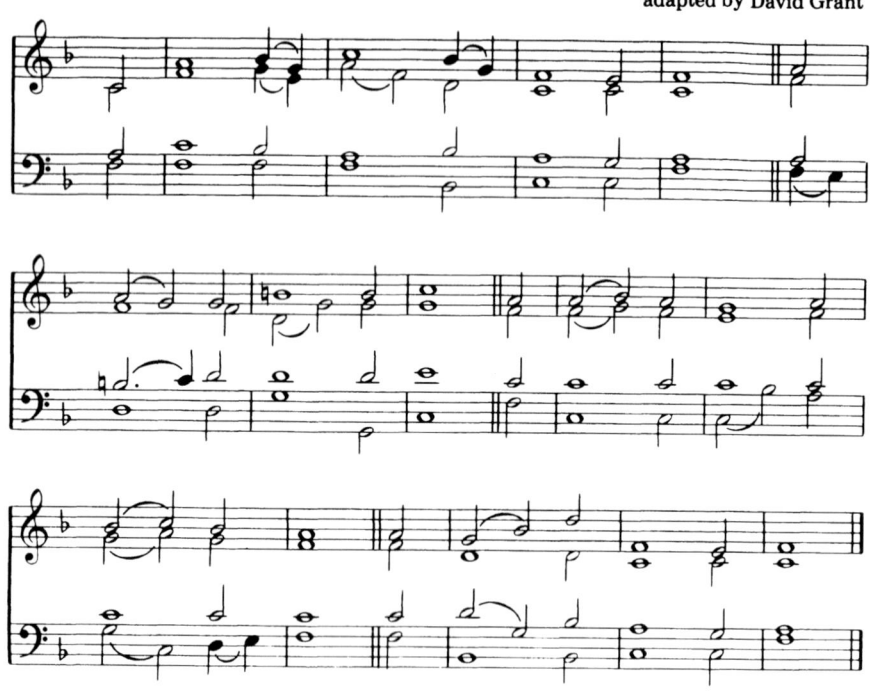

The Lord's my Shepherd, I'll not want,
   He makes me down to lie
In pastures green, he leadeth me
   The quiet waters by.

My soul he doth restore again;
   And me to walk doth make
Within the paths of righteousness,
   E'en for his own name's sake.

Yea, though I walk in death's dark vale,
   Yet will I fear no ill;
For thou art with me, and thy rod
   And staff me comfort still.

My table thou hast furnishèd
   In presence of my foes;
My head thou dost with oil anoint,
   And my cup overflows.

Goodness and mercy all my life
   Shall surely follow me;
And in God's house for evermore
   My dwelling-place shall be.

Scottish Psalter

THE JUDAEO-CHRISTIAN HERITAGE

67 In Praise of Wisdom

LLEF L.M. Griffith H. Jones (Gutyn Arfon), 1849-1919

Wisdom has riches which exceed
The treasured bounty of the earth;
The jewelled objects of our greed
Can never match her priceless worth.

Although the ruby glows like fire,
And gold is precious when refined,
Yet wisdom we should more desire
Than all the riches we have mined.

For length of days is hers to give;
With honour she shall crown your head;
In peace she counsels us to live
And pleasant are her paths to tread.

Who seeks her in the common strife,
And, having found her, holds her fast,
To such she is a tree of life,
And hers the fruits which ever last.

Get wisdom, she shall serve you well;
Make love of her your highest goal;
Within her temple safely dwell
Till understanding floods your soul.

For wisdom is the greatest thing;
In humble longing seek her face,
And she will crown you as a king
And give an ornament of grace.

John Andrew Storey, 1935—
Used by permission

THE JUDAEO-CHRISTIAN HERITAGE

68 Praise the Great and Famous

ST.COLUMBA   87.87. Iambic   Irish Melody

Now praise we great and famous men
   And women named in story;
And praise our God who now as then
   Reveals, in all, true glory.

Praise we the wise and brave and strong,
   Who graced their generation:
Who helped the right and fought the wrong,
   And made our folk a nation.

Praise we the great of heart and mind,
   The singers sweetly gifted,
Whose music, like a mighty wind,
   The souls of all uplifted.

THE JUDAEO-CHRISTIAN HERITAGE

Praise we the peaceful hand of skill
   Which builded homes of beauty,
And, rich in art, made richer still
   The fellowship of duty.

Praise we the glorious names we know;
   And they whose names are perished,
Lost in the haze of long ago,
   In silent love be cherished.

In peace their sacred ashes rest;
   Fulfilled their day's endeavour;
They blessed the earth, and they are blessed
   Of God and us for ever.

From William George Tarrant, 1853-1928

LEONI 66.84.D.

From a Hebrew Melody
noted by Thomas Olivers, 1725-99

THE JUDAEO-CHRISTIAN HERITAGE

69 Praise to the Living God!

Praise to the living God!
  All praisèd be the name,
Who was, and is, and is to be,
  For aye the same!
The one eternal God
  Ere aught that now appears:
The first, the last, beyond all thought,
  God's timeless years!

Formless, all lovely forms
  Declare this loveliness;
Holy, no holiness of earth
  Can God express.
Lo, God is over all!
  Creation speaks in praise,
And everywhere, above, below,
  This will obeys.

The Spirit floweth free,
  High surging where it will:
In prophet's word it spoke of old —
  And speaketh still.
Established is God's law,
  And changeless it shall stand,
Deep writ upon the human heart,
  On sea, or land.

Eternal life hath been
  Implanted in the soul;
God's love shall be our strength and stay
  While ages roll.
Praise to the living God!
  All praisèd be the name,
Who was, and is, and is to be,
  For aye the same!

Daniel Ben Judah, 14th Century
from tr. Newton Mann, 19th Century
and William Channing Gannett, 1840-1923

THE JUDAEO-CHRISTIAN HERITAGE

70 O Worship the King

HANOVER 10 10. 11 11. Probably by William Croft, 1678-1727

O worship the King, all glorious above;
O gratefully sing his power and his love;
Our shield and defender, the Ancient of Days,
Pavilioned in splendour and girded with praise.

O tell of his might, O sing of his grace,
Whose robe is the light, whose canopy space;
His chariots of wrath the deep thunder-clouds form,
And dark is his path on the wings of the storm.

The earth with its store of wonders untold,
Almighty, thy power hath founded of old;
Hath stablished it fast by a changeless decree,
And round it hath cast, like a mantle, the sea.

Thy bountiful care what tongue can recite?
It breathes in the air, it shines in the light;
It streams from the hills, it descends to the plain,
And sweetly distils in the dew and the rain.

Frail children of dust, and feeble as frail,
In thee do we trust, nor find thee to fail;
The humbler creation, though feeble their lays,
With true adoration shall sing to thy praise.

from Robert Grant, 1779-1838

THE JUDAEO-CHRISTIAN HERITAGE

71 Praise to the Lord, the Almighty

LOBE DEN HERREN 14 14. 4. 7. 8. *Stralsund Gesangbuch,* 1665

Praise to the Lord, the Almighty, the King of creation;
O my soul, praise him, for he is thy health and salvation:
    All ye who hear,
    Now to his temple draw near,
  Joining in glad adoration.

Praise to the Lord, who o'er all things so wondrously reigneth,
Shelters thee under his wings, yea, so gently sustaineth:
    Hast thou not seen
    How thy entreaties have been
  Granted in what he ordaineth?

Praise to the Lord, who doth prosper thy work and defend thee;
Surely his goodness and mercy shall daily attend thee:
    Ponder anew
    What the Almighty can do,
  Who with his love doth befriend thee.

Praise to the Lord! O let all that is in me adore him!
All that hath life and breath come now with praises before him!
    Let the Amen
    Sound from his people again:
  Gladly for aye we adore him!

Joachim Neander, 1650-80
tr. Catherine Winkworth, 1827-78, and others

THE JUDAEO-CHRISTIAN HERITAGE

LUCKINGTON 10 4. 6 6. 6 6. 10 4.   Basil Harwood, 1859-1949
By permission of the Executors of the late Dr. Basil Harwood

THE JUDAEO-CHRISTIAN HERITAGE

72 My God and King

Let all the world in every corner sing
    "My God and King!"
The heavens are not too high;
His praise may thither fly:
The earth is not too low;
His praises there may grow.
Let all the world in every corner sing
    "My God and King!"

Let all the world in every corner sing
    "My God and King!"
The Church with psalms must shout,
No door can keep them out:
But, above all, the heart
Must bear the longest part.
Let all the world in every corner sing
    "My God and King!"

George Herbert, 1593-1632

73 A Mighty Fortress

EIN' FESTE BURG   87. 87. 66. 667.   Melody by Martin Luther, 1483-1546

A mighty fortress is our God,
    A bulwark never failing;
Our helper still, amid the flood
    Of mortal ills prevailing.
For still our ancient foe
Doth seek to work us woe;
With craft and power great,
And, armed with cruel hate,
On earth there is no equal.

God's word above all earthly powers—
    No thanks to them— abideth;
The spirit and the gifts are ours,
    Through God, who with us sideth.
Let goods and kindred go,
This mortal life also;
The body they may kill;
God's truth abideth still,
And reigns in love for ever.

Martin Luther, 1483-1546
tr. Frederic Henry Hedge, 1805-90

THE JUDAEO-CHRISTIAN HERITAGE

74   We are the Earth

We are the earth, upright and proud;
  In us the earth is knowing:
Its winds are music in our mouth,
  In us its rivers flowing.
The sun is our hearth-fire,
Warm with the earth's desire,
And with its purpose strong,
We sing earth's pilgrim song:
  In us the earth is growing.

We lift our voices, fill the skies
  With our exultant singing.
We dedicate our minds and hearts,
  Beauty and order bringing.
Our labour is our strength;
Our love will win at length;
Our minds will find the ways
To live in peace and praise:
  Our day is just beginning.

                Kenneth L. Patton, 1911—
                    Used by permission

AUSTRIA 8 7. 8 7. D. Franz Josef Haydn, 1732-1809

THE JUDAEO-CHRISTIAN HERITAGE

75 God of Ages and of Nations

God of ages and of nations!
  Every race and every time
Hath received thine inspirations,
  Glimpses of thy truth sublime.
Ever spirits, in rapt vision,
  Passed the heavenly veil within;
Ever hearts, bowed in contrition,
  Found salvation from their sin.

Reason's noble aspiration
  Truth in growing clearness saw;
Conscience spoke its condemnation,
  Or proclaimed the eternal law.
While thine inward revelations
  Told the saints their prayers were heard,
Prophets to the guilty nations
  Spoke thine everlasting word.

God, that word abideth ever;
  Revelation is not sealed;
Answering unto our endeavour,
  Truth and right are still revealed.
That which came to ancient sages,
  Greek, Barbarian, Roman, Jew,
Written in the heart's deep pages,
  Shines today, for ever new!

from Samuel Longfellow, 1819-92

THE JUDAEO-CHRISTIAN HERITAGE

76 Immortal, Invisible

ST. DENIO   11 11. 11 11.

Welsh Hymn Melody
Caniadau y Cyssegr (1839) of John Roberts (Henllan)

  Immortal, invisible, God only wise,
  In light inaccessible hid from our eyes,
  Most blessèd, most glorious, the Ancient of Days,
  Almighty, victorious, thy great name we praise.

  Unresting, unhasting, and silent as light,
  Nor wanting, nor wasting, thou rulest in might:
  Thy justice like mountains high soaring above
  Thy clouds, which are fountains of goodness and love.

  To all life thou givest — to both great and small;
  In all life thou livest, the true life of all;
  We blossom and flourish as leaves on the tree,
  And wither and perish; but nought changeth thee.

  Great Spirit of glory, pure source of all light,
  Thine angels adore thee, all veiling their sight;
  All laud we would render: O help us to see
  'Tis only the splendour of light hideth thee.

from Walter Chalmers Smith, 1824-1908

THE JUDAEO-CHRISTIAN HERITAGE

77 Our Parents' Faith

DOMINUS REGIT ME　　87.87. Iambic.　　John Bacchus Dykes, 1823-76

Our parents' faith, we'll sing of thee,
　Dear faith, which still we cherish:
Nor may their children's children see
　That faith decay and perish.

We may not think our parents' thought;
　Their creeds our lips may alter;
But in the faith they dearly bought
　Our hearts shall never falter.

O may that faith our hearts inspire
　To earnest thought and labour,
That we may share its heavenly fire
　With every friend and neighbour:

'Tis faith in God, and in ourselves,
　'Tis faith in truth and beauty,
In freedom's might and reason's right,
　And all-controlling duty.

from John White Chadwick, 1840-1904

THE JUDAEO-CHRISTIAN HERITAGE

78 Honourable Saints

EVELYNS 65. 65. D.
William Henry Monk, 1823-89

We will honour Michael
For his quest in God,
Challenging convention
Everywhere he trod.
When he reached Geneva
He was cast in gaol,
Sentenced, burned and damned, but
All to no avail.

THE JUDAEO-CHRISTIAN HERITAGE

Next we honour Faustus
  For his reasoning mind,
Which—applied to scripture—
  Insights there refined.
From his southern homeland
  Europe he did roam,
Till the Polish Brethren
  Gave him welcome home.

Now we honour Francis
  For debating skill;
Who in land beyond the trees
  Is remembered still.
Faith to faith he travelled
  On until he came,
Searching scripture's pages,
  To the simple name.

Praising you, our Father,
  God in unity;
Honouring our Jesus
  In humanity.
We who now acclaim these
  Stars for work begun,
Also still proclaim in
  Faith that God is one.

Andrew McKean Hill, 1942—
Used by permission

Michael Servetus (1511-1553) was born in Spain, studied medicine in Paris and anticipated William Harvey's discovery of the circulation of the blood. He was interested in theology, and wrote on the errors of the trinity. He was burned at Geneva on 27 October 1553, insisting that Jesus was the son of the eternal God and not the eternal son of God.

Faustus Socinus (1539-1604) was an Italian who settled in Poland with the Polish Brethren whose successors became known as Socinians because of his influence among them. He argued that Jesus saved people, not by dying for them, but by setting an example to follow.

Francis Dávid (1520-1579) lived and worked in Transylvania (the land beyond the trees) now in north-western Romania. Born a Catholic, he became a Lutheran, then a Calvinist, and eventually a Unitarian. Through debating skill, he carried many with him, including the Transylvanian ruler, John Sigismund. Following a change in ruler, he was sentenced to perpetual imprisonment and died in prison on 15 November 1579. The Hungarian-speaking Unitarian Church in Romania, of which Dávid was the first Bishop, is the oldest organised Unitarian church in the world. 'The simple name' refers to the assertion that God is one as distinct from the complex three.

THE JUDAEO-CHRISTIAN HERITAGE

79 For All The Saints

SINE NOMINE   10 10 10. 4.   Ralph Vaughan Williams, 1872-1958
Voices in Unison   *From the English Hymnal, by permission of Oxford University Press*

    For all the saints, who from their labours rest,
    Who thee by faith before the world confessed,
    Thy name, O Jesus, be for ever blest:
        Alleluia, Alleluia!

    Thou wast their rock, their fortress, and their might;
    Thou, Lord, their captain in the well-fought fight;
    Thou, in the darkness drear, their one true light:
        Alleluia, Alleluia!

    And when the strife is fierce, the warfare long,
    Steals on the ear the distant triumph-song,
    And hearts are brave again, and arms are strong:
        Alleluia, Alleluia!

    O may thy soldiers, faithful, true, and bold,
    Fight as the saints who nobly fought of old,
    And win, with them, the victor's crown of gold:
        Alleluia, Alleluia!

                                          William Walsham How, 1823-97

THE JUDAEO-CHRISTIAN HERITAGE

80 The Child is Promise

ENGELBERG 10 10 10. 4 Charles Villiers Stanford, 1852-1924

We celebrate the holy gift of light
That grows concealed in winter's tomb of night;
In human form it bursts forth shining bright:
    Alleluia!

In hidden mangers now the child is born
To weary souls, who, anxious and forlorn,
Awake to joys they once believed outworn:
    Alleluia!

The child is promise: love will come to birth
And lessen hatred's hold upon the earth
By softening hardened hearts with simple mirth:
    Alleluia!

The darkened world no longer dulls the heart,
The crystal star has new light to impart;
With each new life, all life anew will start:
    Alleluia!

Don Wayne Vaughn
Used by permission

THE JUDAEO-CHRISTIAN HERITAGE: ADVENT

WACHET AUF 898.D. 664. 88.   Melody attributed to Philipp Nicolai, 1556-1608
adpt. and har. Johann Sebastian Bach, 1685-1750

THE JUDAEO-CHRISTIAN HERITAGE: ADVENT

81   Advent Hymn

Here's the time of preparation;
Our hearts now know anticipation
As Christmas Day draws near once more.
Dying sun, midwinter coldness;
Yet we shall see the festal boldness
Of evergreens around the door.
   Our memories will stir
   As lights adorn the fir,
     Come this season.
Our gifts we'll choose, bright cards peruse,
As greetings flow from shore to shore.

Listen now to carol-singing;
Hark to the herald-angels bringing
The word to shepherds long ago.
Candles gleam and fires are lighted,
And travellers coming home are sighted,
To share their gifts with those they know.
   We shall prepare the way,
   So this belovèd day
     Knows a welcome.
With open heart we'll make the start
Of this glad time our love to show.

Soon the hours of merry-making,
For giving and for humbly taking,
As Christmas sharings grace our ways.
God of love, we'll know your presence;
And God of joy, you are the essence
Of all true pleasure and of praise.
   And we shall hope until
   The morning brings the thrill
     Of a vision
Of peace on earth, its symbol, birth!
To make bright joy of future days.

                                      John Andrew Midgley, 1939—
                                          Used by permission

BESANCON CAROL 87. 98. 87

French Carol
har. John Stainer, 1840-1901

THE JUDAEO-CHRISTIAN HERITAGE: ADVENT

82 People, Look East

People, look east! The time is near
Of the crowning of the year.
Make your house fair as you are able,
Trim the hearth, and set the table.
   People, look east, and sing today:
   Love, the guest, is on the way.

Furrows, be glad! Though earth is bare,
One more seed is planted there:
Give up your strength the seed to nourish,
That, in course, the flower may flourish.
   People, look east, and sing today:
   Love, the rose, is on the way.

Stars, keep the watch! When night is dim,
One more light the bowl shall brim,
Shining beyond the frosty weather,
Bright as sun and moon together.
   People, look east, and sing today:
   Love, the star, is on the way.

Eleanor Farjeon, 1881-1965
From the Oxford Book of Carols
by permission of David Higham Associates, Ltd.

83 These Festive Days

CAROL C.M.D. Richard Storrs Willis, 1819-1900

Our festival is here again
 To lift the darkening year,
And celebrate the Feast of Lights
 'Mid glow of Christmas cheer.
For not alone was Jesus sought
 By wise men, from afar:
The joy of other hallowed births
 Glows with the wondrous star.

And Hanukkah is freedom's shrine
 To all 'neath tyranny;
The lamps are lit within our hearts,
 For faith can make us free.
Joy to the world, these festive days;
 Nowhere may hope be dim;
And as the gladsome spirit glows,
 Sing carol, song and hymn!

John Irving Daniel, 1903—
Used by permission

THE JUDAEO-CHRISTIAN HERITAGE: HANUKKAH

84 While Shepherds Watched

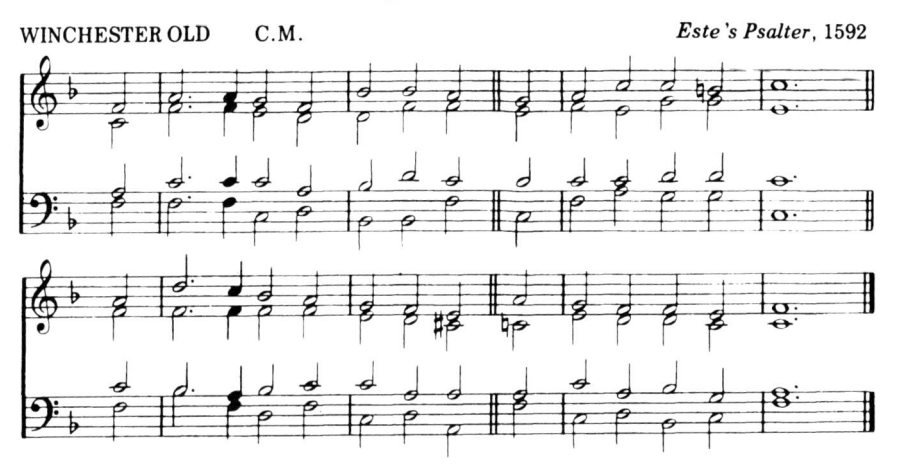

WINCHESTER OLD   C.M.   *Este's Psalter*, 1592

While shepherds watched their flocks by night,
   All seated on the ground,
The angel of the Lord came down,
   And glory shone around.

"Fear not," said he (for mighty dread
   Had seized their troubled mind),
"Glad tidings of great joy I bring
   To you and all mankind.

"To you, in David's town, this day
   Is born of David's line
A Saviour, who is Christ the Lord;
   And this shall be the sign:

"The heavenly Babe you there shall find
   To human view displayed,
All meanly wrapped in swathing bands,
   And in a manger laid."

Thus spake the seraph; and forthwith
   Appeared a shining throng
Of angels, praising God, and thus
   Addressed their joyful song:

"All glory be to God on high,
   And to the earth be peace;
Goodwill henceforth from heaven to men
   Begin and never cease!"

Nahum Tate, 1652-1715

THE JUDAEO-CHRISTIAN HERITAGE: CHRISTMAS

85 O Little Town of Bethlehem

FOREST GREEN   C.M.D.   English Traditional Melody
Coll., Adapt. and arr. Ralph Vaughan Williams, 1872-1958
From the English Hymnal, by permission of Oxford University Press

O little town of Bethlehem,
How still we see thee lie!
Above thy deep and dreamless sleep
The silent stars go by;
Yet in thy dark street shineth
The everlasting light;
The hopes and fears of all the years
Are met in thee tonight.

THE JUDAEO-CHRISTIAN HERITAGE: CHRISTMAS

O morning stars, together
  Proclaim the holy birth,
And praises sing to God the King,
  And peace throughout the earth:
For Christ is born of Mary—
  And gathered all above,
While mortals sleep, the angels keep
  Their watch of wondering love.

How silently, how silently,
  The wondrous gift is given!
So God imparts to human hearts
  The peace and joy of heaven.
No ear may hear his coming;
  But in this world of sin,
Where meek souls will receive him, still
  The dear Christ enters in.

From Phillips Brooks, 1835-93

86 In the Lonely Midnight

LAWNSWOOD   65. 65. D.

David Dawson

Used by permission

In the lonely midnight,
  On the wintry hill,
Shepherds heard the angels
  Singing, "Peace, goodwill."
Listen, O ye weary,
  To the angels' song:
Unto you the tidings
  Of great joy belong.

Though in David's city
  Angels sing no more,
Love makes angel music
  On earth's darkest shore:
Though no heavenly glory
  Meet your wondering eyes,
Love can make your dwelling
  Bright as paradise.

Though the child of Mary,
  Heralded on high,
In his manger cradle
  May no longer lie,
Love is queen for ever,
  Though the proud world scorn:
If we truly seek him,
  Christ for us is born!

from Theodore Chickering Williams, 1855-1915

THE JUDAEO-CHRISTIAN HERITAGE: CHRISTMAS

87 In the Bleak Midwinter

CRANHAM 6 5. 6 5. D.

Gustav Theodore Holst, 1874-1934

In the bleak mid-winter
　Frosty wind made moan,
Earth stood hard as iron,
　Water like a stone;
Snow had fallen, snow on snow,
　Snow on snow,
In the bleak mid-winter
　Long ago.

In the ancient story
　Of the infant's birth
Angels in their glory
　Promised peace on earth;
But only his mother,
　With a mother's bliss,
Worshipped the belovèd
　With a kiss.

Christ was homeless stranger,
　So the gospels say,
Cradled in a manger
　And a bed of hay:
In the bleak mid-winter
　Stable-place sufficed
Mary and her baby
　Jesus Christ.

Once more child and mother
　Weave their magic spell,
Touching hearts with wonder
　Words can never tell:
In the bleak mid-winter,
　In this world of pain,
Where our hearts are open
　Christ is born again.

Christina Georgina Rossetti, 1830-94
with additions

THE JUDAEO-CHRISTIAN HERITAGE: CHRISTMAS

88 Silent Night

STILLE NACHT   6 6. 7 7 5.   adapted from Franz Grüber, 1787-1863

Silent night! peaceful night!
All things sleep, shepherds keep
Watch on Bethlehem's silent hill,
And unseen, while all is still,
    Angels watch above,
    Angels watch above.

Bright the star shines afar,
Guiding travellers on their way;
Who their gold and incense bring,
Offerings to the promised King,
    Child of David's line,
    Child of David's line.

Light around! joyous sound!
Angel voices wake the air:
Glory be to God in heaven,
Peace on earth to you is given:
    Lo! the Christ is born!
    Lo! the Christ is born!

tr. from Joseph Mohr, 1792-1848

THE JUDAEO-CHRISTIAN HERITAGE: CHRISTMAS

89 Long Ago, in Manger Low

NATIVITY C.M. Henry Lahee, 1826-1912

Long, long ago, in manger low
  Was cradled from above
A little child, in whom God smiled,
  A Christmas gift of love.

When hearts were bitter and unjust,
  And cruel hands were strong,
The noise he hushed with hope and trust,
  And peace began her song.

But, sometimes, when God's Christmas gifts
  Seem only frost and snow,
And anxious stress and loneliness
  And poverty and woe;

Straightway provide a welcome wide,
  Nor wonder why they came;
They stand outside our hearts and bide,
  Knocking in Jesus' name.

For trouble, cold, and dreary care
  Are angels in disguise;
And, greeted fair with trust and prayer,
  As peace and love they rise!

They are the manger, rude and low,
  In which a Christ-child lies:
O welcome guest, thy cradle nest
  Is always God's surprise!

From Jane Andrews and
William Channing Gannett, 1840-1923

THE JUDAEO-CHRISTIAN HERITAGE: CHRISTMAS

MENDELSSOHN 7 7. 7 7. D. and refrain. Felix Mendelssohn-Bartholdy, 1809-47
arr. by William H. Cummings, 1831-1915

Organ Pedals

THE JUDAEO-CHRISTIAN HERITAGE: CHRISTMAS

90 Hark! the Herald Angels Sing

Hark! the herald angels sing
Glory to the new-born King!
Peace on earth and mercy mild
Cometh with the holy child.
  Joyful, all ye nations rise!
  Join the triumph of the skies!
  With the angelic host proclaim,
  "Christ is born in Bethlehem!"
  Hark! the herald angels sing
  Glory to the new-born King!

Hail, the holy Prince of Peace!
Hail the Sun of Righteousness!
Light and life to all he brings,
Comes with healing in his wings.
  Veiled in flesh the Godhead see!
  Hail the indwelling Deity!
  Born to raise upon the earth
  All who yearn for love's rebirth.
  Hark! the herald angels sing
  Glory to the new-born King!

From Charles Wesley, 1707-88

THE JUDAEO-CHRISTIAN HERITAGE: CHRISTMAS

91   Midnight Clear

NOEL   C.M.D.

Traditional Air
adapted by Arthur Seymour Sullivan, 1842-1900

It came upon the midnight clear,
That glorious song of old,
From angels bending near the earth
To touch their harps of gold:
"Peace to the earth, goodwill to all,
From heaven's all-gracious King!"
The world in solemn stillness lay
To hear the angels sing.

THE JUDAEO-CHRISTIAN HERITAGE: CHRISTMAS

Still through the cloven skies they come,
   With peaceful wings unfurled;
And still their heavenly music floats
   O'er all the weary world.
Above its sad and lowly plains
   They bend on hovering wing,
And ever o'er its babel sounds
   The blessèd angels sing.

Yet with the woes of sin and strife
   The world has suffered long:
Beneath the angel-strain have rolled
   Two thousand years of wrong;
And those who are at war hear not
   The love-song which they bring:
O hush the noise, all ye of strife,
   And hear the angels sing!

And ye, beneath life's crushing load,
   Whose forms are bending low,
Who toil along the climbing way
   With painful steps and slow:
Look now! for glad and golden hours
   Come swiftly on the wing;
O rest beside the weary road,
   And hear the angels sing!

For lo! the days are hastening on,
   By prophet-bards foretold,
When, with the ever-circling years,
   Comes round the age of gold;
When peace shall over all the earth
   Its ancient splendours fling,
And the whole world send back the song
   Which now the angels sing.

from Edmund Hamilton Sears, 1810-76

THE FIRST NOWELL Irregular

English Traditional Melody
Har. by John Stainer, 1840-1901

THE JUDAEO-CHRISTIAN HERITAGE: CHRISTMAS

92   The First Nowell

The first Nowell the angel did say
Was to certain poor shepherds in fields as they lay;
In fields where they lay keeping their sheep,
On a cold winter's night that was so deep.
Nowell, Nowell, Nowell, Nowell,
Born is the King of Israel.

They lookèd up and saw a star
Shining in the east, beyond them far,
And to the earth it gave great light,
And so it continued both day and night.
Nowell, Nowell, Nowell, Nowell,
Born is the King of Israel.

And by the light of that same star
Three wise men came from country far;
To seek for a king was their intent,
And to follow the star wherever it went.
Nowell, Nowell, Nowell, Nowell,
Born is the King of Israel.

This star drew nigh to the north-west;
O'er Bethlehem it took its rest,
And there it did both stop and stay,
Right over the place where Jesus lay.
Nowell, Nowell, Nowell, Nowell,
Born is the King of Israel.

Then entered in those wise men three,
Full reverently upon their knee,
And offered there, in his presence,
Both gold and myrrh and frankincense.
Nowell, Nowell, Nowell, Nowell,
Born is the King of Israel.

Traditional
From W. Sandys' Christmas Carols Ancient and Modern, 1833

93 Ding Dong! Merrily on High

BRANLE DE L'OFFICIAL 7 7. 7 7. 10 10.

from Thoinot Arbeau's *Orchésographie*, 1588
har. Charles Wood, 1866-1926

Ding dong! merrily on high
In heav'n the bells are ringing:
Ding dong! verily the sky
Is riv'n with angel singing.
   Gloria, Hosanna in excelsis!
   Gloria, Hosanna in excelsis!

E'en so here below, below,
Let steeple bells be swungen,
And i-o, i-o, i-o,
By priest and people sungen.
   Gloria, Hosanna in excelsis!
   Gloria, Hosanna in excelsis!

Pray you, dutifully prime
Your matin chime, ye ringers;
May you beautifully rime
Your eve-time song, ye singers.
   Gloria, Hosanna in excelsis!
   Gloria, Hosanna in excelsis!

George Ratcliffe Woodward, 1848-1934

94. I Heard the Bells

CHURCH TRIUMPHANT L.M. James William Elliott, 1833-1915

I heard the bells on Christmas Day
Their old familiar carols play,
    And wild and sweet
    The words repeat,
"Goodwill to all, and peace on earth!"

I thought how, as the day had come,
The belfries of all Christendom
    Had rolled along
    The unbroken song,
"Goodwill to all, and peace on earth!"

Till, ringing, singing on its way,
The world revolved from night to day,
    A voice, a chime,
    A chant sublime:
"Goodwill to all, and peace on earth!"

And in despair I bowed my head:
"There is no peace on earth," I said.
    "For hate is strong
    And mocks the song:
Goodwill to all and peace on earth!"

Then pealed the bells more loud and deep:
"God is not dead, and doth not sleep!
    The wrong shall fail,
    The right prevail—
Goodwill to all, and peace on earth!"

from Henry Wadsworth Longfellow, 1807-82

THE JUDAEO-CHRISTIAN HERITAGE: CHRISTMAS

95 O Come, all ye Faithful

ADESTE FIDELES (Irregular) Probably by John Francis Wade, c. 1711-86

Without Pedals

Pedals

O come, all ye faithful,
Joyful and triumphant,
O come ye, O come ye to Bethlehem:
Come and behold him
Born this happy morning:
O come, let us adore him,
O come, let us adore him,
O come, let us adore him,
Christ, the Lord.

THE JUDAEO-CHRISTIAN HERITAGE: CHRISTMAS

See how the shepherds,
Summoned to his cradle,
Leaving their flocks draw nigh with lowly fear;
We too will thither
Bend our joyful footsteps:
O come, let us adore him,
O come, let us adore him,
O come, let us adore him,
Christ, the Lord.

Lo, star-led chieftains,
Wise men, Christ adoring,
Offer him incense, gold and myrrh;
We to the Christ-child
Bring our hearts' oblations:
O come, let us adore him,
O come, let us adore him,
O come, let us adore him,
Christ, the Lord.

Sing, choirs of angels,
Sing in exultation,
Sing, all ye citizens of heaven above:
Glory to God
In the highest:
O come, let us adore him,
O come, let us adore him,
O come, let us adore him,
Christ, the Lord.

Latin, 18th Century
from tr. Frederick Oakeley, 1802-80

ANTIOCH   8 6. 8. 6 6 8.   Lowell Mason, 1792-1872

Let peace and free-dom reign! Let peace and free-dom reign! Let love and free-dom reign!

THE JUDAEO-CHRISTIAN HERITAGE: CHRISTMAS

96   Joy to the World

Joy to the world, for peace shall come:
  Let this be our refrain!
In every heart, in every land,
  Let peace and freedom reign!
  Let peace and freedom reign!
Let peace and love and freedom reign!

Joy to the earth where truth is all,
  And justice our domain!
In every mind, in every word,
  Let peace and freedom reign!
  Let peace and freedom reign!
Let peace and love and freedom reign!

Joy to our hearts, good-will to all!
  The earth, the world shall ring
With deeds of love, with songs of praise:
  Let peace and freedom reign!
  Let peace and freedom reign!
Let peace and love and freedom reign!

from William Wolff
after Isaac Watts, 1674-1748
by permission of The Hodgin Press, Los Angeles

97 The Universal Incarnation

SOLOTHURN   L.M.

Swiss Traditional Melody
har. David Dawson
Used by permission

Around the crib all peoples throng
In honour of the Christ-child's birth,
And raise again the ancient song:
'Goodwill to all, and peace on earth.'

But not alone on Christmas morn
Was God made one with humankind:
Each time a girl or boy is born,
Incarnate deity we find.

This Christmastide let us rejoice
And celebrate our human worth,
Proclaiming with united voice
The miracle of every birth.

Round every crib all people throng
To honour God in each new birth,
And raise again the ancient song:
'Goodwill to all, and peace on earth.'

John Andrew Storey, 1935—
Used by permission

THE JUDAEO-CHRISTIAN TRADITION: CHRISTMAS

98 The Son of Man

GONFALON ROYAL L.M.
Percy Carter Buck, 1871-1947
By permission of Oxford University Press

Where cross the crowded ways of life,
Where sound the cries of race and clan,
Above the noise of selfish strife,
We hear thy voice, O Son of Man.

In haunts of wretchedness and need,
On shadowed thresholds dark with fears,
From paths where hide the lures of greed,
We catch the vision of thy tears.

From tender childhood's helplessness,
From woman's grief, man's burdened toil,
From famished souls, from sorrow's stress,
Thy heart has never known recoil.

O Jesus, from the mountain side,
Make haste to heal these hearts of pain;
Among these restless throngs abide,
O tread the city's streets again.

Frank Mason North, 1850-1935

THE JUDAEO-CHRISTIAN HERITAGE: THE MINISTRY OF JESUS

KINGSFOLD C.M.D.

English Traditional Melody
Coll. Lucy Broadwood, 1858-1929
Har. and arr. by Ralph Vaughan Williams, 1872-1958
From the English Hymnal, by permission of Oxford University Press

THE JUDAEO-CHRISTIAN HERITAGE: THE MINISTRY OF JESUS

When Jesus Walked

When Jesus walked upon the earth
  He never talked with kings;
He talked with simple people
  Of doing friendly things.
He never praised the conquerors
  And all their hero host;
He said the very greatest were
  The ones who loved the most.

His words were not of mighty deeds;
  But many times he spoke
Of feeding hungry people
  And cheering lonely folk.
I'm glad his words were simple words
  Just meant for me and you;
The things he asked were simple things
  That you and I can do.

From Marion Brown Shelton
From Pilgrim Elementary Teacher
by permission of the United Church Press,
Philadelphia

100 The Presence Everywhere

DRAKE'S BOUGHTON   87. 87.   Edward Elgar, 1857-1934

Long ago the lilies faded
   Which to Jesus seemed so fair,
But the love that bade them blossom
   Still is working everywhere.

On the moors and in the valleys,
   By the streams we love so well,
There is greater glory blooming
   Than the human tongue can tell.

Long ago in sacred silence
   Died the accents of his prayer;
Still the souls that seek God's spirit
   Find that presence everywhere.

In the multitude adoring,
   In the chamber sad and lone,
God is there to help and comfort,
   As they pray, "Thy will be done!"

Let us seek, then, still believing
   God, who works around us yet,
Clothing lilies in the meadows,
   Will earth's children ne'er forget.

from William George Tarrant, 1853-1928

THE JUDAEO-CHRISTIAN HERITAGE: THE MINISTRY OF JESUS

101 Dear Lord and Father
REPTON 86. 886

Charles Hubert Hastings Parry, 1848-1918

Dear Lord and Father of mankind,
  Forgive our foolish ways!
Reclothe us in our rightful mind;
  In purer lives thy service find,
In deeper reverence, praise.

In simple trust, like theirs who heard
  Beside the Syrian sea
The gracious calling of the Lord,
Let us, like them, without a word,
  Rise up and follow thee.

O Sabbath rest by Galilee!
  O calm of hills above!
Where Jesus knelt to share with thee
The silence of eternity
  Interpreted by love!

With that deep hush subduing all
  Our words and works that drown
The tender whisper of thy call,
As noiseless let thy blessing fall
  As fell thy manna down.

Drop thy still dews of quietness,
  Till all our strivings cease:
Take from our souls the strain and stress,
And let our ordered lives confess
  The beauty of thy peace.

John Greenleaf Whittier, 1807-92

THE JUDAEO-CHRISTIAN HERITAGE: THE MINISTRY OF JESUS

102 Hosanna in the Highest

CRÜGER 76. 76. D.

William Henry Monk, 1823-89
from a Chorale by Johann Crüger, 1598-1662

Hosanna in the highest!
  Our eager hearts acclaim
The prophet of the kingdom,
  Who bears Messiah's name.
O bold, O foolish peasants,
  To deem that he should reign!
The temple and the palace
  Look down in high disdain.

Long ages dim the message,
  And custom has sufficed
For merchants and for princes
  To bow, and own him Christ.
But when a kindred spirit
  Arises from the plain,
The seats of power tremble
  And crucify again.

O first of many prophets
  Who come of simple folk
To free us from our bondage,
  To break oppression's yoke,
Restore our eyes from blindness,
  Make clear the life, the way
That leads through love and justice
  Unto the peace-crowned day!

John Howland Lathrop, 1880-1967

THE JUDAEO-CHRISTIAN HERITAGE: THE MINISTRY OF JESUS

103   O Sacred Head, Now Wounded

PASSION CHORALE   76. 76. D.   Hans Leo Hassler, 1564-1612
har. Johann Sebastian Bach, 1685-1750

O sacred head, now wounded,
   With grief and shame bowed down,
Now scornfully surrounded
   With thorns, thy only crown:
How art thou pale with anguish,
   With sore abuse and scorn!
How doth that visage languish
   Which once was bright as morn!

What language shall I borrow
   To thank thee, dearest friend,
For this, thy dying sorrow,
   Thy pity without end?
Let me be thine for ever;
   And, should I fainting be,
O, let me never, never,
   Outlive my love to thee.

Bernard of Clairvaux, 1091-1153
from tr. James Waddell Alexander, 1804-59
of German version by Paulus Gerhardt, 1607-76

THE JUDAEO-CHRISTIAN HERITAGE: PASSIONTIDE

104 Beneath the Shadow of the Cross

ST. SAVIOUR   C.M.   Frederick George Baker, 1821-77

Beneath the shadow of the Cross,
As earthly hopes remove,
His new commandment Jesus gives,
His blessèd word of love.

O bond of union, strong and deep!
O bond of perfect peace!
Not e'en the lifted cross can harm,
If we but hold to this.

Then, Jesus, be thy spirit ours;
And swift our feet shall move
To deeds of pure self-sacrifice,
And the sweet tasks of love.

Samuel Longfellow, 1819-92

THE JUDAEO-CHRISTIAN HERITAGE: PASSIONTIDE

105   Now in the Tomb is Laid

CAMPIAN 2   66.66.   Thomas Campian, 1567-1620

Now in the tomb is laid,
Who in the wide world walked
And talked with one and all:
Now in the tomb is laid.

Now in the tomb is laid,
Who told the sparrow's worth,
The lily's praises said:
Now in the tomb is laid.

Perfect, no wound nor mark!
By thine own darkened hour,
Do live within my heart:
Perfect, no wound nor mark!

Padraic Colum, 1881-1972
By permission of The Devin-Adair Co.

THE JUDAEO-CHRISTIAN HERITAGE: PASSIONTIDE

106   The Brave of Old

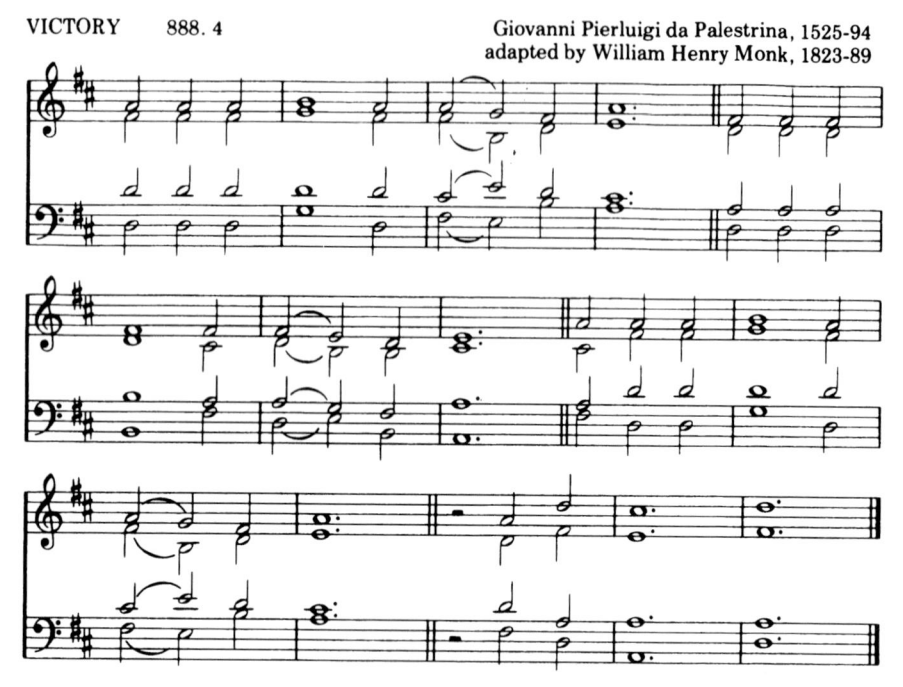

VICTORY   888. 4   Giovanni Pierluigi da Palestrina, 1525-94
                                          adapted by William Henry Monk, 1823-89

Now sing we of the brave of old
Who would not sell themselves for gold,
Yet left us riches manifold;
    Alleluia!

Of those who fought a goodly fight
For liberty, for truth and right,
Their patient love their chiefest might;
    Alleluia!

Of men and women, weak, obscure,
Whose faith was great, whose lives were pure,
Who scorned the world's resplendent lure;
    Alleluia!

Who, when no gleam did point the way,
Pressed ever on, by night and day,
And, spite of pain, did ever say
    Alleluia!

Who long the world's dark sorrows bore
And toiled and loved and suffered sore,
And, being dead, live evermore;
    Alleluia!
                         Albert M. P. Dawson, 1880-1963
by permission of the Beacon Press, Boston, Mass.

THE JUDAEO-CHRISTIAN HERITAGE: EASTER

107 Brightly Breaks the Easter Morn

VULPIUS 8 8 8. 4. with Alleluias

Melchior Vulpius, c.1560-1616
har. Henry George Ley, 1887-1962

From Songs of Praise, by permission of Oxford University Press

Past are the cross, the scourge, the thorn,
The scoffing tongue, the gibe, the scorn,
And brightly breaks the Easter morn.
Alleluia, Alleluia, Alleluia!

Gone are the gloomy clouds of night:
The shades of death are put to flight;
And from the tomb beams heavenly light.
Alleluia, Alleluia, Alleluia!

And so, in sorrow dark and drear,
Though black the night, the morn is near:
Soon shall the heavenly day appear.
Alleluia, Alleluia, Alleluia!

And when death's darkness dims our eyes,
From out the gloom our souls shall rise
In deathless glory to the skies.
Alleluia, Alleluia, Alleluia!

Then let us raise the glorious strain,
Love's triumph over sin and pain,
Faith's victory over terror's reign!
Alleluia, Alleluia, Alleluia!

Alfred Charles Jewitt, 1845-1925

THE JUDAEO-CHRISTIAN HERITAGE: EASTER

EASTER HYMN   77. 77. with Alleluias.   Adapted from melody in *Lyra Davidica*, 1708

THE JUDAEO-CHRISTIAN HERITAGE: EASTER

108 Death's Dominion is Past

Thou whose love has given us birth, *Alleluia!*
Pilgrims on the gladsome earth, *Alleluia!*
Evermore our souls defend, *Alleluia!*
Steadfast, trusting, to the end. *Alleluia!*

They whose life is hid in God, *Alleluia!*
Shepherded with staff and rod, *Alleluia!*
Singing in the shadowed vale, *Alleluia!*
Know that death shall not prevail. *Alleluia!*

Hearts are strong, and voices sing, *Alleluia!*
Where, O death, is now thy sting? *Alleluia!*
When God taketh what God gave, *Alleluia!*
Where thy victory, O grave? *Alleluia!*

Thine the love that shall endure, *Alleluia!*
Ours to trust that promise sure; *Alleluia!*
Death's dominion now is past, *Alleluia!*
In thy love we rest at last! *Alleluia!*

from Henry Wilder Foote, 1875-1964
by permission of the Beacon Press, Boston, Mass.

THE JUDAEO-CHRISTIAN HERITAGE: EASTER

109 Life's Rebirth

MELITA 88.88.88. John Bacchus Dykes, 1823-76

A day like many other days
Has seen us gather here to sing
And offer words which reach for thoughts
That lie beyond their capturing;
   Yet may those prayers our lives renew:
   From rocks of thought a vision hew.

THE JUDAEO-CHRISTIAN HERITAGE: EASTER

We tell from land to land our tales
Where powers of hope shape life from death,
In differing words that share a dream—
With glorying shout, or whispered breath;
   To caves of cold, dark unconcern
   We bring our lights of love to burn.

Such warmth can melt a winter's cold
In human hearts, as flower and field,
And push aside the blocking stone
With which so many a heart is sealed;
   May I be never shut inside
   The tomb of selfishness and pride.

This day, like many other days,
May see us roll the stone to find
A kindred soul who thirsts for light
Yet to the darkness was resigned;
   So may we stretch our hands to lead
   To life's rebirth all those we've freed.

                              Frank R. Clabburn, 1947—
                                  Used by permission

110 Through Human Means

GUTER HIRTE 87. 87.

From the *Geistreiches Gesangbuch* (1705)
of Johann August Freylinghausen, 1670-1739
Harmony by permission of the Beacon Press, Boston, Mass.

Jesus died, but Christ has triumphed,
   Broken now the chains of death:
From the tomb comes God's anointed,
   Kindling cold hearts with his breath.

Now at last we see his purpose,
   Breaking through like sunburst bright:
Liberation for God's people
   Ends humanity's long night.

For there is a Spirit greater,
   Who has now the victory;
And our God indwells the human,
   Striving for our liberty.

And that Spirit dwelt in Jesus,
   Teaching us that love redeems;
How God, through a man's compassion,
   Gains great ends by human means.

But for love and life undying
   Death of self must be the key;
Jesus died to bear this witness
   And Christ rose to make us free.

Clifford Martin Reed, 1947—
Used by permission

THE JUDAEO-CHRISTIAN HERITAGE: EASTER

111 Mighty Spirit, Gracious Guide

CHARITY 777.5. John Stainer, 1840-1901

Mighty Spirit, gracious guide,
Let thy light in us abide;
Light supreme o'er all beside—
Holy, heavenly love.

Faith that mountains could remove,
Tongues of earth and heaven above,
Knowledge—all things—empty prove,
Without heavenly love.

Though I as a martyr bleed,
Give my goods the poor to feed,
All is vain if love I need;
Therefore give me love.

Love is kind, and suffers long;
Love is meek, and thinks no wrong;
Love than death itself more strong;
Therefore give us love.

Prophecy will fade away,
Melting in the light of day;
Love will ever with us stay:
Therefore give us love.

Faith will vanish into sight,
Hope be emptied in delight;
Love in heaven will shine more bright;
Therefore give us love.

Faith and hope and love we see
Joining hand in hand agree:
But the greatest of the three,
And the best, is love.

from Christopher Wordsworth, 1807-85

THE JUDAEO-CHRISTIAN HERITAGE: WHITSUNTIDE

112 The Holy Spirit

ST. MAGNUS   C.M.   Probably by Jeremiah Clarke, c.1670-1707

We look no more for tongues of fire,
  We seek no heavenly dove,
We gather now with one desire
  To know the power of love.

The holy spirit which it brings
  Is nurtured as we share
That fellowship which ever springs
  From ministries of care.

For wounded souls it is a balm,
  For guilty minds, a purge;
To restless hearts it brings a calm,
  To slothful ones an urge.

Its manifold resources give
  New power for the strife:
We rise refreshed, and hence can live
  A more effective life.

John Andrew Storey, 1935—
Used by permission

THE JUDAEO-CHRISTIAN HERITAGE: WHITSUNTIDE

113 Flame of Living Fire

TRURO L.M. *Psalmodia Evangelica* (1789) of Thomas Williams

O for that flame of living fire
Which shone so bright in saints of old;
Which bade their souls to heaven aspire,
Calm in distress, in danger bold.

O for the spirit which of old
Proclaimed thy love and taught thy ways,
Forth in Isaiah's thunder rolled,
Breathed in the psalmist's tenderest lays.

O for that spirit, God, which dwelt
In Jesus' mind and sealed him thine;
Which made Paul's heart with sorrow melt,
And glow with energy divine.

Is not thy word as mighty now
As when the prophets felt its power?
The ancient days remember thou,
The ancient inspiration shower.

from William Hiley Bragge-Bathurst, 1796-1877

THE JUDAEO-CHRISTIAN HERITAGE: WHITSUNTIDE

114 Let There be Light!

MOSCOW 664. 666. 4.   Adapted from Felice Giardini, 1716-96

Thou, whose almighty word
Chaos and darkness heard,
   And took their flight,
Hear us, we humbly pray;
And where the gospel's day
Sheds not its glorious ray,
   Let there be light!

Thou who didst come to bring
On thy redeeming wing
   Healing and sight,
Health to the sick in mind,
Sight to the inly blind,
Now to all humankind
   Let there be light!

Spirit of truth and love,
Life-giving holy dove,
   Speed forth thy flight;
Move on the waters' face,
Bearing the lamp of grace,
And in earth's darkest place
   Let there be light!

from John Marriott, 1780-1825

THE JUDAEO-CHRISTIAN HERITAGE: WHITSUNTIDE

115 Christ Cometh not a King

ST. STEPHEN C.M. William Jones, 1726-1800

Christ cometh not a king to reign,
   The world's long hope is dim;
The weary centuries watch in vain
   The clouds of heaven for him.

But not for signs in heaven above
   Or earth below they look,
Who know with John his smile of love,
   With Peter his rebuke.

In joy of inward peace, or sense
   Of sorrow over sin,
He is his own best evidence,
   His witness is within.

And warm, sweet, tender, even yet
   A present help is he;
And faith has still its Olivet,
   And love its Galilee.

The healing of his seamless dress
   Is by our beds of pain;
We touch him in life's throng and press,
   And we are whole again.

John Greenleaf Whittier, 1807-92

THE JUDAEO-CHRISTIAN HERITAGE

PRAISE, MY SOUL 87. 87. 87. John Goss, 1800-80

THE JUDAEO-CHRISTIAN HERITAGE

116   Praise, My Soul

Praise, my soul, the King of Heaven,
   To his feet thy tribute bring;
Ransomed, healed, restored, forgiven,
   Evermore his praises sing:
Alleluia, Alleluia!
   Praise the everlasting King.

Praise him for his grace and favour
   To our forebears in distress;
Praise him still the same for ever,
   Slow to chide and swift to bless:
Alleluia, Alleluia!
   Glorious in his faithfulness.

Tenderly, he guides and spares us;
   Well our feeble frame he knows;
In his hands he gently bears us,
   Rescues us from all our foes:
Alleluia, Alleluia!
   Widely yet his mercy flows.

Angels in the height, adore him;
   Ye behold him face to face;
Sun and moon, bow down before him,
   Dwellers all in time and space:
Alleluia, Alleluia!
   Praise with us the God of grace.

from Henry Francis Lyte, 1793-1847

BEETHOVEN 87. 87. D   Adapted from Ludwig van Beethoven, 1770-1827

THE JUDAEO-CHRISTIAN HERITAGE

17 Joyful, Joyful, We Adore Thee

Joyful, joyful, we adore thee,
    God of glory, God of love;
Hearts unfold like flowers before thee,
    Hail thee as the sun above!
Field and forest, vale and mountain,
    Blooming meadow, flashing sea,
Chanting bird and flowing fountain
    Call us to rejoice in thee.

Thou art giving and forgiving,
    Ever blessing, ever blest,
Well-spring of the joy of living,
    Ocean depth of happy rest!
Thou our Parent, Christ our Brother,
    All who live in love are thine;
Teach us how to love each other,
    Lift us to the joy divine.

Mortals join the mighty chorus,
    Which the morning stars recall;
Parent love is reigning o'er us,
    Kindred love binds each to all.
Ever singing, march we onward,
    Victors in the midst of strife;
Joyful music lifts us sunward
    In the triumph song of life.

from Henry van Dyke, 1852-1933
by permission of Charles Scribner's Sons, New York

THE JUDAEO-CHRISTIAN HERITAGE

118 All Loves Excelling

LOVE DIVINE 8 7. 8 7. John Stainer, 1840-1901

Love divine, all loves excelling,
  Joy of heaven, to earth come down,
Fix in us thy humble dwelling,
  All thy faithful mercies crown.

Thou, O God, art all compassion,
  Pure unbounded love thou art;
Visit us with thy salvation,
  Enter every trembling heart.

Come, Almighty, to deliver,
  Let us all thy grace receive;
Suddenly return and never,
  Never more thy temples leave.

Thee we would be always blessing,
  Serve thee as thy hosts above;
Pray and praise thee without ceasing,
  Glory in thy perfect love.

Finish then thy new creation,
  Pure and spotless let us be;
Let us see thy great salvation,
  Perfectly restored in thee —

Changed from glory into glory,
  Till in heaven we take our place,
Till we cast our crowns before thee,
  Lost in wonder, love and praise.

from Charles Wesley, 1707-88

THE JUDAEO-CHRISTIAN HERITAGE

World-Wide Heritage

119 O'er Continent and Ocean

LLANGLOFFAN 7 6. 8 6. D. *Hymnau a Thônau* (1865) of Daniel Evans

O'er continent and ocean,
   From city, field and wood,
Still speak, O Lord, thy messengers
   Of peace and brotherhood.
In Athens and Benares,
   In Rome and Galilee,
They fronted kings and conquerors,
   And taught mankind of thee.

WORLD-WIDE HERITAGE

We hear, O Lord, these voices,
    And hail them as thine own,
They speak as speak the winds and tides
    On planets far and lone:
One God, the Life of Ages,
    One rule, his will above,
One realm, our wide humanity,
    One law, the law of love.

The tribes and nations falter
    In rivalries of fear;
The fires of hate to ashes turn,
    To dust the sword and spear.
Thy word alone remaineth—
    That word we speak again,
O'er sea and shore and continent,
    To all the sons of men.

                        John Haynes Holmes, 1879-1964
                        by permission of the Author's family

WORLD-WIDE HERITAGE

120 Life of Ages, Richly Poured

UNIVERSITY COLLEGE 77. 77.   Henry John Gauntlett, 1805-76

Life of Ages, richly poured,
Love of God, unspent and free,
Flowing in the prophet's word,
And the people's liberty!

Never was to chosen race
That unstinted tide confined;
Thine is every time and place,
Fountain sweet of heart and mind:

Breathing in the thinker's creed,
Pulsing in the hero's blood,
Nerving simplest thought and deed,
Freshening time with truth and good;

Consecrating art and song,
Holy book and pilgrim track,
Hurling floods of tyrant wrong
From the sacred limits back!

Life of Ages, richly poured,
Love of God, unspent and free,
Flow still in the prophet's word,
And the people's liberty!

Samuel Johnson, 1822-82

WORLD-WIDE HERITAGE

121 City of God

RICHMOND C.M.   Thomas Haweis, 1734-1820

City of God, how broad and far
   Outspread thy walls sublime!
The true thy free in spirit are
   Of every age and clime.

One holy church, one army strong,
   One steadfast high intent,
One working band, one harvest song,
   One King Omnipotent.

How purely hath thy speech come down
   From our primeval youth!
How grandly hath thine empire grown
   Of freedom, love, and truth!

How gleam thy watchfires through the night
   With never-fainting ray!
How rise thy towers, serene and bright,
   To meet the dawning day!

In vain the surge's angry shock,
   In vain the drifting sands;
Unharmed upon the Eternal Rock
   The Eternal City stands.

from Samuel Johnson, 1822-82

WORLD-WIDE HERITAGE

122 One Holy Church

ST. PETER   C.M.   Alexander Robert Reinagle, 1799-1877

One holy Church of God appears
   Through every age and race,
Unwasted by the lapse of years,
   Unchanged by changing place.

From oldest time, on farthest shores,
   Beneath the pine or palm,
One unseen presence she adores,
   With silence or with psalm.

The truth is her prophetic gift,
   The soul her sacred page;
And feet on mercy's errand swift
   Do make her pilgrimage.

O living Church, thine errand speed,
   Fulfil thy task sublime;
With bread of life earth's hunger feed;
   Redeem the evil time!

Samuel Longfellow, 1819-92

WORLD-WIDE HERITAGE

123 Where is our Holy Church?

DOMINICA S.M. Herbert Stanley Oakeley, 1830-1903

Where is our holy church?
Where race and class unite
As equal persons in the search
 For beauty, truth and right.

Where is our holy writ?
Where'er a human heart
A sacred torch of truth has lit,
 By inspiration taught.

Where is our holy one?
A mighty host respond;
The people rise in every land
 To break the captive's bond.

Where is our holy land?
Within the human soul,
Wherever free minds truly seek
 With character the goal.

Where is our paradise?
In aspiration's sight,
Wherein we hope to see arise
 Ten thousand years of light.

Edwin Henry Wilson, 1898—
Used by permission

WORLD-WIDE HERITAGE

124   Past, Present, Future

GALILEE   L.M.   Philip Armes, 1836-1908

O thou, to whom our parents built
Their altars in the ancient days,
Upon our worship we invoke
The benediction of their praise.

As then their reverent hearts received
The Spirit's gift of flame from thee,
So on our altars kindle now
Fires of ancestral piety.

WORLD-WIDE HERITAGE

Thou living, radiant, inward light,
Whom we today, though dimly, see —
Our guide amid the world we know,
Our hope for what is yet to be —

Break now, in greater majesty,
Upon the minds and hearts that crave
With widening knowledge of the truth
Triumphant power to seek and save.

God of the ages yet unborn
Whose clearer presence then shall shine,
When each of us shall live in peace,
And human life become divine —

O touch our lips that we may be
The messengers of thine accord,
And with prophetic power proclaim
The growing purpose of thy word.

Adapted by Beth Ide, 1921 —
from Frederick May Eliot, 1889-1958
by permission of the Religious Arts Guild, Boston, Mass.

125 One Human Commonwealth

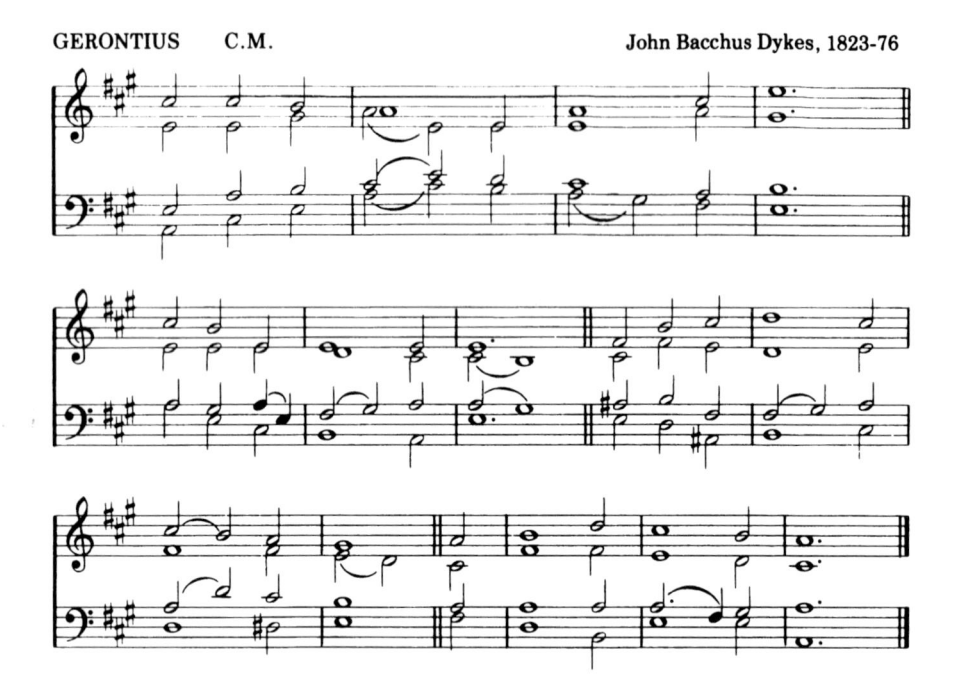

GERONTIUS C.M. John Bacchus Dykes, 1823-76

Let freedom span both east and west,
　And love both south and north,
In universal fellowship
　Throughout the whole wide earth.

In beauty, wonder, everywhere,
　Let us communion find;
Compassion be the golden cord
　Close-binding humankind.

Beyond all barriers of race,
　Of colour, caste or creed,
Let us make friendship, human worth,
　Our common faith and deed.

Then east and west will meet and share,
　And south shall build with north,
One human commonwealth of good
　Throughout the whole wide earth.

Jacob Trapp, 1899—
Used by permission

WORLD-WIDE HERITAGE

126 The Larger View

STENKA RAZIN   87. 87. D.

Traditional Russian Melody
Arr. David Dawson
Used by permission

In their ancient isolation
  Races framed their moral codes,
And the peoples of each nation
  Trod their solitary roads.
Now the distances are shrinking;
  Travel, and the printed page,
All earth's many lands are linking,
  Spreading knowledge of each sage.

Now new times demand new measures,
  And new ways we must explore;
Let each faith bring its own treasures
  To enrich the common store.
Then no more will creeds divide us—
  Though we love our own the best—
For the larger view will guide us
  As we join in common quest.

John Andrew Storey, 1935—
Used by permission

WORLD-WIDE HERITAGE

127 Gather Us In

WOODLANDS 10 10. 10 10. Walter Greatorex, 1877-1949
From Enlarged Songs of Praise, by permission of Oxford University Press

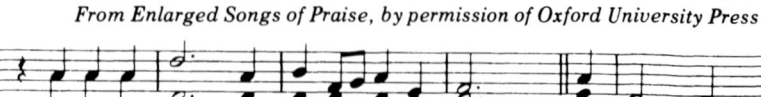

Gather us in, thou Love that fillest all:
Gather the rival faiths within thy fold;
Throughout the nations, sound the clarion call:
Beneath Love's banner all shall be enrolled!

Gather us in, we worship only thee;
In varied names we stretch a common hand;
In diverse forms a common soul we see;
In many ships we seek one promised land.

Thine is the mystic life great India craves;
Thine is the Parsee's sin-destroying beam;
Thine is the Buddhist's rest from tossing waves;
Thine is the empire of vast China's dream.

Thine is the Roman's strength without the pride;
Thine is the Greek's glad world without its graves;
Thine is the Law that is the Jew's life-guide;
Thine is the Christian's faith, the grace that saves.

Gather us in, thou Love that fillest all;
Gather thy rival faiths within thy fold;
Throughout the nations, sound the clarion call:
Beneath Love's banner all shall be enrolled!

after George Matheson, 1842-1906

WORLD-WIDE HERITAGE

128 Heritage

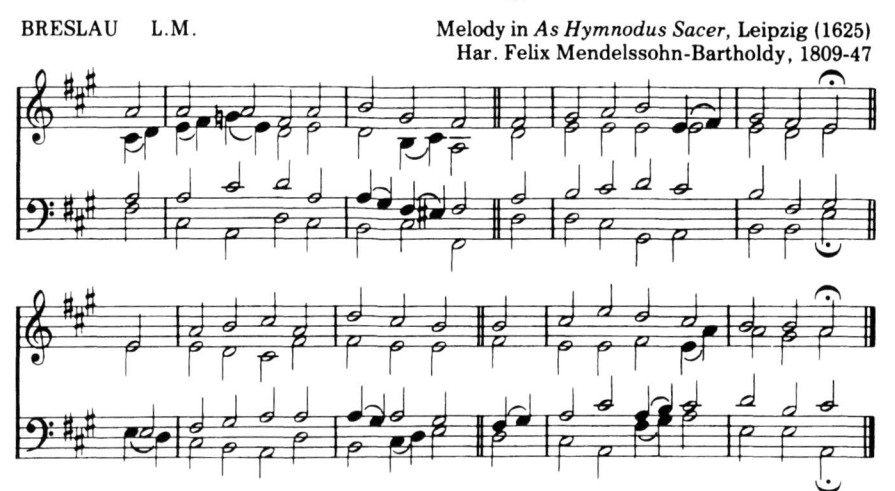

BRESLAU L.M.

Melody in *As Hymnodus Sacer*, Leipzig (1625)
Har. Felix Mendelssohn-Bartholdy, 1809-47

The art, the science, and the lore
Of those through ages long since dust,
Their hard-won wisdom, slowly grown,
Come down to us a sacred trust.

From Sinai and from Bethlehem,
From China, India, Greece and Rome,
Their music, symbols, songs and prayers
Enrich and beautify our home.

The golden splendour of the sun,
The beauty of the living earth,
The far-flung galaxies of stars,
The need to love, attend our birth;

And all the hopes and prophecies
Of freedom, peace, the coming day
Of life more deeply, grandly lived,
Shine luminous upon our way.

Ours for the present, to increase,
Ours for the future and its care,
A heritage of growing light,
To live, transmit, and greatly share.

Jacob Trapp, 1899 —
Used by permission

WORLD-WIDE HERITAGE

129 It Sounds Along the Ages

FAR OFF LANDS 7 6. 7 6. D. Melody of the Bohemian Brethren, *Hemlandssanger*, Rock Island, Illinois, 1892
arr. by permission of the Beacon Press, Boston, Mass.

It sounds along the ages,
   Soul answering to soul;
It kindles on the pages
   Of every Bible scroll;
The psalmist heard and sang it,
   From martyr lips it broke,
The prophet tongues out-rang it
   Till sleeping nations woke.

From Sinai's cliffs it echoed,
   It breathed from Buddha's tree,
It charmed in Athens' market,
   It hallowed Galilee;
The hammer stroke of Luther,
   The Pilgrims' seaside prayer,
The testament of Torda
   One holy word declare.

It calls—and lo, new justice!
   It speaks—and lo, new truth!
In ever nobler stature
   And unexhausted youth.
Forever on resounding,
   And knowing nought of time,
Our laws but catch the music
   Of its eternal chime.

from William Channing Gannett, 1840-1923

WORLD-WIDE HERITAGE

130 All Faiths

DANBY L.M.

English Traditional Melody
coll. and arr. Ralph Vaughan Williams, 1872-1958
From the English Hymnal, by permission of Oxford University Press

Our faith is but a single gem
Upon a rosary of beads;
The thread of truth which runs through them
Supports our varied human needs.

Confucian wisdom, Christian care,
The Buddhist way of self-control,
The Muslim's daily call to prayer
Are proven pathways to the goal.

From many lips, in every age,
The truth eternal is proclaimed,
By Western saint, and Eastern sage,
And all the good, however named.

Beside the noblest of our race
Our lives as yet cannot compare:
May we at length their truth embrace
And in their sacred mission share.

John Andrew Storey, 1935—
Used by permission

WORLD-WIDE HERITAGE

LONDON (ADDISON'S)   L.M.D.   John Sheeles, c. 1720
                                                (shortened version)

WORLD-WIDE HERITAGE

131 All Earth's Children

For all the paths which guide our ways
We lift our hearts in joyful praise.
For Akhenaton, by whose hand
New light was brought to Egypt's land:
For Moses, and Judaic seers,
And every Hebrew psalm which cheers,
For Jesus Christ of lowly birth,
Who sought to found God's reign on earth:

For Hindu's varied paths to God
Which many noble souls have trod:
For Buddha's path, which, like the Jain,
Has shown the way to conquer pain:
For Guru Nanak, Punjab's son,
And all that noble Sikhs have done:
For Japanese and Chinese lore,
Confucian wisdom, Shinto awe:

For Zarathustra, Parsi sage,
The fount of Persia's golden age:
For Islam's Prophet, who by grace
Transformed a wayward desert race:
For Stoic souls of Rome and Greece,
Whose fame on earth shall never cease,
For all great souls, with common voice,
Let all earth's children now rejoice!

John Andrew Storey, 1935—
Used by permission

WORLD-WIDE HERITAGE

132 Children of the Universe

SPANISH HYMN   7 7. 7 7. D.   Arr. Benjamin Carr, 1768-1831

Children of the human race,
Offspring of our Mother Earth,
Not alone in endless space
Has our planet given birth.
Far across the cosmic skies
Countless suns in glory blaze,
And from untold planets rise
Endless canticles of praise.

Should some sign of others reach
This, our lonely planet Earth,
Differences of form and speech
Must not hide our common worth.
When at length our minds are free,
And the clouds of fear disperse,
Then at last we'll learn to be
Children of the Universe.

John Andrew Storey, 1935—
Used by permission

WORLD-WIDE HERITAGE

The Free Spirit

SINGING   8 7. 8 7. D. Iambic   American Gospel Tune

THE FREE SPIRIT

133 How Can I Keep from Singing!

My life flows on in endless song
　　Above earth's lamentation:
I hear the real though far-off hymn
　　That hails a new creation.
Through all the tumult and the strife
　　I hear the music ringing:
It sounds an echo in my soul—
　　How can I keep from singing!

What though the tempest round me roar,
　　I know the truth, it liveth.
What though the darkness round me close,
　　Songs in the night it giveth.
No storm can shake my inmost calm
　　While to that rock I'm clinging:
Since love prevails in heaven and earth,
　　How can I keep from singing!

When tyrants tremble, sick with fear,
　　And hear their death-knells ringing;
When friends rejoice, both far and near,
　　How can I keep from singing!
To prison cell and dungeon vile
　　Our thoughts of love are winging:
When friends by shame are undefiled,
　　How can I keep from singing!

Early Quaker Song

THE FREE SPIRIT

MIT FREUDEN ZART 87. 87. 887. Later form of hymn melody of
the Bohemian Brethren, Kirchengeseng, 1566

THE FREE SPIRIT

Faith of the Free

Faith of the larger liberty,
  Source of the light expanding,
Law of the church that is to be,
  Old bondage notwithstanding:
    Faith of the free!
    By thee we live—
By all thou givest and shalt give
  Our loyalty commanding.

Heroes of faith in every age,
  Far-seeing, self-denying,
Wrought an increasing heritage,
  Monarch and priest defying.
    Faith of the free!
    In thy dear name
The costly heritage we claim:
  Their living and their dying.

Faith for the people everywhere,
  Whatever their oppression,
Of all who make the world more fair,
  Living their faith's confession:
    Faith of the free!
    Whate'er our plight,
Thy law, thy liberty, thy light
  Shall be our blest possession.

Vincent Brown Silliman, 1894-1979
by permission of the Beacon Press, Boston, Mass.

THE FREE SPIRIT

135 Sing in Celebration

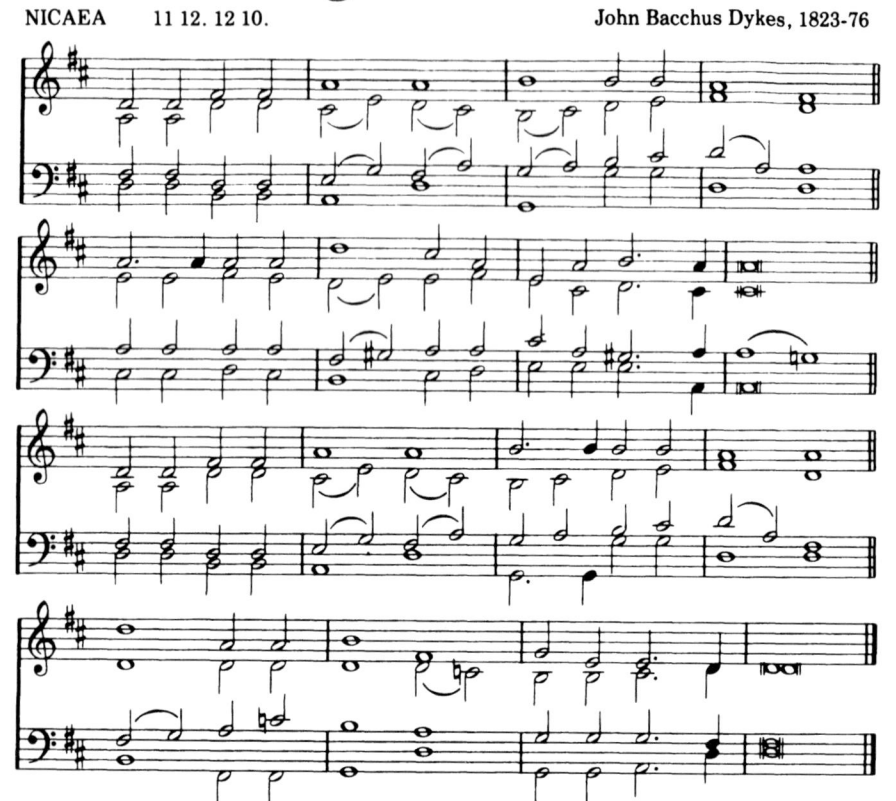

NICAEA 11 12. 12 10. John Bacchus Dykes, 1823-76

Sing in celebration, time to remember
Those who in past ages kept love of truth alive;
Now, in dedication, as we pay them homage,
We too would pledge for truth and love to strive.

Pioneers undaunted, upheld by courage,
Freed the mind from fetters and set the conscience free;
By the tyrant taunted, for their faith derided,
They yet stood firm in love and liberty.

We who share their vision must share their labour,
Marching to the future — a new world yet to be.
This shall be our mission — to extol compassion
Till humankind become one family.

John Andrew Storey, 1935 –
Used by permission

THE FREE SPIRIT

136 Our Kindred Fellowships

MARYTON L.M. Henry Percy Smith, 1825-98

As tranquil streams that meet and merge
And flow as one to seek the sea,
Our kindred fellowships unite
To build a church that shall be free—

Free from the bonds that bind the mind
To narrow thought and lifeless creed;
Free from a social code that fails
To serve the cause of human need;

A freedom that reveres the past,
But trusts the dawning future more;
And bids the soul, in search of truth,
Adventure boldly and explore.

Prophetic church, the future waits
Thy liberating ministry;
Go forward in the power of love,
Proclaim the truth that makes us free.

Marion Franklin Ham, 1867-1956
by permission of the Beacon Press, Boston, Mass.

THE FREE SPIRIT

PEN-LAN 76. 76. D.   David Jenkins, 1848-1915

THE FREE SPIRIT

137 We Shall be Strong and Free

We lift our hearts in yearning
  From bondage to be free,
To break the ages' learning
  That what has been must be—
And not alone from tyrants
  Of church or state or class,
But from our own reliance
  On habits of the past.

From centuries' affliction
  By custom, rule and word,
With courage of conviction
  Let now our voice be heard.
And let our deeds be worthy
  Of moral insight gained,
When minds by truth are lightened
  And hearts by love inflamed.

So may our firm foundation
  Be knowledge of the right,
Each life a new creation,
  Each day a new delight.
By ancient dominations
  And helpless destiny,
We will not be o'erburdened:
  We shall be strong and free.

Robert C. Palmer, 1911—
used by permission

THE FREE SPIRIT

138 O Help the Prophet to be Bold

BRISTOL C.M.

Melody from the *Psalter* (1621) of
Thomas Ravenscroft, 1592- c.1640

O help the prophet to be bold,
   The poet to be true!
It yet remains for us to learn
   What human love can do,

With faith not pent within a book,
   Or buried in a creed,
But growing with expanding thought
   And deepening with the need:

A faith whose sacred strength is sure,
   And needs no priest to tell;
Its law — 'Be kind, be pure, be just;'
   Its promise — 'Thence be well.'

For joy shall one with feeling be,
   And feeling, planet-wide,
Where many folk have done their best,
   And, doing it, have died.

O help the prophet to be bold,
   The poet to be true!
It yet remains for us to learn
   What human love can do.

from Louise Guggenberger

THE FREE SPIRIT

139 The Golden Heresy of Truth

VOM HIMMEL HOCH L.M.

Later form of melody in
Valentin Schumann's *Gesangbuch*, 1539

The generations as they rise
May live the life as lived before,
Still hold the thought once held as wise,
Go in and out by the same door.

We leave the easy peace it brings;
The few we are shall still unite
In fealty to unseen kings
Or unimaginable light.

We hold the vision in the heart
More than the land our eyes have seen,
And love the goal for which we start
More than the tale of what has been.

No blazoned banner we unfold—
One charge alone we give to youth:
Against the sceptred myth to hold
The golden heresy of truth.

from George William Russell, 1867-1935

THE FREE SPIRIT

140 The Love of God is Broader

ST. OSWALD   87. 87.   John Bacchus Dykes, 1823-76

There's a wideness in God's mercy
    Like the wideness of the sea;
There's a kindness in God's justice
    Which is more than liberty.

If we render love too narrow
    With false limits of our own,
Then we magnify the strictness
    With a zeal God will not own.

For the love of God is broader
    Than the measures of our mind,
And the heart of the Eternal
    Is most wonderfully kind.

from Frederick William Faber, 1814-63

THE FREE SPIRIT

141 The World Stands Out

ALSTONE L.M.   Christopher Edwin Willing, 1830-1904

The world stands out on either side
No wider than the heart is wide;
Above the world is stretched the sky
No higher than the soul is high.

The heart can push the sea and land
Farther away on either hand;
The soul can split the sky in two
And let the face of God shine through.

Edna St.Vincent Millay, 1892-1950
by permission of Norma Millay Ellis

THE FREE SPIRIT

142 Freedom Is the Finest Gold

ST. PHILIP 77. 6. William Henry Monk, 1823-89

Freedom is the finest gold
That the sun strews o'er the mould:
 Treasure it for ever.

From the freedom-loving heart
Honour cannot live apart:
 None the twain can sever.

Freedom is the city blest
Whose calm life no hates molest:
 Neighbour there loves neighbour.

Though all love their family name,
They let others do the same:
 Each for all there labour.

from Thomas Simonsson of Strängnäs, Sweden, d.1443
tr. or arr. by Elias Gordon
in W.R.Benét and N.Cousins' *The Poetry of Freedom*, 1945.

THE FREE SPIRIT

143   Die Gedanken Sind Frei

DIE GEDANKEN SIND FREI   12 12. 12 11.   Traditional German, c. 1500
vv. 2 & 3

Die Gedanken sind frei, my thoughts freely flower,
Die Gedanken sind frei, my thoughts give me power.
No scholar can map them, no hunter can trap them,
   No one can deny: Die Gedanken sind frei!

So I think as I please, and this gives me pleasure,
My conscience decrees this right I must treasure.
My thoughts will not cater to duke or dictator,
   No one can deny: Die Gedanken sind frei!

And if tyrants take me and throw me in prison,
My thoughts will burst free, like blossoms in season.
Foundations will crumble, the structure will tumble,
   And people will cry: Die Gedanken sind frei!

German Folk Song
English version by Arthur Kevess
by permission of the Hodgin Press, Los Angeles

Die Gedanken sind frei (pronounced Dee guh-dank'-en zint fry) means "Thought is free."

THE FREE SPIRIT

WOLVERCOTE 76. 76. D. William Harold Ferguson, 1874-1950
By permission of Oxford University Press

THE FREE SPIRIT

Sunrise to Freedom

This world has been a prison
  Too long for me and mine;
It's time the sun were risen,
  I mean to see it shine.
One night I dreamt my daughter
  Was just as free as you,
And when I woke I taught her
  To dream of freedom too.

My veins have nursed your meadow;
  My tears have washed your lawn.
Too long I thirst in shadow,
  It's time I shared the dawn.
Too long in midnight mining
  I've coaxed your fires with coal;
Inside me there's a pining—
  It's time I fed my soul.

I dreamt my son was breaking
  His bondage, limb from limb;
As soon as I awakened
  I taught that dream to him.
This world has been a prison
  Too long for me and mine;
It's time the sun were risen—
  I mean to make it shine.

Aaron Kramer, 1921—
Used by permission

SALVATION   C.M.D.   Melody from Ananias Davisson's *Kentucky Harmony*, c.1815
Har. David Dawson
Used by permission

THE FREE SPIRIT

145 Unrest

A fierce unrest seethes at the core
   Of all existing things:
It was the eager wish to soar
   That gave the gods their wings.
There throbs through all the worlds that are
   This heart-beat, hot and strong,
And shaken systems, star by star,
   Awake and glow in song.

But for the urge of this unrest
   These joyous spheres are mute;
But for the rebel in our breast,
   Had we remained a brute.
When baffled lips demanded speech,
   Speech trembled into birth—
One day the lyric word shall reach
   From earth to laughing earth.

From deed to dream, from dream to deed,
   From daring hope to hope,
The restless wish, the instant need,
   Still drove us up the slope.
Sing we no governed firmament,
   Cold, ordered, regular—
We sing the stinging discontent
   That leaps from star to star.

Don Marquis, 1878-1937
From Dreams and Dust
by permission of Doubleday & Co., Inc.

SHAKER SONG   P.M.

Traditional Melody, arr. David Dawson
Used by permission

THE FREE SPIRIT

146 True Simplicity

'Tis the gift to be simple, 'tis the gift to be free;
'Tis the gift to know just where we want to be;
And when we find ourselves in the place just right,
'Twill be in the valley of love and delight.

> When true simplicity is gained,
> To greet all as friend we shan't be ashamed:
> To turn, turn, will be our delight,
> Till by turning, turning, we come round right.

'Tis the gift to be simple, 'tis the gift to be free;
'Tis the gift to share our common destiny;
And when we find ourselves in the place just right,
'Twill be in the valley of love and delight.

> When true simplicity is gained,
> To greet all as friend we shan't be ashamed:
> To turn, turn, will be our delight,
> Till by turning, turning, we come round right.

Traditional Shaker Song

147 Free from the World's Cares

WAREHAM   L. M.   William Knapp, 1698-1768

How happy are they born or taught,
Who do not serve another's will;
Whose armour is their honest thought,
And simple truth their highest skill;

Whose passions not their rulers are;
Whose souls are still, and free from fear,
Not tied unto the world with care
Of public fame or private ear;

Who God doth late and early pray
Far more of grace than goods to lend;
And walk with each, from day to day,
As with a comrade and a friend.

All such are freed from servile bands
Of hope to rise, or fear to fall;
They rule themselves, but rule not lands,
And, having nothing, yet have all.

adapted from Henry Wotton, 1568-1639

THE FREE SPIRIT

148   The Miracle

NUN DANKET ALL   C. M.   *Praxis Pietatis Melica*, 1653

O what a piece of work are we,
   How marvellously wrought;
The quick contrivance of the hand,
   The wonder of our thought.

Why need to look for miracles
   Outside of nature's law?
Humanity we wonder at
   With every breath we draw!

But give us room to move and grow,
   But give our spirit play,
And we can make a world of light
   Out of the common clay.

from Malvina Reynolds

Copyright 1971 Schroeder Music Co., assigned to TRO Essex Music Ltd., 19/20 Poland Street, London W1V 3DD. International Copyright secured. Used by permission. British Commonwealth [excluding Canada]. Also Republics of Ireland and South Africa.

THE FREE SPIRIT

WALK IN THE LIGHT P.M.

Sydney Carter
arr. David Dawson
by permission of Stainer & Bell

Intro., Interludes & Postlude

v. 1

vv. 1, 2 & 3

v. 3

v. 4

Chorus

THE FREE SPIRIT

149 Walk in the Light

There's a light that was shining when the world began,
And a light that is shining in the heart of Man;
There's a light that is shining in the Turk and the Jew,
And a light that is shining, friend, in me and in you.
    Walk in the light, wherever you may be,
    Walk in the light, wherever you may be!
    In my old leather breeches and my shaggy, shaggy locks,
    I am walking in the glory of the light, said Fox.

With a book and a steeple and a bell and a key
They would bind it for ever—but they can't, said he.
O, the book, it will perish, and the steeple will fall,
But the light will be shining at the end of it all.
    Walk in the light, wherever you may be,
    Walk in the light, wherever you may be!
    In my old leather breeches and my shaggy, shaggy locks,
    I am walking in the glory of the light, said Fox.

"Will you swear on the Bible?" "I will not," said he,
"For the truth is as holy as the Book to me."
"If we give you a pistol, will you fight for the Lord?"
"You can't kill the devil with a gun or a sword."
    Walk in the light, wherever you may be,
    Walk in the light, wherever you may be!
    In my old leather breeches and my shaggy, shaggy locks,
    I am walking in the glory of the light, said Fox.

There's an ocean of darkness and I drowned in the night
Till I came through the darkness to the ocean of light;
And the light is forever, and the light will be free,
And I'll walk in the glory of the light, said he.
    Walk in the light, wherever you may be,
    Walk in the light, wherever you may be!
    In my old leather breeches and my shaggy, shaggy locks,
    I am walking in the glory of the light, said Fox.

Sydney Carter
by permission of Stainer & Bell

George Fox (1624-91) founded the Religious Society of Friends. At nineteen he followed a divine call to wander through Britain, teaching his idea of the 'inner light', opposing sacerdotalism and formalism in religion, and preaching against social convention. He denounced amusements, and God forbade him to put off his hat to any, high or low. Many of his followers were gaoled for refusing to take the oath of abjuration. He was an amiable man with love for his fellows, who started the Quaker tradition of concern for education and social welfare.

THE FREE SPIRIT

Personal Commitment

150 Pilgrim's Hymn

MONKS GATE 65. 65. 6 6 6 5.

Coll., adpt. and arr. Ralph Vaughan Williams, 1872-1958
From the English Hymnal, by permission of Oxford University Press

Who would true valour see
  Let him come hither;
One here will constant be
  Come wind, come weather.
There's no discouragement
Shall make him once relent
His first avowed intent
  To be a pilgrim.

Whoso beset him round
  With dismal stories,
Do but themselves confound:
  His strength the more is.
No lion can him fright,
He'll with a giant fight,
But he will have a right
  To be a pilgrim.

Hobgoblin nor foul fiend
  Can daunt his spirit:
He knows he at the end
  Shall life inherit.
Then fancies flee away,
He'll fear not what they say,
He'll labour night and day
  To be a pilgrim.

John Bunyan, 1628-88

PERSONAL COMMITMENT

51. Be Thou My Vision

LANE 10 10. 10 10. Dactylic

Irish Traditional Melody
Har. by David Evans, 1874-1948

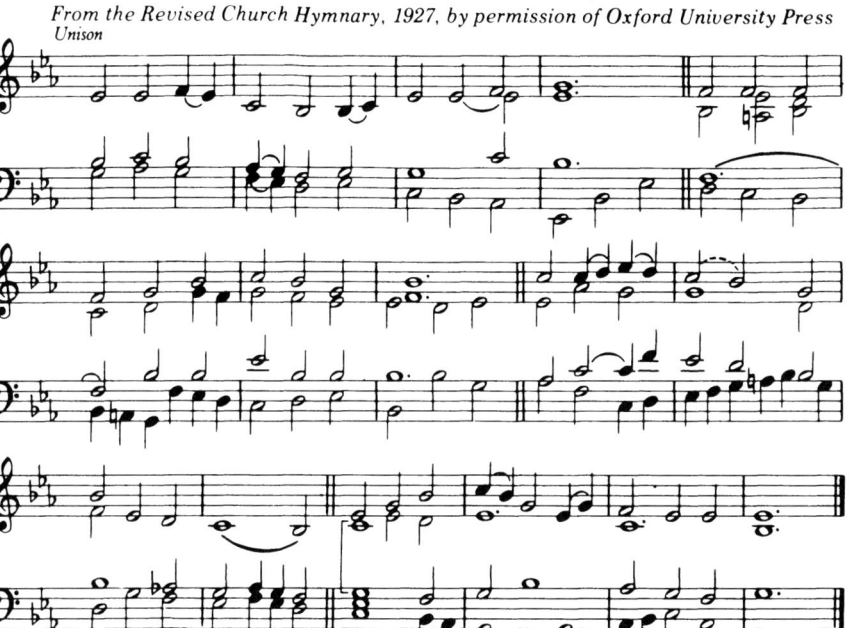

From the Revised Church Hymnary, 1927, by permission of Oxford University Press

Be thou my vision, O God of my heart;
Naught be all else to me, save that thou art;
Thou my best thought, by day or by night,
Waking or sleeping, thy presence my light.

Be thou my wisdom and thou my true word,
I ever with thee and thou with me, God;
Thou my soul's shelter, thou my high tower,
Raise thou me heavenward, O Power of my power.

Riches I heed not, nor world's empty praise,
Thou my inheritance, now and always;
Thou and thou only, first in my heart,
Sovereign of heaven, my treasure thou art.

Sovereign of heaven, my victory won,
May I reach heaven's joys, O bright heaven's Sun.
Heart of my own heart, whatever befall,
Still be my vision, O Ruler of all.

From *A Prayer* from *The Poem Book of the Gael*
Selected and edited by Eleanor Henrietta Hull, 1860-1935
*by permission of the Editor's Literary Estate
and Chatto and Windus, Ltd.*

PERSONAL COMMITMENT

ST. PATRICK L. M. D. Irish Melody
From A Student's Hymnal, by permission of Oxford University Press

PERSONAL COMMITMENT

152 I Bind Unto Myself Today

I bind unto myself today
The virtues of the star-lit heaven,
The glorious sun's life-giving ray,
The whiteness of the moon at e'en,
The flashing of the lightning free,
The whirling wind's tempestuous shocks,
The stable earth, the deep salt sea
Around the old eternal rocks.

I bind unto myself today
The power of God to hold and lead,
God's eye to watch, God's might to stay,
An ear to hearken to my need;
The wisdom of my God to teach,
A hand to guide, a shield to ward;
The word of God to give me speech,
A heavenly host to be my guard.

St. Patrick, c.385-c.461
tr. Cecil Frances Alexander (née Humphreys), 1823-95

PERSONAL COMMITMENT

153 We Must Be True

WYNNSTAY 8 4. 8 4. 8 8 8 4. John Ambrose Lloyd, 1815-74

Winning not, though ever striving,
  We must be true!
Onward pressing, ne'er arriving,
  We must be true!
Though success may never greet us,
Failure ever come to meet us,
All things seeming to defeat us,
  We must be true!

PERSONAL COMMITMENT

Following where our light shall lead us,
  We must be true!
Helping all, whene'er they need us,
  We must be true!
Reaching always for the better,
Trust the spirit, not the letter;
Think high thoughts without a fetter,
  And e'er be true.

Then our lives will be worth living,
  If we are true;
Helping, serving, loving, giving,
  And always true;
Journeying down life's road together,
In the bright or cloudy weather,
Make these words our blessèd tether —
  We must be true!

Althea A. Ogden
By permission of the Hodgin Press,
Los Angeles

PERSONAL COMMITMENT

154 I Would Be True

STRENGTH AND STAY 11 10. 11 10. John Bacchus Dykes, 1823-76

I would be true, for there are those who trust me;
I would be pure, for there are those who care;
I would be strong, for there is much to suffer;
I would be brave, for there is much to dare.

I would be friend of all—the foe, the friendless;
I would be giving, and forget the gift;
I would be humble, for I know my weakness;
I would look up, and laugh, and love, and lift.

Howard Arnold Walter, 1883-1918

PERSONAL COMMITMENT

155 Be True, Live Truly
HERONGATE L. M.

English Traditional Melody
Coll., arr. and har. Ralph Vaughan Williams, 1872-1958
From the English Hymnal, by permission of Oxford University Press

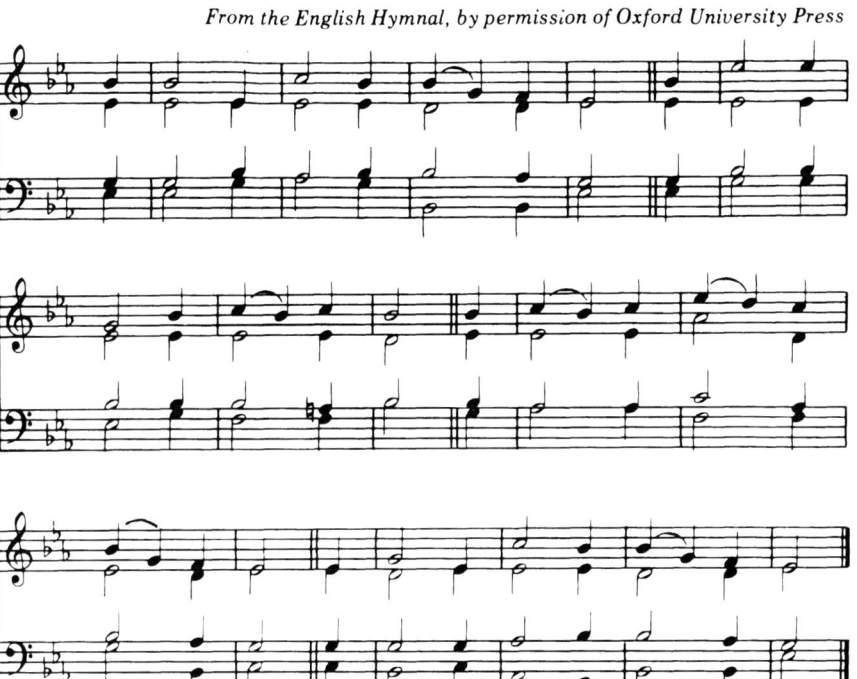

You must be true unto yourself
If truth to others you would teach;
Your soul must overflow with love
If you another's soul would reach.

Think wisely, truly, and your thoughts
This hungry world shall help to feed;
Speak truly, and your every word
Shall yet become a fruitful seed.

Let lips be full of gentle speech,
Your heart respond to human need;
Live truly, and your life shall be
A glorious and a noble creed.

after Horatius Bonar, 1808-89

PERSONAL COMMITMENT

156 The Harvest of Truth

RIMINGTON L. M. Francis Duckworth, b. 1862

O live each day and live it well—
All else is life but flung away;
Who lives a life of love can tell
Of true things truly done each day.

Be what thou seemest; live thy creed;
Hold up to earth the torch divine;
Be what thou prayest to be made;
The thirst for righteousness be thine.

Fill up each hour with what will last;
Use well the moments as they go;
Into life's soil thy seed is cast—
Thy deeds into a harvest grow.

Sow truth, if thou the true wouldst reap;
Who sows the false shall reap the vain;
Erect and sound thy conscience keep,
From hollow words and deeds refrain.

Sow love, and taste its fruitage pure;
Sow peace, and reap its harvest bright;
Sow sunbeams on the rock and moor,
And find a harvest-home of light.

from Horatius Bonar, 1808-89

PERSONAL COMMITMENT

157 The Golden Rule

KESTEVEN C. M.

Traditional Melody
Har. David Dawson
Used by permissioin

Grieve not your heart for want of place,
   Nor yearn for easy praise;
But fit yourself some task to do,
   And well employ your days.

From wise and foolish both alike
   We should all try to learn,
For one can show us how to live,
   The other what to spurn!

Be fair to people when they err,
   When good, your pleasure show;
Their faults be quick to understand,
   In judging them, be slow.

But this above all else obey,
   It is the best of goals,
What you would wish not done to you
   Do not to other souls.

Confucius, 551-479 B.C.
recast by John Andrew Storey, 1935—
Used by permission

PERSONAL COMMITMENT

158   Dare to Think

ORIENTIS PARTIBUS   77. 77.   From the *Beauvais Liturgical Play*, 13th Century

Dare to think, though others frown;
Dare in words your thoughts express;
Dare to rise, though oft cast down;
Dare the wronged and scorned to bless.

Dare from custom to depart;
Dare the priceless pearl possess;
Dare to wear it in your heart;
Dare, when others curse, to bless.

Dare what conscience says is right;
Do what reason says is best;
Do with all your mind and might;
Do your duty and be blest.

Anonymous

PERSONAL COMMITMENT

159 We Will Speak Out!

TALLIS' ORDINAL   C. M.   Thomas Tallis, c. 1505-85

We will speak out, we will be heard!
    Though all earth's systems crack,
We will not bate a single word,
    Nor take a letter back!

Let liars fear, let cowards shrink,
    Let traitors turn away;
Whatever we have dared to think,
    That dare we also say.

We speak the truth, and what care we
    For hissing and for scorn,
While some faint gleaming we can see
    Of freedom's coming morn.

We will speak out, we will be heard!
    Though all earth's systems crack,
We will not bate a single word,
    Nor take a letter back!

                       James Russell Lowell, 1819-91

PERSONAL COMMITMENT

160 It Is Something to Have Been

KEITH   11 10. 11 10.   Robert L. Sanders, 1906-74
By permission of the Beacon Press, Boston, Mass.

It is something to have wept, as we have wept,
   And something to have done as we have done;
It is something to have watched when all have slept,
   And seen the stars which never see the sun.

It is something to have smelt the mystic rose,
   Although it break and leave the thorny rods;
It is something to have hungered once as those
   Must hunger who have ate the bread of gods.

PERSONAL COMMITMENT

To have known the things that from the weak are furled,
   The fearful ancient passions, strange and high;
It is something to be wiser than the world,
   And something to be older than the sky.

Lo, and blessèd are our ears for they have heard;
   Yea, blessèd are our eyes for they have seen:
Let the thunder break on people, beast and bird,
   And lightning. It is something to have been.

From Gilbert Keith Chesterton, 1874-1936
From 'The Great Minimum' in The Collected Poems of
G. K. Chesterton
By permission of Miss D. E. Collins

PERSONAL COMMITMENT

161 The Sun of Hope Within

SURSUM CORDA   10 10. 10 10.   Alfred Morton Smith, b.1879

When I recall the hopes which almost died
And how I suffered to keep them alive—
Why, then I know they always in me cried
To be fulfilled, and always still shall call.

To find a place which truly seemed to be
Stretched on a road which surely would be mine,
To know which way to climb, to find this Me—
That was the hope that somehow would not die.

Now I know not what Future beckons on,
Nor what my life will be, full years from now,
But I know that I cannot kill that Sun—
That Sun of Hope within me presses on.

Linda Carol Morrison, 1947—
by permission of the Religious Arts Guild, Boston, Mass.

PERSONAL COMMITMENT

162 The Star of Truth

DEO GRACIAS (AGINCOURT)   L. M.   The Agincourt Tune, 1415

The star of truth but dimly shines
Behind the veiling clouds of night,
But every searching eye divines
Some partial glimmer of its light.

The certainty for which we crave
No mortal ones can ever know;
Uncharted waters we must brave,
And face whatever winds may blow.

Though for safe harbour we may long,
We must not let our courage fail,
And, though the winds of doubt blow strong,
Upon the trackless ocean sail.

From honest doubt we shall not flee,
Nor fetter the inquiring mind,
For where the hearts of all are free,
A truer faith we there shall find.

John Andrew Storey, 1935—
Used by permission

PERSONAL COMMITMENT

163 Those Who Seek Wisdom

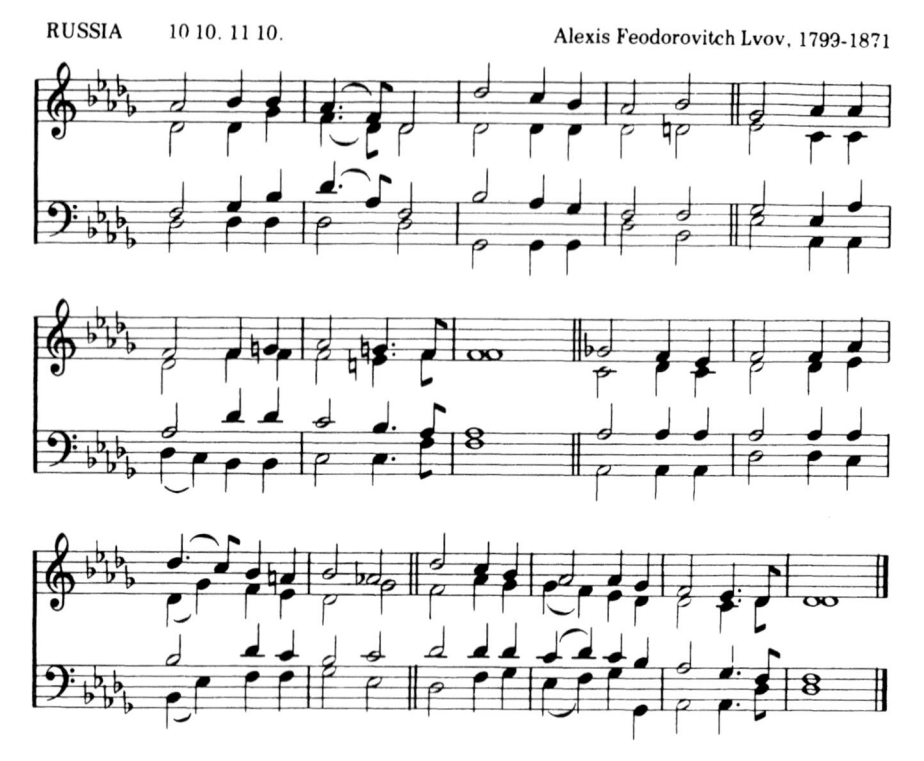

RUSSIA 10 10. 11 10.

Alexis Feodorovitch Lvov, 1799-1871

Those who seek wisdom
Seek truth and courage,
Walk through the darkness,
Endure through the storm.
Those who meet wisdom
In youth or in old age
Know that the wonder
Is always new-born.

They know the vision
In words is spoken.
They live the vision
Without words in deed.
Touching with loving
In healing the broken,
Touching with dreaming,
With vision they lead.

Rise out of weeping,
Joy in this hour.
Sing out our greeting
In this new-born day.
Now may our meeting
Rekindle the power
Of truth and courage
To walk in the Way.

Richard Frederick Boeke, 1931—
Used by permission

PERSONAL COMMITMENT

164 The Choice in Life

GRAGARETH 888.

David Dawson
Used by permission

The pen is greater than the sword :
To wield a blade or write a word
We need the skill which hands accord.

A surgeon takes a knife to heal :
Assassins do the same to kill.
Each acts according to their will.

I can pick cherries from a tree,
Or break the branch and let it die :
For good or ill, my hands are free.

With fingers I can soothe a brow,
Or make a fist and strike a blow,
Kindness or cruelty bestow.

Then let us now this lesson see :
Like life itself our hands can be
For evil used, or charity.

John Andrew Storey, 1935—
Used by permission

PERSONAL COMMITMENT

165   **Inasmuch**   Leonard P. Breedlove, d. c. 1879
CROSS OF CHRIST   C.M.D.   har. Robert L. Sanders, 1906-74
by permission of the Beacon Press, Boston, Mass.

The world is full of poverty,
  The world is full of care,
And people in extremity
  Are driven to despair.
In hope the poor stretch out their hands;
  The hungry we must feed;
We do not live the faith we teach
  Until we meet their need.

The lonely and companionless,
  The prisoner in the cell,
The sick and dying in distress
  With fears they can't dispel;
The homeless and the destitute,
  For whom our hearts should bleed;
We do not live the faith we teach
  Until we meet their need.

John Andrew Storey, 1935—
Used by permission

PERSONAL COMMITMENT

166 All Heroic Lives Remind Us

BETHANY   87. 87. D.   Henry Smart, 1813-79

All heroic lives remind us
    We can make our lives sublime,
And, departing, leave behind us
    Footprints on the sands of time;
Footprints that perhaps another,
    Sailing o'er life's solemn main,
Forlorn sister or lost brother,
    Seeing, shall take heart again.

Let us then be up and doing,
    With a heart for any fate;
Still achieving, still pursuing,
    Learn to labour and to wait.
Not enjoyment, and not sorrow,
    Is our destined end or way;
But to act that each tomorrow
    Finds us further than today.

from Henry Wadsworth Longfellow, 1807-82

PERSONAL COMMITMENT

167 True Freedom

ABERYSTWYTH 77. 77. D.   Joseph Parry, 1841-1903

Though it is our boast that we
Come of parents brave and free,
If there breathe on earth a slave,
Are we truly free and brave?
If we do not feel the chain
When it works another's pain,
Are we not base slaves indeed,
Slaves unworthy to be freed?

PERSONAL COMMITMENT

Is true freedom but to break
Fetters for our own dear sake,
And with leathern hearts forget
That we owe the world a debt?
No, true freedom is to share
All the chains our comrades wear,
And with heart and hand to be
Earnest to make others free.

They are slaves who fear to speak
For the fallen and the weak;
They are slaves who will not choose
Hatred, scoffing, and abuse,
Rather than in silence shrink
From the truth they needs must think;
They are slaves who dare not be
In the right with two or three.

from James Russell Lowell, 1819-91

PERSONAL COMMITMENT

EBENEZER 87. 87. D. Thomas John Williams, 1869-1944
By permission of Mrs. Dilys Evans

PERSONAL COMMITMENT

168 The Moment to Decide

Once to every man and nation
    Comes the moment to decide,
In the strife of Truth with Falsehood,
    For the good or evil side;
Some great cause, God's new Messiah,
    Offers each the bloom or blight,
And the choice goes by for ever
    'Twixt that darkness and that light.

Then to side with Truth is noble,
    When we share her wretched crust,
Ere her cause bring fame and profit,
    And 'tis prosperous to be just;
Then it is the brave soul chooses,
    While the coward stands aside,
Till the multitude make virtue
    Of the faith they had denied.

Though the cause of evil prosper,
    Yet 'tis Truth alone is strong;
Though her portion be the scaffold,
    And upon the throne be Wrong;
Yet that scaffold sways the future,
    And behind the dim unknown,
Standing there within the shadow,
    Keeping watch, is God alone.

from James Russell Lowell, 1819-91

PERSONAL COMMITMENT

169 The Voice of God

MISSIONARY 76. 76. D.   Lowell Mason, 1792-1872

The voice of God is calling
Its summons unto men;
As once he spoke in Zion,
So now he speaks again.
Whom shall I send to succour
My people in their need?
Whom shall I send to loosen
The bonds of shame and greed?

PERSONAL COMMITMENT

I hear my people crying
   In cot and mine and slum;
No field or mart is silent,
   No city street is dumb.
I see my people falling
   In darkness and despair.
Whom shall I send to shatter
   The fetters which they wear?

We heed, O Lord, thy summons,
   And answer : Here are we!
Send us upon thine errand;
   Let us thy servants be.
Our strength is dust and ashes,
   Our years a passing hour,
But thou canst use our weakness
   To magnify thy power.

From ease and plenty save us,
   From pride of place absolve;
Purge us of low desire,
   Lift us to high resolve.
Take us, and make us holy,
   Teach us thy will and way,
Speak, and, behold, we answer,
   Command, and we obey!

                John Haynes Holmes, 1879-1964
                By permission of the Author's family

PERSONAL COMMITMENT

170 The Goal

ANGELUS   L. M.

Johann Scheffler (Silesius Angelus), 1624-77
From *Heilige Seelenlust*, 1657

Creative Love, our thanks we give
That this, thy world, is incomplete,
That struggle greets our will to live,
That work awaits our hands and feet;

That we are not yet fully wise,
That we are in the making still —
As friends who share one enterprise,
And strive to blend with nature's will.

Beyond the present sin and shame,
Wrong's bitter, cruel, scorching blight,
We see the beckoning vision flame,
The commonwealth of truth and right.

What though the future long delay,
And still with faults we daily cope?
It gives us that for which to pray,
A field for toil and faith and hope.

Since what we choose is what we are,
And what we love we yet shall be,
The goal may ever shine afar —
The will to reach it makes us free.

adapted by Beth Ide, 1921 —
from William De Witt Hyde, 1858-1917
by permission of the Religious Arts Guild, Boston, Mass.

PERSONAL COMMITMENT

Love and Community

171 What Love Can Do

PRINCETHORPE   6 5. 6 5. D.   William Pitts, 1829-1903

When this day is over,
  Darkness in the sky,
Still of lives uncertain
  Will the lonely cry;
Yet we know this one dream,
  Simple, warm and bright :
Love can fill the darkest
  Loneliness with light.

Though the world's divided
  Nations, churches, creeds
Separate and sadden —
  Flowers turned to weeds :
And, though small truths deaden,
  Yet one truth we know :
Love can make what seems but
  Desert flower and grow.

So once more we gather,
  Fellowship to share,
Seek an understanding
  Trust with far and near;
And, though ideas differ,
  In this thought rejoice :
Love can form from all our
  Songs, one song, one voice.

Frank R. Clabburn, 1947—
Used by permission

LOVE AND COMMUNITY

172 All are Welcome Here

WESTMINSTER C.M.
James Turle, 1802-82

Now open wide your hearts, my friends,
   And I will open mine,
And let us share all that is fair,
   All that is true and fine.

We gather in this meeting house —
   People of many kinds :
Let us, below the surface, seek
   A meeting of true minds.

For in our company shall be
   Great witnesses of light :
The Buddha, Krishna, Jesus — those
   Gifted with clearest sight.

Like them, we seek to know ourselves,
   To seek, in spite of fear;
To open wide, to all, our hearts —
   For all are welcome here.

Peter Galbraith
Used by permission

LOVE AND COMMUNITY

173 The Fellowship of the Church

PETERSHAM C.M.D. Clement William Poole, 1828-1924

The Church is not where altar stands
  Within the hallowed walls,
But where the strong reach out their hands
  To raise the one who falls;
Not stately building, standing fair,
  Where people sing their creeds,
But fellowship of loving care
  Which serves all human needs.

The Church is not where ancient rite
  Is seen on Sabbath days,
But wisdom's constant beam of light
  To guide our common ways;
The Church is me, the Church is you,
  Not mortar, brick and stone;
It is with all who love the true,
  And where true love is shown.

John Andrew Storey, 1935—
Used by permission

LOVE AND COMMUNITY

174 A Church is a Living Fellowship

LANCASTER 9 6.9 6.
David Dawson
Used by permission

vv. 1, 2 & 5

A church is a living fellowship
   More than a holy shrine,
Where people can share their hopes and fear
   Less of the yours and mine;

Where bonded by trust we search for Truth
   Beyond the chains of creeds,
And thought can aspire to shine with fire
   From all our deepest needs.

Let's stretch out the open hand of Love,
   Conquer the fists of hate,
Divided no more by voices of war,
   Greeds of our mindless state;

We'll take all our building bricks of Truth,
   Make of them homes of Life,
A future to face the shame and disgrace
   In all our past of strife.

A church is a place of human trust
   More than of brick and stone;
Of Love we will sing to make it ring
   In every joyous tone.

Frank R.Clabburn, 1947—
Used by permission

LOVE AND COMMUNITY

BREAK BREAD TOGETHER   10 10. 7 8. 9.

Traditional Melody
adpt. Trevor Howarth Jones, 1932—
Used by permission

Slow and Strong

LOVE AND COMMUNITY

175 Let us Break Bread Together

Let us break bread together every day,
Let us break bread together every day.
If we break bread together,
If we share all we have to share,
We will make a blessing come our way.

Let us all sing together every day,
Let us all sing together every day.
If we all sing together,
If we share all we have to share,
We will make a blessing come our way.

Let us all pray together every day,
Let us all pray together every day.
If we all pray together,
If we share all we have to share,
We will make a blessing come our way.

Let us all work together every day,
Let us all work together every day.
If we all work together,
If we share all we have to share,
We will make a blessing come our way.

Negro Spiritual
Adapted by Trevor Howarth Jones, 1932—
Used by permission

LOVE AND COMMUNITY

176 Come Together in Love

COME TOGETHER   P.M. Dorothy Grover, arr. Douglas L. Butler

O come together in truth;
O come together in peace;
O come together in joy and sharing,
Come together in knowing and caring;
   Come together,
   O come together,
   O come together in love.

We come together in search
Of new beginnings for all,
Where understanding and trust surround us—
Gone the hate and fear that bound us;
   Come together,
   O come together,
   O come together in love.

Dorothy Grover
By permission of the Religious Arts Guild,
Boston

LOVE AND COMMUNITY

177 We Can Become

AMAZING GRACE C. M.

Traditional, adpt. by David Dawson
Used by permission

    Community, supporting friends,
       Hands joined in unity...
    Rejoice, my friend, in fellowship,
       In living, full and free.

    O let us live with humankind
       As sisters, brothers, true.
    We'll share our joys, our sorrows share,
       Becoming as we do.

    We all can grow. We can become
       Our finer selves set free...
    Risk what we are, sure in our faith
       In what we yet can be.

                          Doris Jeanine Stevens
              Used by permission of the author
              and the Hodgin Press, Los Angeles.

LOVE AND COMMUNITY

ALCUIN   L. M. D.

David Dawson
Used by permission

LOVE AND COMMUNITY

178 A Shelter From the Vast

A shelter from the vast we win
In homely hearths, and make therein
The glow of light, the sound of mirth,
That bind all children of the earth
In fellowship ; and when the rain
Beats loud upon the window-pane,
The shadows of the firelight fall
Across the floor and on the wall,

We know that countless hearth-lights burn
In darkened places, and discern—
Inwoven with the troubled plan
Of worlds and ways unknown to Man—
The shelter at the heart of life,
The refuge beyond doubt and strife,
The rest for every soul out-cast :
The homely hidden in the vast.

Amid the boundless and unknown,
We call some darkened spot our own;
Though all without is unexplored,
Uncharted lands and seas and world,
We doubt not that whatever fate
May lie beyond us, soon or late,
However far afield we roam
The unknown way will lead us home.

from Sidney Royse Lysaght, 1856-1941

179   A Noble Life

BELMONT   C. M.   Gardiner's *Sacred Melodies*, 1812

A noble life, a simple faith,
  An open heart and hand—
These are the lovely litanies
  Which all may understand;

These are the firm-knit bonds of grace,
  Though hidden to the view,
Which bind in sacred fellowship
  All folk the whole world through.

from A.S.Isaacs, 1914

LOVE AND COMMUNITY

180 This Old World

RESTORATION 87. 87.

American Folk Melody
Har. David Dawson
Used by permission

This old world is full of sorrow,
    Full of sickness, weak and sore;
If you love your neighbour truly,
    Love will come to you the more.

We're all children of one family;
    We're all brothers, sisters too;
If you cherish one another,
    Love and friendship come to you.

This old world can be a garden,
    Full of fragrance, full of grace;
If we love our neighbours truly,
    We must meet them face to face.

It is said now, 'Love thy neighbour',
    And we know well that is true;
This the sum of human labour,
    True for me as well as you.

Adapted from American Folk Song

LOVE AND COMMUNITY

181 Can I See Another's Woe?

ST. BEES 77.77. John Bacchus Dykes, 1823-76

Can I see another's woe,
And not be in sorrow too?
Can I see another's grief,
And not seek for kind relief?

Can I see a falling tear,
And not feel my sorrow's share?
Can a father see his child
Weep, nor be with sorrow filled?

Can a mother sit and hear
Infant groan, an infant fear?
No, no, never can it be!
Never, never can it be!

William Blake, 1757-1827

LOVE AND COMMUNITY

182 All Are Our Neighbours

NIAGARA L. M. Robert Jackson, 1842-1914

We must be one with all who found
Life's brilliant morning turned to tears,
Or who by sin and suffering bound,
Pass on in sorrow down the years.

The ploughman working in his field,
The anxious mother worn with toil,
The serf who finds in faith revealed
Strength rising from his native soil;

And those who lie, for conscience' sake
Forgotten in a distant jail,
Or who to nobler thoughts awake,
And custom's guarded towers assail.

All are our neighbours, far and near,
In whom there throbs a human heart:
Their hopes and fears to each are dear,
In all they are, we have our part.

So, as the sense of kinship grows,
Our own disordered fears abate :
As life with fellow feeling flows,
We reach at last our full estate.

Wilfrid Edward Reeve, 1909—
Used by permission

LOVE AND COMMUNITY

183 With Your Neighbour Share

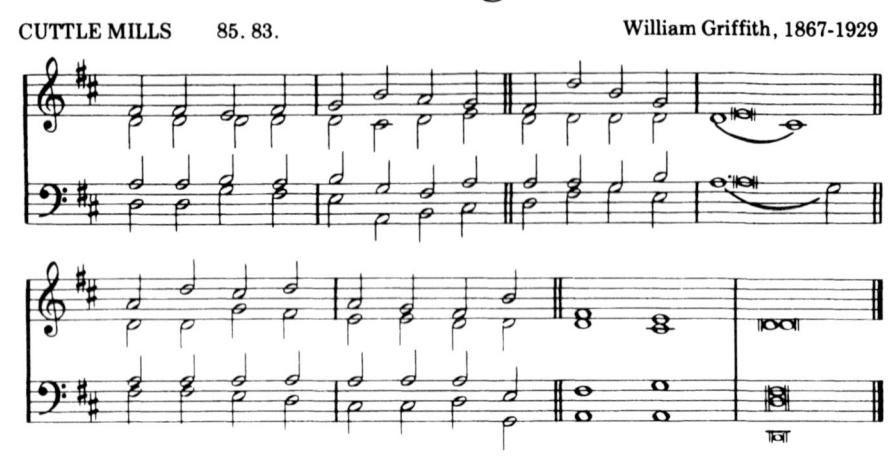

CUTTLE MILLS 85. 83. William Griffith, 1867-1929

When your heart, with joy o'erflowing,
  Sings a thankful prayer,
In your joy, O let your neighbour
    With you share.

When the harvest sheaves ingathered
  Fill your barns with store,
To your God and to your neighbour
    Give the more.

If your soul, with power uplifted,
  Yearn for glorious deed,
Give your strength to serve your neighbour's
    Every need.

Have you borne a secret sorrow
  In your lonely breast?
Take to you your sorrowing neighbour
    For a guest;

Share in full your bread of blessing,
  Sorrow's burden share;
When your heart enfolds a neighbour,
    God is there.

After Theodore Chickering Williams, 1855-1915

LOVE AND COMMUNITY

184 The Best Things

CROMER L. M.

John Ambrose Lloyd, 1815-74

I learned it in the meadow path,
I learned it on the mountain stairs—
The best things any mortal hath
Are those which every mortal shares.

The air we breathe, the sky, the breeze,
The light without us and within;
Life with its unlocked treasuries,
God's riches, are for all to win.

The grass is softer to my tread
Because it rests unnumbered feet;
Sweeter to me the wild rose red
Because she makes the whole world sweet.

Wealth won by others' poverty—
Not such be mine! Let me be blest
Only in what they share with me,
And what I share with all the rest.

We learn it in the meadow path,
We learn it on the mountain stairs—
The best things any mortal hath
Are those which every mortal shares.

Lucy Larcom, 1826-93

LOVE AND COMMUNITY

185 The Power of Love

INTERCESSOR 11 10. 11 10. Charles Hubert Hastings Parry, 1848-1918

We know that this life brings its share of sorrow
To us, and men and women everywhere;
The knowledge of the world floods in unceasing—
Too much to match with equal love and care.

We stand before the threat of world pollution,
We live in shame that half the world is poor,
We look out from our homes upon the homeless
And wish we had the power to love them more.

We know the power of love can move a nation,
We know that love creates more of itself;
We know the human needs which need attention,
We know the drugs of affluence and wealth.

O power of love already here within us!
Help us to trust—be not afraid to live
In love which works its miracles in details
Of thought and feeling and the will to give.

Bruce Findlow, 1922—
Used by permission

LOVE AND COMMUNITY

186 The Law of Love

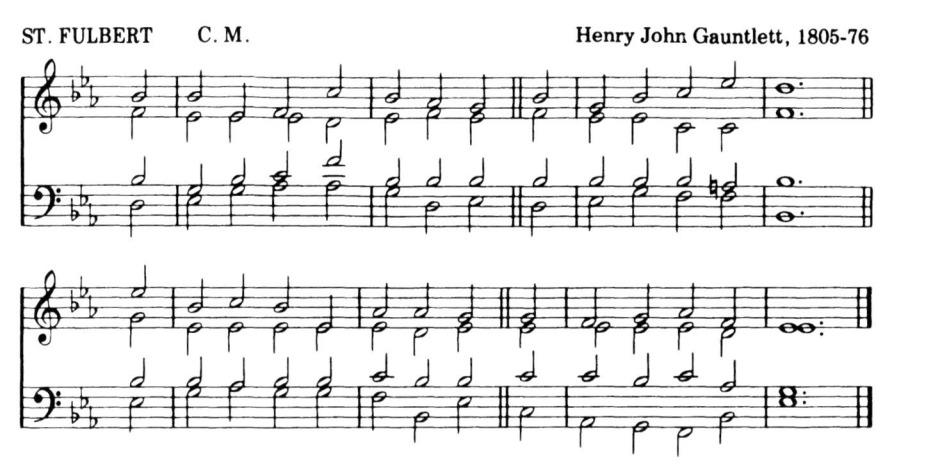

ST. FULBERT C. M. Henry John Gauntlett, 1805-76

Make channels for the streams of love,
  Where they may broadly run;
For love has overflowing streams
  To fill them, every one.

But if at any time we cease
  Such channels to provide,
The very founts of love for us
  Will soon be parched and dried.

For we must share if we would keep
  That blessing from above;
Ceasing to give we cease to have—
  This is the law of love.

Richard Chenevix Trench, 1825-97

LOVE AND COMMUNITY

187 Human Kindness

LUX EOI   8 7. 8 7. D.   Arthur Seymour Sullivan, 1842-1900

We believe in human kindness
   Large amid the human race,
Turning from indifferent blindness
   To compassion's healing grace.
We believe in self-denial
   In the cause of greater joy;
In the love that lives through trial,
   Dying not, though death destroy.

We believe in love renewing
   All that sin has swept away,
Leaven-like its work pursuing
   Night by night and day by day.
In its patience, its endurance,
   To forbear and to retrieve,
In the large and full assurance
   Of its triumph—we believe.

from an anonymous hymn

LOVE AND COMMUNITY

188 Let Love Continue Long

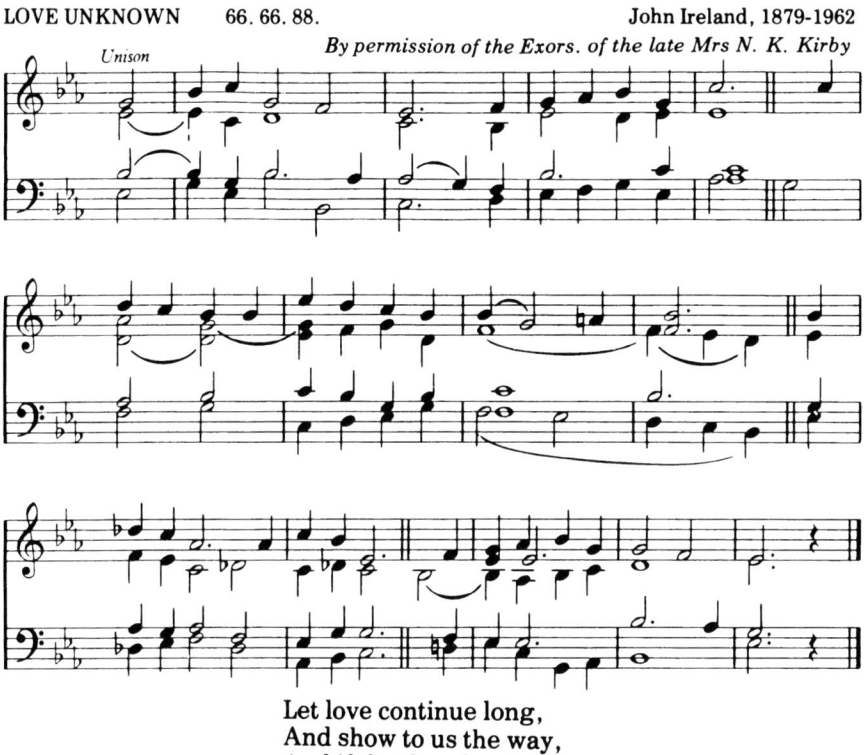

LOVE UNKNOWN 66. 66. 88. John Ireland, 1879-1962

By permission of the Exors. of the late Mrs N. K. Kirby

Let love continue long,
And show to us the way,
And if that love be strong
No hurt can have a say;
And if that love remain but strong,
No hurt can ever have a say.

If love can not be found,
Though common faith prevail,
When love does not abound,
A common faith will fail.
When human love does not abound,
A common faith will always fail.

If we in love unite,
Debate can cause no strife :
For with this love in sight
Disputes enrich our life.
For with this bond of human love,
Disputes can mean a richer life.

May love continue long,
And lead us on our way :
For if that love be strong
No hurt can have a say.
For if that love remain but strong
No hurt can ever have a say.

from traditional American words

LOVE AND COMMUNITY

189 True Religion

O WALY, WALY L.M.

Somerset Folk Song
arr. David Dawson
Used by permission

Religion needs to permeate
The common life of every day;
Each to the other must relate
To build the world for which we pray.

Our forms and customs will not meet
The spirit's needs we deeply feel,
Unless our hearts with quickened beat
Match outward show with inner zeal.

When thoughts are pure, and words are kind,
Compassionate our every deed,
With selfishness put from the mind
Our lives become a worthy creed.

The Dalai Lama
recast by John Andrew Storey, 1935–
Used by permission

LOVE AND COMMUNITY

190 To Mercy, Pity, Peace and Love

EPSOM C. M. William Tans'ur, 1706-83

To Mercy, Pity, Peace and Love
All pray in their distress,
And to these virtues of delight
Return their thankfulness.

For Mercy, Pity, Peace, and Love
Is God our Father dear;
And Mercy, Pity, Peace, and Love
Is man, his child and care.

For Mercy has a human heart;
Pity, a human face;
And Love, the human form divine;
And Peace, the human dress.

Then every man, of every clime,
That prays in his distress,
Prays to the human form divine :
Love, Mercy, Pity, Peace.

William Blake, 1757-1827

LOVE AND COMMUNITY

191 To Worship Rightly

LONDONDERRY AIR 11 10. 11 10. D.

Irish Traditional Melody
Arr. David Dawson
Used by permission

LOVE AND COMMUNITY

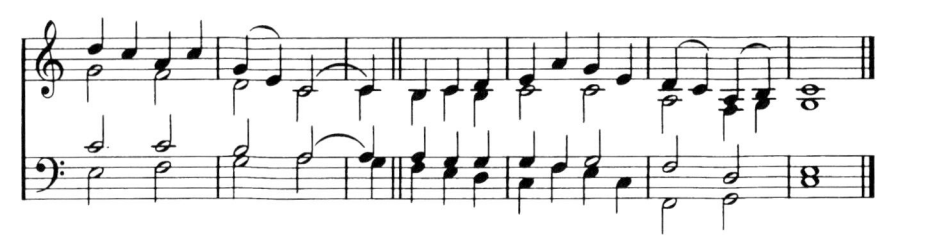

Now let us sing in loving celebration :
   The holier worship, which our God may bless,
Restores the lost, binds up the spirit broken,
   And feeds the widowed and the parentless.
Fold to thy heart thy sister and thy brother;
   Where pity dwells, the peace of God is there;
To worship rightly is to love each other;
   Each smile a hymn, each kindly deed a prayer.

Follow with reverent steps the great example
   Of those whose holy work was doing good :
So shall the wide earth seem our daily temple,
   Each loving life a psalm of gratitude.
Then shall all shackles fall; the stormy clangour
   Of wild war-music o'er the earth shall cease;
Love shall tread out the baleful fire of anger,
   And in its ashes plant the tree of peace.

from John Greenleaf Whittier, 1807-92

LOVE AND COMMUNITY

192 A New Community

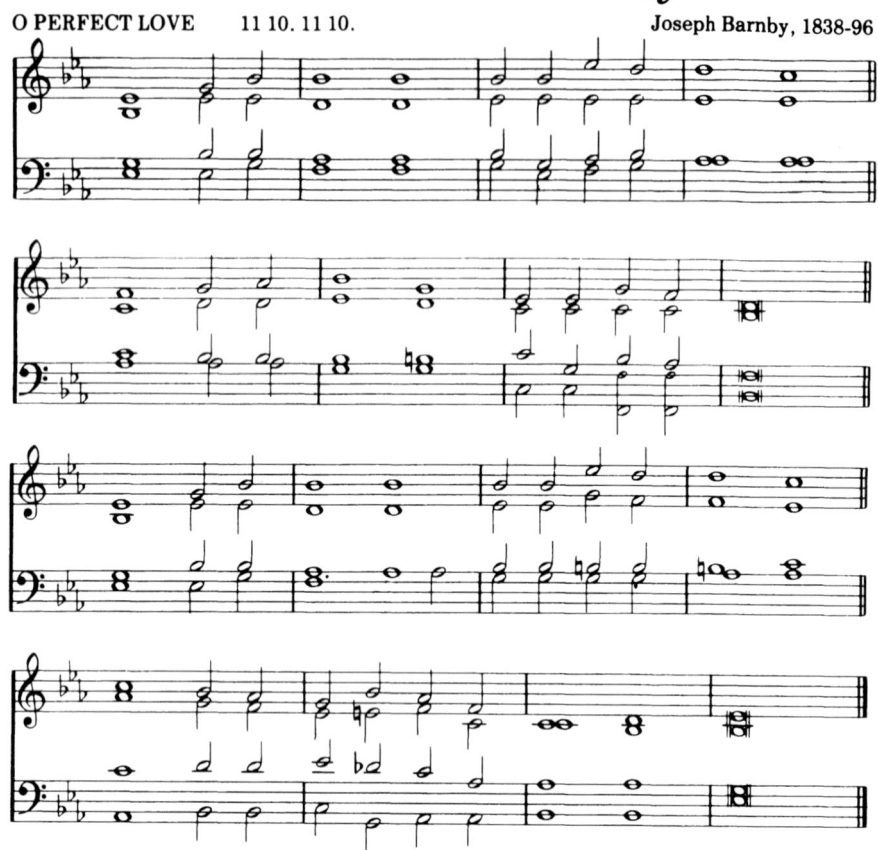

O PERFECT LOVE 11 10. 11 10. Joseph Barnby, 1838-96

We would be one as now we join in singing
Our hymn of love, to pledge ourselves anew
To that high cause of greater understanding
Of who we are, and what in us is true.

We would be one in building for tomorrow
A greater world than we have known today;
We would be one in searching for that meaning
Which binds our hearts and points us on our way.

We would be one in living for each other,
With love and justice strive to make all free;
As one, we pledge ourselves to greater service,
To show the world a new community.

From Samuel Anthony Wright, 1919—
Used by permission

LOVE AND COMMUNITY

A Better World

193 Wisdom and Courage

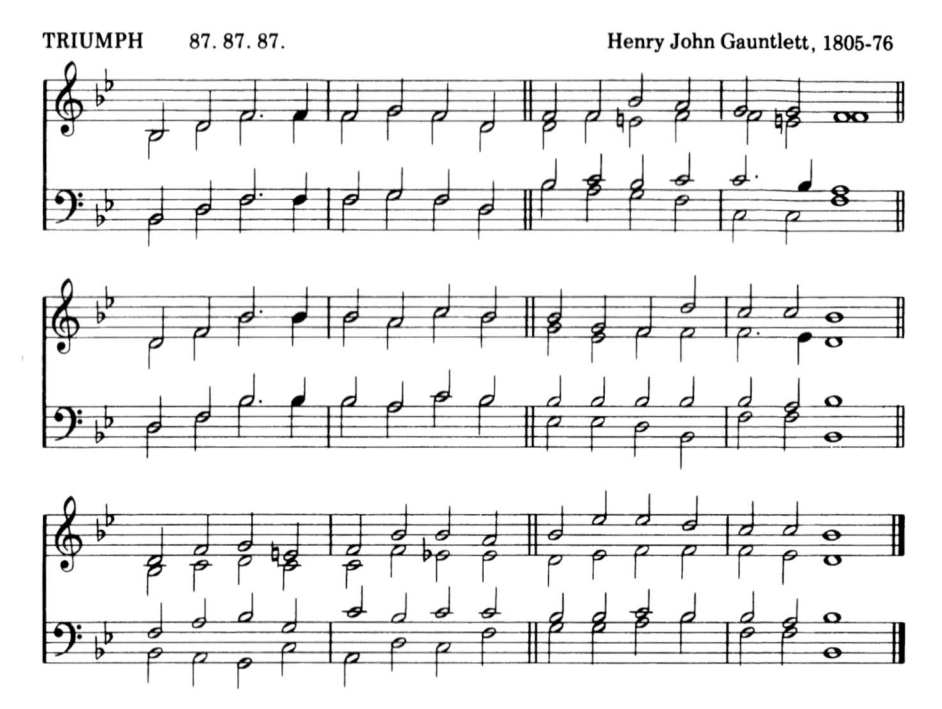

TRIUMPH 87. 87. 87. Henry John Gauntlett, 1805-76

God of grace and God of glory,
On thy people pour thy power;
Crown thine ancient church's story;
Bring her bud to glorious flower.
Grant us wisdom,
Grant us courage,
For the facing of this hour.

Heal thy children's warring madness;
Bend our pride to thy control;
Shame our wanton, selfish gladness,
Rich in things and poor in soul.
Grant us wisdom,
Grant us courage,
Lest we miss thy kingdom's goal.

Save us from weak resignation
To the evils we deplore;
Let the search for thy salvation
Be our glory evermore.
Grant us wisdom,
Grant us courage,
Serving thee whom we adore.

Harry Emerson Fosdick, 1878-1969
Used by permission of Riverside Church, New York

A BETTER WORLD

194 What Purpose Burns

ANGEL'S SONG (SONG 34)   L. M.   Orlando Gibbons, 1583-1625

What purpose burns within our hearts
   That we together here should stand
Pledging each other mutual vows,
   And ready hand to join in hand?

We see in vision fair a time
   When evil shall have passed away;
And thus we dedicate our lives
   To hasten on that blessed day.

To seek the truth whate'er it be,
   To follow it where'er it leads;
To turn to facts our dreams of good,
   And coin our lives in loving deeds:

For this we gather here today;
   To such a church of God we bring
Our utmost love and loyalty,
   And make our souls an offering.

Minot Judson Savage, 1841-1918

A BETTER WORLD

195 We Limit Not the Truth of God

ELLACOMBE   C. M. D.   *Mainz Gesangbuch*, 1833

We limit not the truth of God
  To our poor reach of mind,
By notions of our day and sect,
  Crude, partial and confined.
No, let a new and better hope
  Within our hearts be stirred:
The Lord hath yet more light and truth
  To break forth from his word.

A BETTER WORLD

Who dares to bind to partial sense
   The oracles of heaven,
For all the nations, tongues and climes,
   And all the ages given?
That universe, how much unknown!
   That ocean unexplored!
The Lord hath yet more light and truth
   To break forth from his word.

Darkling our noble forbears went
   The first steps of the way;
'Twas but the dawning, yet to grow
   Into the perfect day.
And grow it shall; our glorious sun
   More fervid rays afford;
The Lord hath yet more light and truth
   To break forth from his word.

The valleys past, ascending still,
   Our souls would higher climb,
And look down from supernal heights
   On all the bygone time.
Upward we press; the air is clear,
   And the sphere-music heard:
The Lord hath yet more light and truth
   To break forth from his word.

From George Rawson, 1807-1889

A BETTER WORLD

196 The Spirit Conquers All

BIRMINGHAM 10 10. 10 10.
From F. Cunningham's *A Selection of Psalm Tunes, 1834*

The mighty elm tree falls before the storm,
Uprooted from the earth, its pride laid low;
The fragile harebell flutters in the wind
To greet the dawn with strength no elm can know.

Put not your trust in rigid edifice,
Nor panoplied parade of earthly power,
Nor fortress built to brave the elements,
For none of these is stronger than the flower.

Vast empires walled with steel and rigid rule,
Fearful of change, invoke suppression blind:
And fall at last before some new idea,·
Some vision great to fire the human mind.

Armies in conquest, vast in numbered power,
In fearful might hold multitudes in thrall:
The voice of Buddha or some lonely Christ
Speaks gentleness and love to conquer all.

Though tyrant-power on earth may seem supreme,
The Spirit's fruits have greater power in store:
Truth, beauty, goodness, faith and hope and love
Shall outlast all and live for evermore.

Sydney Henry Knight, 1923—
Used by permission

A BETTER WORLD

197 Westward, Look

LES COMMANDEMENS DE DIEU 9 8. 9 8.

Louis Bourgeois, c. 1523-1600
from the *Genevan Psalter*, 1543

Say not, "The struggle nought availeth,
  The labour and the wounds are vain,
The enemy faints not nor faileth
  And as things have been they remain."

If hopes were dupes, fears may be liars;
  It may be, in yon smoke concealed,
Your comrades chase e'en now the fliers,
  And, but for you, possess the field.

For while the tired waves vainly breaking
  Seem here no painful inch to gain,
Far back, through creeks and inlets making,
  Comes silent, flooding in, the main.

And not by eastern windows only,
  When daylight comes, comes in the light;
In front the sun climbs slow, how slowly,
  But westward, look, the land is bright.

Arthur Hugh Clough, 1819-61

A BETTER WORLD

CWM RHONDDA 8 7. 8 7. 8 7.   John Hughes, 1873-1932
By permission of Mrs. Dilys S. Webb

A BETTER WORLD

198 The Healing of the Nations

For the healing of the nations,
  God, we pray with one accord;
For a just and equal sharing
  Of the things that earth affords.
To a life of love in action
  Help us rise and pledge our word,
  Help us rise and pledge our word.

Lead us ever into freedom,
  From despair your world release;
That, redeemed from war and hatred,
  All may come and go in peace.
Show us how through care and goodness
  Fear will die and hope increase,
  Fear will die and hope increase.

All that kills abundant living,
  Let it from the earth depart;
Pride of status, race or schooling,
  Dogmas keeping us apart.
May our common quest for justice
  Be our brief life's hallowed art,
  Be our brief life's hallowed art.

Fred Kaan, 1929—
by permission of Stainer & Bell, Ltd.

A BETTER WORLD

199 When a Deed is Done for Freedom

AN DIE FREUDE   87. 87. D.   German Melody
for Schiller's *Hymn to Joy*, 1799

When a deed is done for freedom,
   Through the broad earth's aching breast
Runs a thrill of joy prophetic,
   Trembling on from east to west;
And the slaves, where'er they cower,
   Feel the soul within them climb
To achieve new independence
   With an energy sublime.

New occasions teach new duties;
   Time makes ancient good uncouth;
We must upward still and onward,
   Who would keep abreast of truth—
Launch our vessel and steer boldly
   Through the desperate winter sea,
Nor attempt the future's portal
   With the past's blood-rusted key!

For we are now one in spirit,
   And an instinct bears along,
Round the earth's electric circle,
   The swift flash of right or wrong;
All earth's ocean-sundered fibres
   Feel the gush of joy or shame;
In the gain or loss of one race
   All the rest have equal claim.

from James Russell Lowell, 1819-91

A BETTER WORLD

200   Courage Shall Conquer

EPIPHANY HYMN   11 10. 11 10. Dactylic.   Joseph Francis Thrupp, 1827-67

"Onward and upward for ever and ever,"
Hopes once we cherished are fading away,
Saving them should be our common endeavour—
Times are so urgent they brook no delay.

Learn then to labour for human salvation,
Build from the ashes the dreams we have lost,
Shrink not from hardship nor scorn tribulation,
Spurn no endeavour nor reckon the cost.

For though our hopes may have faltered and dwindled,
Heights still call upwards and beckon us on;
Courage shall conquer when hearts are rekindled,
Dreams find fulfilment in victories won.

John Andrew Storey, 1935—
Used by permission

A BETTER WORLD

201 Tomorrow is a Highway

TOMORROW IS A HIGHWAY   10 10. 10 9. 6. (Irregular)   Melody by Pete Seeger

Tomorrow is a highway broad and fair,
And we are the many who'll travel there.
Tomorrow is a highway broad and fair,
And we are the hands who'll build it there,
   And we will build it there.

Come, let us build a way for humankind,
A way to leave all hate and wrong behind;
And travel onward to a better year,
Where love is, and there will be no fear,
   Where love is, and no fear.

O come then friend, and travel on with me,
We'll go to a time of liberty.
Come, let us walk together, hand in hand,
From darkness, into a happy land,
   From dark to sunlit land.

Tomorrow is a highway broad and fair,
And hate and greed shall never travel there;
But only they who've learned the peaceful way
Of fellowship to bring a better day;
   We'll see that coming day!

From Lee Hays
Words and music reprinted by permission of Harmony Music Ltd.

A BETTER WORLD

202 Children of a Bright Tomorrow

CROSS OF JESUS   87. 87.   John Stainer, 1840-1901

Now we gather here to worship,
   Each with but one life to live;
Each with gifts and each with failings,
   Each with but one heart to give.

In our longing, here we gather,
   With warm voices for a friend;
Two or three, or tens, or thousands,
   Heart and hand to all extend.

May our circle grow still wider;
   May we see as others see:
Standing in the others' sandals
   Shows us they, too, would be free.

Children of a bright tomorrow,
   Every race and every creed;
Men and women of all nations,
   Each a glory, each in need.

Small are we, and small our planet,
   Hidden here among the stars:
May we know our timeless mission—
   Universal avatars.

Roger Taylor Walke, 1924—
by permission of the Religious Arts Guild, Boston, Mass.

A BETTER WORLD

203 These Things Shall Be!

SIMEON L. M.
Samuel Stanley, 1767-1822

These things shall be! a loftier race
Than e'er the world hath known shall rise,
With flame of freedom in their souls
And light of knowledge in their eyes.

They shall be gentle, brave, and strong
To spill no drop of blood, but dare
All that may make them stewards true
Of earth and fire and sea and air.

Nation with nation, land with land,
Inarmed shall live as comrades free;
In every heart and brain shall throb
The pulse of one community.

New arts shall bloom of loftier mould,
And mightier music thrill the skies,
And every life shall be a song,
When all the earth is paradise.

There shall be no more sin nor shame,
Though pain and passion may not die;
For all shall be at one with God
In bonds of firm necessity.

A BETTER WORLD   from John Addington Symonds, 1840-93

204 We Shall Overcome

WE SHALL OVERCOME 557. 97.

Slowly – Strongly accented
Unison

We shall overcome,
We shall overcome,
We shall overcome some day;
O, deep in my heart, I do believe
We shall overcome some day.

We'll walk hand in hand,
We'll walk hand in hand,
We'll walk hand in hand some day;
O, deep in my heart, I do believe
We'll walk hand in hand some day.

We shall live in peace,
We shall live in peace,
We shall live in peace some day;
O, deep in my heart, I do believe
We shall live in peace some day.

Truth shall make us free,
Truth shall make us free,
Truth shall make us free some day;
O, deep in my heart, I do believe
Truth shall make us free some day.

We shall overcome,
We shall overcome,
We shall overcome some day;
O, deep in my heart, I do believe
We shall overcome some day.

Guy Carawan, Pete Seeger, Zilphia Horton and Frank Hamilton

Words and music copyright 1960, 1963 Ludlow Music Inc., assigned to TRO Essex Music Ltd., 19/20 Poland Street, London W1V 3DD. International copyright secured. Used by permission. British Empire and Commonwealth [excluding Canada and Australasia] and Republics of Ireland and South Africa.

A BETTER WORLD

ST. CATHERINE   88. 88. 88.   Melody by Henri F. Hémy, 1818-88

A BETTER WORLD

205 In Braver Mould

From out of time's immortal hand,
The centuries fall like grains of sand.
The years have passed, an era's done,
And now a new day has begun;
   We meet today where freedom stands,
   To join in love our hearts and hands.

For art and labour met in truce,
And beauty made the bride of use,
We thank our forbears :   still we crave
The austere virtues, strong to save,
   The honour proof to place or gold,
   The courage never bought or sold!

May we be through the ages long
In peace secure, in justice strong;
Around our gift of freedom draw
The safeguards of a righteous law;
   And cast our age in braver mould,
   To let the new years shame the old.

Adpt. by William Wolff
from John Greenleaf Whittier, 1807-92
Copyright 1960, The Hodgin Press, Los Angeles
Used by permission

A BETTER WORLD

MERTHYR TYDFIL   L. M. D.   Joseph Parry, 1841-1903

A BETTER WORLD

The Choice is Ours

O earth, you are surpassing fair,
From out your store we're daily fed,
We breathe your life-supporting air
And drink the water that you shed.
Yet greed has made us mar your face,
Pollute the air, make foul the sea:
The folly of the human race
Is bringing untold misery.

Our growing numbers make demands
That e'en your bounty cannot meet;
Starvation stalks through hungry lands
And some die hourly in the street.
The Eden-dream of long ago
Is vanishing before our eyes;
Unwise, unheeding, still we go,
Destroying hopes of paradise.

Has evolution been in vain
That life should perish ere its prime?
Or will we from our greed refrain
And save our planet while there's time?
We must decide without delay
If we're to keep our race alive:
The choice is ours, and we must say
If we're to perish or survive.

John Andrew Storey, 1935—
Used by permission

A BETTER WORLD

MOUNTAIN ALONE   89. 87. D   Waldemar Hille, 1908—
                                            Used by permission

A BETTER WORLD

207 Stranger on the Mountain

In the branches of the forest,
In the petals of the marigold,
On the shoulder of the mountain,
   In the vastness of the sea,
You will find a brooding sadness
Over all the ancient watershed;
You will see it written plainly
   On the wind and in the sand.

In the green world of the forest,
In the stillness of the tide-land pool,
There is fear and there is trembling
   For a certain stranger there ;
Now he walks upon the mountain
Like a warlock of the countryside,
And he spoils the ancient meadow,
   Laying waste the forest green.

There's a blight upon the mountain,
There's a sickness in the evening sky,
And we ask the age-old question—
   Can we purge us of this sin?
Can we save the little nestling
From the venom of the cankerworm?
Can we clear the look of anguish
   From the soft eyes of the doe?

In the thunder, new commandments
Sound a warning through the wilderness—
Let the forest be untainted,
   Let the streams be undefiled;
Let the waters of the river,
As they flow down to the ocean,
Be as sweet as in the old days,
   When the mountain stood alone!

David Arkin, 1934—
By permission of the Hodgin Press,
Los Angeles

A BETTER WORLD

ST. GERTRUDE 65. 65. T. Arthur Seymour Sullivan, 1842-1900

Move the faith - ful spir - its at the call di - vine.

A BETTER WORLD

208 Forward Through the Ages

Forward through the ages
  In unbroken line,
Move the faithful spirits
  At the call divine:
Gifts in differing measure,
  Hearts of one accord,
Manifold the service,
  One the sure reward.
    Forward through the ages
    In unbroken line,
    Move the faithful spirits
    At the call divine.

Wider grows the kingdom,
  Reign of love and light;
For it we must labour,
  Till our faith is sight.
Prophets have proclaimed it,
  Martyrs testified,
Poets sung its glory,
  Heroes for it died.
    Forward through the ages
    In unbroken line,
    Move the faithful spirits
    At the call divine.

Not alone we conquer,
  Not alone we fall;
In each loss or triumph
  Lose or triumph all.
Bound by God's far purpose
  In one living whole,
Move we on together
  To the shining goal!
    Forward through the ages
    In unbroken line,
    Move the faithful spirits
    At the call divine.

Frederick Lucian Hosmer, 1840-1929

A BETTER WORLD

BLAENWERN 87. 87. D. William Penfro Rowlands, 1860-1937
By permission of Mr. G. A. Gabe

A BETTER WORLD

209   A World Transfigured

Wonders still the world shall witness
   Never known in days of old,
Never dreamed by ancient sages,
   Howsoever free and bold.
Sons and daughters shall inherit
   Wondrous arts to us unknown,
When the dawn of peace its splendour
   Over all the world has thrown.

They shall rule with wingèd freedom
   Worlds of health and human good,
Worlds of commerce, worlds of science,
   All made one and understood.
They shall know a world transfigured,
   Which our eyes but dimly see;
They shall make its towns and woodlands
   Beautiful from sea to sea.

For a spirit then shall move them
   We but vaguely apprehend—
Aims magnificent and holy,
   Making joy and labour friend.
Then shall bloom in song and fragrance
   Harmony of thought and deed,
Fruits of peace and love and justice—
   Where today we plant the seed.

Jacob Trapp, 1899—
Used by permission

A BETTER WORLD

210 Jerusalem

JERUSALEM L.M.D.
Charles Hubert Hastings Parry, 1848-1918

Voices in unison.

1. And did those feet in an-cient time Walk up-on Eng-land's moun-tains green? And was the ho-ly Lamb of

A BETTER WORLD

210 JERUSALEM

... God On England's pleasant pastures seen? And did the countenance divine Shine forth upon our clouded hills? And was Jerusalem builded here Among these

A BETTER WORLD

JERUSALEM

dark sa-tan-ic mills?

2. Bring me my bow of burn-ing gold! Bring me my ar-rows of de-sire! Bring me my spear! O clouds, un-

A BETTER WORLD

210 JERUSALEM

-fold! Bring me my cha-ri-ot of fire! I will not cease from men-tal fight, Nor shall my sword sleep in my hand, Till we have built Je-ru-sa-lem In Eng-land's

A BETTER WORLD

210 Jerusalem

And did those feet in ancient time
Walk upon England's mountains green?
And was the holy Lamb of God
On England's pleasant pastures seen?
And did the countenance divine
Shine forth upon our clouded hills?
And was Jerusalem builded here
Among these dark satanic mills?

Bring me my bow of burning gold!
Bring me my arrows of desire!
Bring me my spear! O clouds, unfold!
Bring me my chariot of fire!
I will not cease from mental fight,
Nor shall my sword sleep in my hand,
Till we have built Jerusalem
In England's green and pleasant land.

William Blake, 1757-1827

A BETTER WORLD

211 All are Architects of Fate

LÜBECK 77.77.

Geistreiches Gesangbuch (1704)
of Johann August Freylinghausen, 1670-1739

All are architects of fate,
Working in these walls of time;
Some with massive deeds and great,
Some with ornaments of rhyme.

Nothing useless is, or low;
Each thing in its place is best;
And what seems but idle show
Strengthens and supports the rest.

For the structure that we raise
Time is with materials filled;
Our todays and yesterdays
Are the blocks with which we build.

Build today, then, strong and sure,
With a firm and ample base;
And ascending and secure
Shall tomorrow find its place.

Henry Wadsworth Longfellow, 1807-82

A BETTER WORLD

HYFRYDOL 8 7. 8 7. D.   Rowland Hugh Prichard, 1811-87

A BETTER WORLD

212 The Golden City

Sing we of the Golden City
    Pictured in the legends old:
Everlasting light shines o'er it,
    Wondrous things of it are told.
Only righteous men and women
    Dwell within its gleaming walls;
Wrong is banished from its borders,
    Justice reigns within its halls.

We are builders of that City,
    All our joys and all our groans
Help to rear its shining ramparts;
    All our lives are building-stones.
For that City we must labour,
    For its sake bear pain and grief;
In it find the end of living,
    And the anchor of belief.

And the work that we have builded,
    Oft with bleeding hands and tears,
Oft in error, oft in anguish,
    Will not perish with our years—
It will last, and shine transfigured
    In the final reign of right:
It will pass into the splendours
    Of the City of the Light.

Felix Adler, 1851-1933

213 A City Which is Ours

DUNDEE C. M. *Scottish Psalter*, 1615

We need a city which is ours,
    A place where we are free —
Not slaves within the place we've made —
    A place where truth can be:

Truth in the plans our leaders make,
    And in their motives too;
Truth in our commerce and our arts —
    In all that people do.

Value for all the ground we take
    And cover with our schemes,
As much of beauty and of health
    As in the hills and streams.

Clear air, clean lives, clean government:
    A city which is ours,
Where all who live can live in love
    And know its finest hours.

Bruce Findlow, 1922 —
Used by permission

A BETTER WORLD

214 Our Nation

LAUS DEO (REDHEAD No. 46)   87. 87.   Richard Redhead, 1820-1901

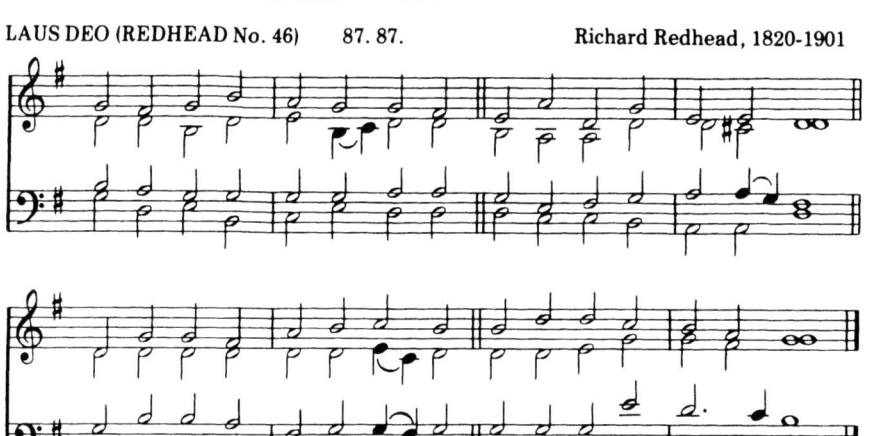

Long ago they came in conquest,
   Stayed to make this land their home:
Viking warrior and Norman,
   Legionnaire from ancient Rome.

Jewish victims of men's hatred,
   Huguenots both rich and poor,
Fled the lands of their oppression,
   Finding here an open door.

From the continent of Europe
   Came Ukrainian and Greek;
And from lands of past dominion
   Hindu, Parsi, Muslim, Sikh.

Many peoples, many customs,
   Many new things all must learn;
Each can make a contribution
   To the common good we yearn.

All our cultures now converging
   Let us learn to understand;
Till in love we've built together
   One great nation in this land.

John Andrew Storey, 1935—
Used by permission

A BETTER WORLD

BLACK AND WHITE   Irregular

Earl Robinson, 1910—
Arr. (by permission) David Dawson

Unison *vv. 2, 3 & 4*

Words and music copyright.
Original Publisher: Templeton Publishing Co. Inc.
Controlled by Durham Music Ltd. for the territory of the World
[excluding USA, Canada and Australasia]

A BETTER WORLD

215   Black and White

The ink is black, the page is white,
Together we learn to read and write,
   To read and write.
And now a child can understand
This is the law of all the land,
   All the land.
The ink is black, the page is white,
Together we learn to read and write,
   To read and write.

The slate is black, the chalk is white,
The words stand out so clear and bright,
   So clear and bright.
And now at last we plainly see
The alphabet of liberty,
   Liberty.
The slate is black, the chalk is white,
Together we learn to read and write,
   To read and write.

A child is black, a child is white,
The whole world looks upon the sight,
   Upon the sight.
For very well the whole world knows
This is the way that freedom grows,
   Freedom grows!
A child is black, a child is white,
Together we learn to read and write,
   To read and write.

The world is black, the world is white,
It turns by day and then by night,
   It turns by night.
It turns so each and every one
Can take their station in the sun,
   In the sun!
The world is black, the world is white,
Together we learn to read and write,
   To read and write.

David Arkin, 1934—

A BETTER WORLD

BREAD AND ROSES 7 6. 7 6. 7 7. 7 8. (Irreg.) Caroline Kohlsaat
*By permission of the Hodgin Press,
Los Angeles*

A BETTER WORLD

216   Bread and Roses

As we come marching, marching,
  In the beauty of the day,
A million darkened kitchens,
  A thousand workshops gray,
Are touched with all the radiance
  That a sudden sun discloses:
For the people hear us singing,
  "Bread and roses, bread and roses!"

As we come marching, marching,
  We battle too for men,
For they are women's children,
  And we mother them again.
Our lives shall not be sweated
  From birth until life closes:
Hearts starve as well as bodies—
  Give us bread, but give us roses!

As we come marching, marching,
  Unnumbered women dead
Go crying, through our singing,
  Their ancient song of bread!
Small art and love and beauty
  Their drudging spirits knew:
Yes, it is bread we fight for,
  But we fight for roses too!

As we come marching, marching,
  We bring the greater days:
The rising of the women
  Means the rising of the race.
No more the drudge and idler,
  Ten that toil where one reposes,
But a sharing of life's glories—
  Bread and roses, bread and roses!

James Oppenheim, 1882-1932
By permission of the Hodgin Press,
Los Angeles

A BETTER WORLD

217 Boldly Live, My Daughter

David Dawson
Used by permission

GREENSIDE 7 10. 11 7.

Come, my daughter, come with me
To where rushing waters flow to the sea;
We'll share what has been and what's still yet to be—
   For now's the time for living.

Tell your story, sing your song,
Seek for gentleness and learn to be strong:
For living it takes now the whole of life long—
   Your life is yours for living.

Learn to give and learn to love,
Nurture all life under heaven above,
And learn of the eagle and learn of the dove:
   For love is yours for giving.

Taste the grapes on distant vine,
Fill your cup with fine and different wine,
And sit at the table with strangers and dine—
   For you must learn of living.

Dance with milkweed, dance with rose,
Let the sun burn sand that drifts through your toes,
The sweat of your body let drench all your clothes—
   For you must do your living.

Daughter dear, you leave today:
Take my love as you go out on your way,
And pass it to those whom you meet on your way—
   And boldly do your living.

from Carolyn McDade
Used by permission

A BETTER WORLD

218   Liberation

HEATON   888   David Dawson
Used by permission

God our Father and our Mother,
Help us to respect each other,
Loving all as sister, brother.

Widen now your daughters' vision,
Break the shackles of tradition,
Let their skills find recognition.

Help your sons to be more tender,
Arrogance at last surrender,
Gentleness in them engender.

Barriers have been erected,
Sister, brother, been rejected,
Human needs too long neglected.

Love for love shall be requited
When these ancient wrongs are righted,
And your children are united.

John Andrew Storey, 1935—
Used by permission

A BETTER WORLD

219 The People's Peace

ST.AGNES   10 10. 10 10.   James Langran, 1835-1909

Peace is the mind's old wilderness cut down—
A wider nation than our parents dreamed.
Peace is the high street in a country town;
Our children named; our parents' lives redeemed.

Not scholar's calm, nor gift of church or state,
Nor everlasting date of death's release;
But careless noon, the houses lighted late,
Harvest and holiday: the people's peace.

The peace not past our understanding falls
Like light upon the soft white table cloth
At winter supper, warm, between four walls:
A thing too simple to be tried as truth.

Days into years, the doorways worn at sill;
Years into lives, the plans for long increase
Come true at last for people of goodwill:
These are the things we mean by saying, Peace.

From John Holmes, 1904-1962
Used by permission of the Beacon Press, Boston, Massachusetts

A BETTER WORLD

220 Break not the Circle

LEYTONEN   10 11. 10 11.

Doreen Potter, 1925-80
Used by permission of Agape, Illinois

Break not the circle of enabling love
Where people grow, forgiven and forgiving;
Break not that circle, make it wider still,
Till it includes, embraces all the living.

Come, wonder at this love that comes to life,
Where words of freedom are with humour spoken,
And people keep no score of wrong and guilt,
But will that human bonds remain unbroken.

Join then the movement of the love that frees,
Till people of whatever race or nation
Will truly be themselves, stand on their feet,
See eye to eye with laughter and elation.

Fred Kaan, 1929—
Copyright 1975 by Agape,
Carol Stream, IL 60187.
International copyright secured.
All rights reserved. Used by permission.

A BETTER WORLD

221 Release from Bitter Things

RHUDDLAN 8 7. 8 7. 8 7. Welsh Traditional Melody

Judge eternal, throned in splendour,
　Lord of lords and King of kings,
With thy living fire of judgement
　Purge this realm of bitter things:
Solace all its wide dominion
　With the healing of thy wings.

Still the weary folk are pining
　For the hour that brings release;
And the city's crowded clangour
　Cries aloud for sin to cease;
And the homesteads and the woodlands
　Plead in silence for their peace.

Crown, O God, thine own endeavour:
　Cleave our darkness with thy sword:
Feed the faint and hungry nations
　With the richness of thy word:
Cleanse the body of this empire
　Through the glory of the Lord.

Henry Scott Holland, 1847-1918

A BETTER WORLD

222 Hush the Sounds of War

IRISH　　C. M.　　　　　　　　　　　*Hymns and Sacred Poems*, Dublin, 1749

O God! the darkness roll away
　Which clouds the human soul,
And let thy bright and holy day
　Speed onward to its goal!

Let every hateful passion die
　Which makes of neighbours foes,
And war no longer raise its cry
　To mar the world's repose.

　How long shall glory still be found
　　In scenes of cruel strife,
　Where misery walks, a giant crowned,
　　Crushing the flowers of life?

　O hush, great God, the sounds of war,
　　And make thy children feel
　That one, with thee, is nobler far
　　Who toils for human weal.

　Let faith, and hope, and charity
　　Go forth through all the earth;
　And we in holy friendship be
　　True to our heavenly birth.

from William Gaskell, 1805-84

A BETTER WORLD

MEIRIONYDD 76. 86. D.   Melody by William Lloyd, 1786-1852

A BETTER WORLD

223 The Vision of a World Set Free

One faith and hope undying
    Henceforth we make our own,
The vision of a world set free
    When war shall be o'erthrown;
When love and law shall vanquish
    The sovereignty of strife,
And found, by human fellowship,
    A commonwealth of life.

The curse of war has darkened
    The way that we have trod,
Has mocked the hopes of human weal
    And scorned the love of God;
Yet to the restless nations
    That love is speaking still,
And bids us build in all the earth
    An empire of goodwill.

Now to the listening peoples
    Come tidings of release,
As on the wings of hope are borne
    The prophecies of peace;
Love's day at last is dawning,
    When covenant and law
Shall bring to peace her victories
    More proud than those of war.

O thou whose love embraces
    All folk beneath the sun,
May peace disarm our hearts of fear
    And bind us all in one:
The peace allied with courage,
    A flame against all wrong,
By truth and honour glorified,
    By righteousness made strong.

from Ernest Dodgshun

A BETTER WORLD

BATTLE HYMN   14 15 15. 7 & Refrain

American Traditional
Arr. David Dawson
Used by permission

Unison

A BETTER WORLD

224 A Glad, Resplendent Day

Mine eyes have seen the glory of a glad, resplendent day,
When the lords of war shall vanish with their blind and brutal sway,
As the women join in marching with their men on freedom's way,
    And the truth goes marching on!

Glory, glory, hallelujah,
Glory, glory, hallelujah,
Glory, glory, hallelujah,
    As the truth goes marching on!

The people have awakened and their eyes must close no more,
They will burn the gibbets, sheathe the sword and still the drums of war,
They will bring the earth to blossom where the desert was before,
    And the truth goes marching on!

Glory, glory, hallelujah,
Glory, glory, hallelujah,
Glory, glory, hallelujah,
    As the truth goes marching on!

Adapted by Waldemar Hille, 1908—
from Caroline M. Sèverance, 1820-1914
Copyright, The Hodgin Press, Los Angeles
Used by permission

A BETTER WORLD

For Guitar accompaniment.

ORKNEY L.M.

Melody by James Waters

For Organ or Piano accompaniment.

HERONGATE L.M.

English Traditional Melody
coll., arr. & har. Ralph Vaughan Williams, 1872-1958
From the English Hymnal, by permission of Oxford University Press

A BETTER WORLD

225 Child of Hiroshima

I come and stand at every door,
But none can hear my silent tread:
I knock, and yet remain unseen,
For I am dead, for I am dead.

I'm only seven, although I died
In Hiroshima long ago;
I'm seven now as I was then:
When children die, they do not grow.

My hair was scorched with swirling flame,
My eyes grew dim, my eyes grew blind;
It came and burned my bones to dust,
And that was scattered by the wind.

I need no fruit, I need no rice,
I need no sweets, nor even bread:
I ask for nothing for myself,
For I am dead, for I am dead.

All that I ask is that for peace
You fight today, you fight today,
So that the children of this world
May live and grow and laugh and play.

Source unknown

FINLANDIA 11 10. 11 10. 11 10. Jean Sibelius, 1865-1957

Used by permission of The Lorenz Corporation, Dayton, Ohio

A BETTER WORLD

226 Song of Peace

This is my song, O God of all the nations,
   A song of peace for lands afar and mine;
This is my home, the country where my heart is,
   Here are my hopes, my dreams, my holy shrine;
But other hearts in other lands are beating
   With hopes and dreams as true and high as mine.

My country's skies are bluer than the ocean,
   And sunlight beams on clover leaf and pine;
But other lands have sunlight, too, and clover,
   And skies are everywhere as blue as mine.
O hear my song, thou God of all the nations,
   A song of peace for their land and for mine.

Lloyd Stone, 1913—
Used by permission of The Lorenz Corporation, Dayton, Ohio

HOLYWELL 87. 87. D. Harold William Spicer, 1888-1977
By permission of Mrs. Muriel Spicer

A BETTER WORLD

227 Sing Your Country's Anthem

People, sing your country's anthem,
   Shout your land's undying fame;
Light the wondrous tale of nations
   With your people's golden name.
Tell your forebears' noble story,
   Raise on high your country's sign:
Join, then, in the final glory—
   Come and lift your flag with mine!

Hail the sun of peace now rising;
   Hold the war-clouds ever furled;
Blend your banners, sister, brother,
   In the rainbow of the world!
Red as blood and blue as heaven,
   Wise as age and proud as youth,
Melt your colours, wonder-woven
   In the glowing light of truth.

Build the road of peace before us,
   Build it wide and deep and long;
Speed the slow and check the eager,
   Help the weak and curb the strong.
None shall push aside another,
   None shall let another fall:
March beside me, sister, brother,
   All for one, and one for all!

Josephine Daskam Bacon
Used by permission pf the Beacon Press, Boston, Mass.

A BETTER WORLD

STAR OF THE COUNTY DOWN   C. M. D.

Irish Traditional Melody
Arr. David Dawson
Used by permission

A BETTER WORLD

228 Till Greed and Hate Cease

Eternal God, whose power upholds
  Both flower and flaming star,
To whom there is no here nor there,
  No time, no near nor far,
No alien race, no foreign shore,
  No child unsought, unknown,
O send us forth, thy prophets true,
  To make all lands thine own!

O God of truth, whom science seeks
  And reverent souls adore,
Who lightest every earnest mind
  Of every clime and shore,
Dispel the gloom of error's night,
  Of ignorance and fear,
Until true wisdom from above
  Shall make life's pathway clear!

O God of beauty, oft revealed
  In dreams of human art,
In speech that flows to melody,
  In holiness of heart,
Teach us to ban all ugliness
  That blinds our eyes to thee,
Till all shall know the loveliness
  Of lives made fair and free.

O God of love, whose spirit wakes
  In every human breast,
Whom love, and love alone, can know,
  In whom all hearts find rest,
Help us to spread thy gracious reign,
  Till greed and hate shall cease,
And kindness dwell in human hearts,
  And all the earth find peace!

Henry Hallam Tweedy, 1868-1953
from Christian Worship and Praise
edited by Henry Hallam Tweedy
and reprinted by permission of
Harper & Row, Publishers, Inc., New York.

A BETTER WORLD

SCHMÜCKE DICH   88. 88. D. (Trochaic)   Melody by Johann Crüger, 1598-1662

A BETTER WORLD

229   One World This

One world this, for all its sorrow;
One world shaping one tomorrow;
One humanity, though riven —
We, to whom a world is given.
From one world there is no turning;
For one world the prophets' yearning.
One, the world of poets, sages;
One world, goal of all the ages.

One, our world from the beginning;
One, the world we would be winning;
World so eagerly expected;
World so recklessly rejected.
One, enfolding every nation;
One, our mightiest creation:
Dream, to guide the mind's endeavour;
Hope, to hold the heart for ever.

One world, land and air and ocean;
One, upheld by our devotion.
One, as common folk have willed it;
One, as government can build it.
World of friendly ways and faces,
Cherished arts and honoured races.
One world, free in word and science;
People free, its firm reliance.

Vincent Brown Silliman, 1894-1979
by permission of the American Ethical Union

230 Earth Shall be Fair

OLD 124TH   10 10. 10 10. 10.   *Genevan Psalter*, 1551

Turn back, O Man, forswear thy foolish ways.
Old now is Earth, and none may count her days,
Yet thou, her child, whose head is crowned with flame,
Still wilt not hear thine inner God proclaim —
"Turn back, O Man, forswear thy foolish ways."

Earth might be fair and all men glad and wise.
Age after age their tragic empires rise,
Built while they dream, and in that dreaming weep:
Would Man but wake from out his haunted sleep,
Earth might be fair and all men glad and wise.

Earth shall be fair, and all her people one;
Nor till that hour shall God's whole will be done.
Now, even now, once more from earth to sky
Peals forth in joy Man's old undaunted cry —
"Earth shall be fair, and all her folk be one!"

Clifford Bax, 1886-1962
Reprinted by permission of A.D. Peters and Co. Ltd.

A BETTER WORLD

The Natural World

RIDDINGS 11 10. 11 10.   David Dawson
                                                         Used by permission

THE NATURAL WORLD

231 The God of Galaxies

The God of galaxies has more to govern
Than once was thought when mountain thundered wrath,
The rainbow stood a sign of mercy given,
And stars were candles for the darkened path.

The God of galaxies is omnipresent
In cosmic host and in the deepest void,
In blazing sun, the new moon's sickled crescent,
A Presence none can speak in mortal word.

Yet, God of galaxies, we bring our praises:
Though what is speech, what homage can we frame?
The light within each distant star that rises,
The furthest world, your habitat and home.

The God of galaxies has more to govern
Than constellations which reward earth's gaze:
Tongues cannot tell the majesty of heaven,
But hearts revere, and silently give praise.

Based on the poem The God of Galaxies
by Mark Van Doren

THE NATURAL WORLD

FIRMAMENT   L.M.D.

Henry Walford Davies, 1869-1941
By permission of Oxford University Press

Small notes V. 3

THE NATURAL WORLD

232 The Spacious Firmament

The spacious firmament on high,
With all the blue ethereal sky,
And spangled heavens, a shining frame,
Their great Original proclaim.
The unwearied sun, from day to day,
Doth his Creator's power display;
And publishes to every land
The work of an almighty hand.

Soon as the evening shades prevail,
The moon takes up the wondrous tale,
And nightly to the listening earth
Repeats the story of her birth;
Whilst all the stars that round her burn,
And all the planets in their turn,
Confirm the tidings as they roll,
And spread the truth from pole to pole.

What though in solemn silence all
Move round the dark terrestrial ball;
What though nor real voice nor sound
Amidst their radiant orbs be found;
In reason's ear they all rejoice,
And utter forth a glorious voice,
For ever singing as they shine,
"The hand that made us is divine."

Joseph Addison, 1672-1719

AURELIA 76.76.D. Samuel Sebastian Wesley, 1810-76

THE NATURAL WORLD

233 Others Call it God

A fire-mist and a planet,
    A crystal and a cell,
A star-fish and a saurian,
    And caves where cave-folk dwell;
The sense of law and beauty,
    A face turned from the clod—
Some call it evolution,
    And others call it God.

Haze on the far horizon,
    The infinite tender sky,
The ripe, rich tints of cornfields,
    And wild geese sailing high;
And over high and lowland,
    The charm of golden rod—
Some people call it nature,
    And others call it God.

Like tides on a crescent sea-beach,
    When the moon is new and thin,
Into our hearts high yearnings
    Come welling, surging in,
Come from the mystic ocean
    Whose rim no foot has trod—
Some people call it longing,
    And others call it God.

A picket frozen on duty,
    A mother starved for her brood,
And Socrates drinking hemlock,
    And Jesus on the rood;
And millions, who, though nameless,
    The straight, hard pathway trod—
Some call it consecration,
    And others call it God.

from William Herbert Carruth, 1859-1924

THE NATURAL WORLD

234 O God of Stars and Sunlight

BREMEN 76.76.D. Johann Georg Christian Störl's *Würtemberg Gesangbuch*, 1710

O God of stars and sunlight,
  Whose wind lifts up a bird,
In marching wave and leaf-fall
  We hear thy patient word.
The colour of thy seasons
  Goes gold across the land:
By green upon the tree-tops
  We know thy moving hand.

O God of cloud and mountain,
  Whose rain on rock is art,
Thy plan and care and meaning
  Renew the head and heart.
Thy word and colour spoken,
  Thy summer noons and showers—
By these and by thy day-shine,
  We know thy world is ours.

O God of root and shading
  Of boughs above our head,
We breathe in thy long breathing,
  Our spirit spirited.
We walk beneath thy blessing,
  Thy seasons and thy way,
O God of stars and sunlight,
  O God of night and day.

John Holmes, 1904-62
By permission of the Beacon Press, Boston, Mass.

THE NATURAL WORLD

235 A Melody of Love

CHILDHOOD 8 8 8. 6.

Henry Walford Davies, 1869-1941
By permission of Oxford University Press

God speaks to us in bird and song,
In winds that drift the clouds along,
Above the din of toil and wrong,
A melody of love.

God speaks to us in far and near,
In peace of home and friends most dear,
From the dim past and present clear,
A melody of love.

God speaks to us in darkest night,
By quiet ways through mornings bright,
When shadows fall with evening light,
A melody of love.

God speaks to us in every land,
On wave-lapped shore and silent strand,
By kiss of child and touch of hand,
A melody of love.

O voice divine, speak thou to me,
Beyond the earth, beyond the sea;
First let me hear, then sing to thee
A melody of love.

Joseph Johnson, 1849-1926

THE NATURAL WORLD

236 Thy Purpose Crowning All

GOSTERWOOD 76.76.D.

English Traditional Melody
Coll., arr. & har. Ralph Vaughan Williams, 1872-1958
From The English Hymnal by permission of Oxford University Press

There hides within the lily
   A strong and tender care,
That wins the earth-born atoms
   To glory of the air;
God weaves the shining garments
   Unceasingly and still,
Along the quiet waters
   In niches of the hill.

THE NATURAL WORLD

We linger at the vigil
   With him who bent the knee
To watch the old-time lilies
   In distant Galilee;
And still the worship deepens
   And quickens into new,
As, brightening down the ages,
   God's secret thrilleth through.

Creator of the lily,
   Thy touch is in us too!
From leaf that dawns to petal
   New realms of life ensue.
The flower horizons open,
   The blossom vaster shows;
We hear thy wide worlds echo:
   "See how the lily grows!"

Shy yearnings of the savage,
   Unfolding thought by thought,
To holy lives are lifted,
   To visions fair are wrought;
The races rise and cluster,
   And evils fade and fall,
Till chaos blooms to beauty,
   Thy purpose crowning all!

from William Channing Gannett, 1840-1923

THE NATURAL WORLD

237 Seek Not Afar for Beauty

LIMPSFIELD 10 10. 10 10. Andrew Freeman

Seek not afar for beauty; lo, it glows
  In dew-wet grasses all about your feet;
  In birds, in sunshine, childlike faces sweet,
In stars and mountain summits topped with snows.

Go not abroad for happiness—for see,
  It is a flower blooming at your door.
  Bring love and justice home, and then no more
You'll wonder in what dwelling joy may be.

Dream not of noble service elsewhere wrought;
  The simple duty that awaits your hand
  Is God's voice speaking with divine command:
Life's common deeds build all that saints have thought.

In wonder-workings, or some bush aflame,
  We look for God who seems to be concealed;
  But in earth's common things God stands revealed,
While grass and flowers and stars spell out the name.

Minot Judson Savage, 1841-1918

THE NATURAL WORLD

238 Source of All

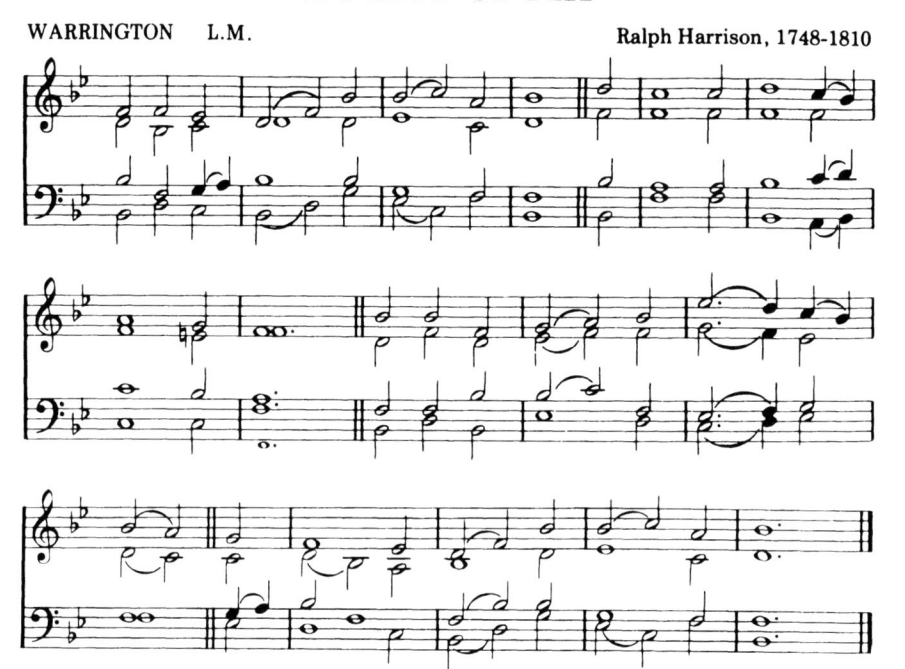

WARRINGTON L.M.   Ralph Harrison, 1748-1810

Mysterious Presence, Source of all,
The world without, the world within,
Fountain of life, O hear our call,
And pour thy living waters in.

Thou breathest in the rushing wind,
Thy spirit stirs in leaf and flower;
Nor wilt thou from the willing mind
Withhold thy light and love and power.

Thy hand unseen to accents clear
Awoke the psalmist's trembling lyre,
And touched the lips of holy seer
With flame from thine own altar-fire.

That touch divine still, God, impart,
Still give the prophet's burning word;
And vocal in each waiting heart
Let living psalms of praise be heard.

Seth Curtis Beach, 1837-1932

THE NATURAL WORLD

239 The Upward Reach

EINTRACHT 7 5. 7 5. D.

Franz Xavier Mathias, 1871-1939
arr. David Dawson

Who thou art I know not,
  But this much I know—
Thou hast set the Pleiades
  In a silver row;
Thou hast sent the trackless winds
  Loose upon their way;
Thou hast reared a coloured wall
  'Twixt the night and day.

Thou hast made the flowers to bloom
  And the stars to shine;
Hid rare gems of richest ore
  In the tunnelled mine;
But chief of all thy wondrous works,
  Supreme in thy design,
Thou hast put an upward reach
  Into this heart of mine.

From Harry Kemp, 1883-1960

THE NATURAL WORLD

240 Daisies are Our Silver

GLENFINLAS 6 5. 6 5.
Kenneth George Finlay, 1882-1974
Used by permission

Daisies are our silver,
Buttercups our gold:
This is all the treasure
We can have or hold.

Raindrops are our diamonds
And the morning dew;
While for shining sapphires
We've the speedwell blue.

These shall be our emeralds—
Leaves so new and green;
Roses make the reddest
Rubies ever seen.

God, who gave these treasures
To your children small,
Teach us how to love them
And grow like them all.

Make us bright as silver:
Make us good as gold;
Warm as summer roses
Let our hearts unfold.

Gay as leaves in April,
Clear as drops of dew—
God, who made the speedwell,
Keep us true to you.

Jan Struther (Mrs. Joyce Anstruther Placzek), 1901-53
*From Enlarged Songs of Praise
by permission of Oxford University Press*

THE NATURAL WORLD

LASST UNS ERFREUEN (EASTER ALLELUIA) L.M. with Alleluias
Kölner Gesangbuch, 1623
From The English Hymnal, by permission of Oxford University Press

THE NATURAL WORLD

241 The Hymn of St. Francis

All creatures of our God and King,
Lift up your voice and with us sing,
   Alleluia, Alleluia!
Thou burning sun with golden beam,
Thou silver moon with softer gleam,
   Sing your praises, sing your praises,
   Alleluia, Alleluia, Alleluia!

Thou rushing wind that art so strong,
Ye clouds that sail in heaven along,
   Sing your praises, Alleluia!
Thou rising morn, in praise rejoice,
Ye lights of evening, find a voice,
   Sing your praises, sing your praises,
   Alleluia, Alleluia, Alleluia!

Thou flowing water, pure and clear,
Make music for thy God to hear,
   Alleluia, Alleluia!
Thou fire so masterful and bright,
That givest us both warmth and light,
   Sing your praises, sing your praises,
   Alleluia, Alleluia, Alleluia!

Dear mother earth, who day by day
Unfoldest blessings on our way,
   Sing your praises, Alleluia!
The flowers and fruit that in thee grow,
Let them God's glory also show:
   Alleluia, Alleluia!
   Alleluia, Alleluia, Alleluia!

Let all things their Creator bless,
And worship God in humbleness;
   Alleluia, Alleluia!
Praise, praise your Maker and your King,
Lift up your voice and with us sing,
   Alleluia, Alleluia!
   Alleluia, Alleluia, Alleluia!

St. Francis of Assisi, 1182-1226
from tr. William Henry Draper, 1855-1933
Used by permission of J. Curwen and Sons, Ltd.

THE NATURAL WORLD

242 For the Strength of the Hills

MOUNTAIN CHRISTIAN 7 6. 7 6. D. (Irreg.) J. Mannin

For the strength of the hills we bless thee,
  Our God, eternal God;
Thou hast made thy people mighty
  By the touch of the mountain sod;
Thou hast fixed our ark of refuge
  Where the spoiler's feet ne'er trod.
For the strength of the hills we bless thee,
  Our God, eternal God.

THE NATURAL WORLD

We are watchers of a beacon
   Whose light can never die,
We are guardians of an altar
   'Mid the silence of the sky.
The rocks yield founts of courage
   Struck forth as by thy rod;
For the strength of the hills we bless thee,
   Our God, eternal God.

For the dark resounding mountains
   Where thy still, small voice is heard,
For the strong pines in the forest,
   Which by thy breath are stirred;
For the storm on whose free pinions
   Thy spirit walks abroad,
For the strength of the hills we bless thee,
   Our God, eternal God.

The eagle proudly darteth
   On her quarry from the height,
And the stag that knows no master
   Seeks there his wild delight.
But we, for thy communion,
   Have sought the mountain sod —
For the strength of the hills we bless thee,
   Our God, eternal God.

                      Felicia Dorothea Hemans (née Browne), 1793-1835

243 All Things Bright and Beautiful

ROYAL OAK   7 6. 7 6. (with Refrain)

English Melody, 17th Century
arr. Martin Fallas Shaw, 1875-1958
Used by permission of J. Curwen & Sons, Ltd.

Quick.

All things bright and beautiful,
All creatures great and small,
All things wise and wonderful—
The Lord God made them all.

Each little flower that opens,
Each little bird that sings,
God made their glowing colours,
And made their tiny wings.

The purple-headed mountain,
The river running by,
The sunset and the morning
That brighten up the sky;

The cold wind in the winter,
The pleasant summer sun,
The ripe fruits in the garden—
God made them, every one.

The tall trees in the greenwood,
The meadows where we play;
The rushes by the water
We gather every day;

God gave us eyes to see them,
And lips that we might tell
How great is God Almighty,
Who has made all things well.

Cecil Frances Alexander (née Humphreys), 1823-95

THE NATURAL WORLD

244 Glad That I Live Am I

WATER END 6 5. 6 5. (Irreg.) Geoffrey Shaw, 1879-1943
From *Songs of Praise*, by permission of Oxford University Press

Glad that I live am I;
That the sky is blue;
Glad for the country lanes,
And the fall of dew.

After the sun, the rain;
After the rain, the sun;
This is the way of life,
Till the work be done.

All that we need to do,
Be we low or high,
Is to see that we grow
Nearer the sky.

Lizette Woodworth Reese
Words from *A Wayside Lute*
Published by Holt, Rinehart and Winston, Inc.
Used by permission of E. J. Dietrich

THE NATURAL WORLD

BARNFIELD 88.88.88. David Dawson
Used by permission

THE NATURAL WORLD

245 All These Things Belong to Me

The sun that shines across the sea,
The wind that whispers in the tree,
The lark that carols in the sky,
The fleecy clouds a-sailing by—
O, I'm as rich as rich can be,
For all these things belong to me!

The raindrops which refresh the earth,
The springtime mantle of rebirth,
The summer days when all things grow,
The autumn mist and winter snow—
O, I'm as rich as rich can be,
For all these things belong to me.

The task well done, the fun of play,
The wise who guide me on my way,
The balm of sleep when each day ends,
The joy of family and friends—
O, I'm as rich as rich can be,
For all these things belong to me.

Verse 1, Dimitri Stepanovitch Bortnianski, 1752-1825
Verses 2 & 3, John Andrew Storey, 1935-

Used by permission

THE NATURAL WORLD

246 Morning, So Fair to See

SCHÖNSTER HERR JESU   6 6 9. 6 6 8.   A.H.Hoffmann von Fallersleben's
Schlesische Volkslieder, 1842
har. by permission of the Beacon Press, Boston, Mass.

Morning, so fair to see,
Night, veiled in mystery—
Glorious the earth and resplendent skies!
Comrades, we march along,
Singing our pilgrim song,
As through an earthly paradise.

Fair are the verdant trees;
Fair are the flashing seas;
Fair is each wonder the seasons bring.
Fairer is faith's surmise
Shining in pilgrim eyes:
Fairer the comradeship we sing.

Age after age arise,
'Neath the eternal skies,
Into the light from the shadowed past:
Still shall our pilgrim song,
Buoyant and brave and strong,
Resound while life and mountains last.

Vincent Brown Silliman, 1894-1979
by permission of the Beacon Press, Boston, Mass.

THE NATURAL WORLD

247 A World of Wonder

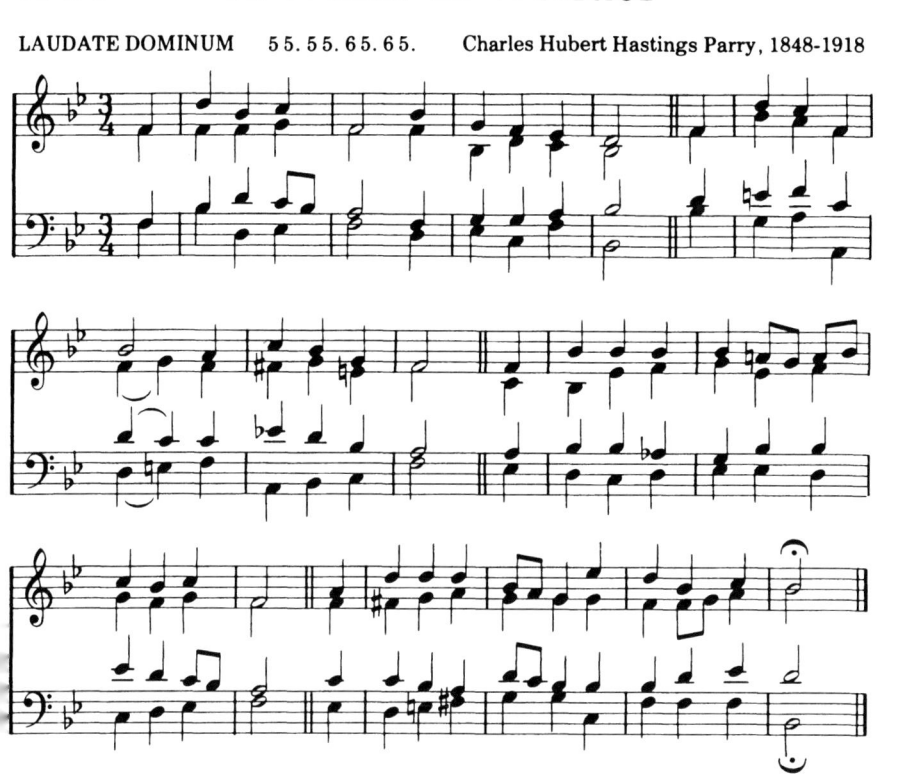

LAUDATE DOMINUM 5 5. 5 5. 6 5. 6 5. Charles Hubert Hastings Parry, 1848-1918

The sun at high noon,
The stars in dark space,
The light of the moon
On our upturned face,
The high clouds, the rain clouds,
The lark-song on high—
We gaze up in wonder
Above to the sky.

The green grassy blade,
The grasshopper's sound,
The creatures of shade
That live in the ground,
The dark soil, the moist soil,
Where plants spring to birth—
We look down at wonder
Below in the earth.

The glad joys that heal
The tears in our eyes,
The longings we feel,
The light of surprise,
Our night dreams, our day dreams,
Our thoughts ranging wide—
We live with a whole world
Of wonder inside.

Sydney Henry Knight, 1923—
used by permission

THE NATURAL WORLD

NORBER 10 10. 10 10. 10 10.   David Dawson
                                          Used by permission

THE NATURAL WORLD

248   Now is the Time

Now is the time to live; now is the time,
As nature may disclose, to savour life:
To know her streams, her woodland hills to climb,
To read her cliffs, engraved with ancient lore;
To share her moods, the carefree and sublime,
And thrill with beauty from her ancient store.

Now is the time, in wonder to explore
From whispering tree and softly answering dove
To storied shells beside the storm-swept shore,
From star-flower to the galaxies above:
Then peace shall flood the restless heart once more
As seasons' beauty fills the woods we love.

Now is the time to live, to look, to see,
To taste that life is good, to share its zest,
And know its patience in the dormant tree,
The budding earth, the motion that is rest;
Creation in each moment flowing free —
Nor dread the sunset in the darkening west.

                                        Robert Terry Weston, 1898 —
                                            Used by permission

249 Life's Great Gifts

BROTHER JAMES'S AIR 8 6. 8 6. 8 6. Melody by James Leith Macbeth Bain, d.1925
arr. David Dawson

Life is the greatest gift of all
  The riches on this earth;
Life and its creatures, great and small,
  Of high and lowly birth:
So treasure it and measure it
  With deeds of shining worth.

We are of life, its shining gift,
  The measure of all things;
Up from the dust our temples lift,
  Our vision soars on wings;
For seed and root, for flower and fruit,
  Our grateful spirit sings.

THE NATURAL WORLD

Mind is the brightest gift of all,
   Its thought no barrier mars;
Seeking creation's hidden plan,
   Its quest surmounts all bars;
It reins the wind, it chains the storm,
   It weighs the outmost stars.

Love is the highest gift of life,
   Our glory and our good;
Kindred and friend, husband and wife,
   It flows in golden flood;
So, hand in hand, from land to land,
   Spread sister-brotherhood.

Adapted by Waldemar Hille, 1908—
from William E. Oliver
Used by permission of the Hodgin Press,
Los Angeles

250 Reverence for Life

DEERHURST 8 7. 8 7. D.

James Langran, 1835-1909

In life's complex web of being
    Each is fitted for its place,
Plants and beasts and all things living,
    Peoples of the human race;
But the balances of nature
    Exploitation has disturbed,
And all creatures she will nurture
    Only when this greed is curbed.

Dolphin leaping through the waters,
    Skylark over lonely fen,
Timid fawn in dappled forest,
    Hungry lion in its den,
Butterfly, the bee and flower,
    Each should have its chance to thrive;
Humankind, restrain your power
    And for wider kinship strive.

John Andrew Storey, 1935—

THE NATURAL WORLD

Used by permission

251 Morning on Morning

STREETS OF LAREDO   11 10. 11 10.   Dactylic

American Folk Tune
arr. David Dawson
Used by permission

Morning on morning I roam the wild meadow,
  Morning on morning I know the wild world,
See how the first sun reveals the wild flowers,
  How one is blighted before it's unfurled:

How one is favoured and lives out its cycle,
  Peeps out in springtime and blooms into fall,
How one that stretches to fill its young promise
  Breaks as it's trodden, and never grows tall.

Now the wind whispers, "The blighted, the trodden
  Give as the favoured one, each has its worth.
Come back in summer and see the bright blossoms,
  Come back in winter and see the dark earth."

Anne Etkin, 1923—
Used by permission

THE NATURAL WORLD

252 Tranquillity

COME, LABOUR ON   4. 10 10 10. 4.   Charles H. Wrigley

By permission of the General Assembly of Unitarian and Free Christian Churches

        Wild waves of storm,
The wonder of the wind and crashing sea,
Nature in power and might and majesty—
Yet wonder more in deep tranquillity,
        Sea, calm and still.

        Migrating birds,
In flocks intent upon far distant shore
Great wonder hold; yet there is wonder more
When lonely eagle, watchful on the tor,
        Sits, calm and still.

        Herds driven on
By urgent instinct, sparing none to flag,
Are wonderful; but see the lonely stag
Over the glen, supreme on rocky crag,
        Majestic, still!

THE NATURAL WORLD

All people one
In urgent haste, on some great enterprise,
Hearts beating fast, great dreams to realise—
Yet in the soul a dream of richer prize,
    Serene and still.

Then striving cease:
From troubled turmoil seek an inward goal;
Tranquillity shall make the spirit whole.
Be still, and know a Presence in the soul,
    Serene, alive.

Sydney Henry Knight, 1923—
Used by permission

253 God Bless the Grass

GOD BLESS THE GRASS Irregular
Malvina Reynolds

> God bless the grass that grows through the crack:
> They roll the concrete over it to try and keep it back.
> The concrete gets tired of what it has to do,
> It breaks and it buckles and the grass grows through;
> > And God bless the grass.
>
> God bless the truth that fights towards the sun:
> They heap lies all over it and think that it is done.
> It moves through the ground and reaches for the air,
> And after a while it is growing everywhere;
> > And God bless the grass.
>
> God bless the grass that grows through cement:
> It's green and very tender, and it's easily bent.
> But after a while it raises up its head,
> For grass is a living thing, and stone is dead;
> > And God bless the grass.
>
> God bless the grass that's gentle and low:
> Its roots are very deep, and its plan wills it to grow,
> God bless the truth, the friend of the poor,
> And the wild grass that's growing at the poor folk's door;
> > And God bless the grass.

Malvina Reynolds

THE NATURAL WORLD

254 Let us Wander where we Will

INNOCENTS 7 7. 7 7. *The Parish Choir,* 1850

Let us wander where we will,
Something kindred greets us still:
Something seen on vale or hill
Falls familiar on the heart.

Dew and rain fall everywhere,
Harvests ripen, flowers are fair,
And the whole round earth is bare
To the moonshine and the sun.

And the live air, fanned with wings,
Bright with breeze and sunshine, brings
Into contact distant things,
And makes all the countries one.

Robert Louis Stevenson, 1850-94

THE NATURAL WORLD

No. 253 God Bless the Grass

Words and music copyright 1964 Schroeder Music Co., assigned to TRO Essex Music Ltd. 19/20 Poland Street, London W1V 3DD. International copyright secured. Used by permission. British Empire and Commonwealth [excluding Canada]. Also Republics of Ireland and South Africa.

THIS IS YOUR LAND   10 10 10. 8. (Irregular)   Woody Guthrie

THE NATURAL WORLD

255 This Land is Your Land

This land is your land, this land is my land,
From lowland pasture to western island,
From teeming city to fen and moorland—
   This land was made for you and me.

As I went walking that ribbon of highway,
I saw above me that endless skyway,
I saw below me that golden valley:
   This land was made for you and me.

I roamed and rambled and followed my footsteps
To sparkling sands of her dunes and beaches,
And all around me a voice was sounding:
   This land was made for you and me.

The sun was shining, as I was strolling
In wheatfields waving, on downlands rolling;
A voice was chanting as mists were lifting:
   This land was made for you and me.

In ancient city, by wall and steeple,
In field and factory, in office and stable,
Cared for or lonely, I sing to people:
   This land was made for you and me.

This land is your land, this land is my land,
From lowland pasture to western island,
From teeming city to fen and moorland—
   This land was made for you and me.

Adapted from Woody Guthrie

Words and music copyright 1956, 1958 Ludlow Music Inc., assigned to TRO Essex Music Ltd., 19/20 Poland Street, London W1V 3DD. International copyright secured. Used by permission. British Commonwealth [excluding Canada and Australasia]. Also the Republics of Ireland and South Africa.

THE NATURAL WORLD

256 I Held the Planets in My Hand

SEABECK L.M. Evangeline Morris Bachelder, 1920—
Used by permission

I held the planets in my hand,
The sun upon my forehead burned,
The moon was cool among my hair,
And earth held still till I returned.

For I had gone, yet never far;
For in the stars there was my name:
My car rode avenues of sun,
There where I left was where I came.

The farther from the homes of all
I wandered, I found them the more;
And where the waste and void expand
I found the threshold of my door.

Go on your journeys where you may,
And travel sea and land and air;
Then when you pause, and where you love,
Will be your temple and your stair.

Kenneth L. Patton, 1911—
Used by permission

THE NATURAL WORLD

The Seasons

DEUS TUORUM MILITUM   L. M.

Grenoble Church Melody, 1868
har. David Dawson
Used by permission

THE SEASONS: OLD YEAR

257   Ring Out, Ring In

Ring out, wild bells, to the wild sky,
   The flying cloud, the frosty light:
   The year is dying in the night;
Ring out, wild bells, and let it die.

Ring out the old, ring in the new,
   Ring, happy bells, across the snow:
   The year is going, let it go;
Ring out the false, ring in the true.

Ring out a slowly dying cause,
   And ancient forms of party strife;
   Ring in the nobler modes of life,
With sweeter manners, purer laws.

Ring out false pride in place and blood,
   The civic slander and the spite;
   Ring in the love of truth and right,
Ring in the common love of good.

Ring out old shapes of foul disease;
   Ring out the narrowing lust of gold;
   Ring out the thousand wars of old,
Ring in the thousand years of peace.

Alfred Tennyson, 1809-92

THE SEASONS: NEW YEAR

258 O Glad New Year of God

UNIVERSITY C.M.   Probably by John Randall, 1715-99

Welcome from God, O glad new year!
  Thy paths all yet untrod,
Another year of life's delight;
  Another year of God!

Another year of setting suns,
  Of stars by night revealed,
Of springing grass, of tender buds
  By winter's snow concealed.

Another year of summer's glow,
  Of autumn's gold and brown,
Of waving fields, and ruddy fruit
  The branches weighing down.

Another year of happy work,
  That better is than play;
Of simple cares, and love that grows
  More sweet from day to day.

Welcome from God, O glad new year!
  Thy paths all yet untrod,
Another year of life's delight—
  O glad new year of God.

John White Chadwick, 1840-1904

THE SEASONS: NEW YEAR

259 The Eternal Now

CAPEL C.M.

English Traditional Melody
Coll. Evelyn Henry Tschudi Broadwood, 1889-1975
arr. Lucy Broadwood, 1858-1929

The ceaseless flow of endless time
　No one can check or stay;
We'll view the past with no regret,
　Nor future with dismay.

The present slips into the past,
　And dream-like melts away;
The breaking of tomorrow's dawn
　Begins a new today.

The past and future ever meet
　In the eternal now:
To make each day a thing complete
　Shall be our New Year vow.

John Andrew Storey, 1935—
used by permission

THE SEASONS: NEW YEAR

260 'Tis Winter Now

PUER NOBIS NASCITUR L.M.

Latin Carol, 15th Century
adpt. Michael Praetorius, 1571-1621

'Tis winter now; the fallen snow
Has left the heavens all coldly clear;
Through leafless boughs the sharp winds blow,
And all the earth lies dead and drear:

And yet God's love is not withdrawn;
For life within the keen air breathes,
A beauty paints the crimson dawn,
And clothes the boughs with glittering wreaths.

And though abroad the sharp winds blow,
And skies are chill, and frosts are keen,
Home closer draws her circle now,
And warmer glows her light within.

O God! who giv'st the winter's cold,
As well as summer's joyous rays,
Us warmly in thy love enfold,
And keep us through life's wintry days.

From Samuel Longfellow, 1819-92

THE SEASONS: WINTER

261 Waiting for the Plough

SUSSEX   8 7. 8 7.

From an English Traditional Melody
Col., adpt. & arr. Ralph Vaughan Williams, 1872-1958
*from the English Hymnal
by permission of Oxford University Press*

By the rutted roads we follow,
  Fallow fields are rested now;
All along the waking country
  Soil is waiting for the plough.

In the yard the plough is ready,
  Ready for the ploughman's hand,
Ready for the crow-straight furrow,
  Farmer's sign across God's land.

God, in this good land you lend us,
  Bless the service of the share;
Light our thinking with your wisdom,
  Plant your patience in our care.

This is first of all our labours,
  We must always plough the earth;
God, be with us at the ploughing,
  Touch our harvest at its birth.

John Arlott, 1914—
Used by permission

THE SEASONS: PLOUGHTIME

262 New Life Beginning

KRISZTUS URUNK 11 11. 11 5.

Hungarian Carol

har. by permission of the Beacon Press, Boston, Mass.

Bells in the high tower, ringing o'er the white hills,
Mocking the winter, singing like the spring rills;
Bells in the high tower, in the cold foretelling
   The spring's up-welling.

Bells in the old tower, like the summer chatter
From darting bright birds, as the grapes turn redder;
Bells in the old tower, now the wine is brimming,
   New life beginning.

Bells in the stone tower, echoing the soft sound
Of autumn's mill wheel, as the wheat is spun round;
Bells in the stone tower, see, the bread is yeasting
   For time of feasting.

Bells in the cold tower, 'midst the snow of winter,
Sound out the spring-song that we may remember;
Bells in the cold tower, after the long snowing
   Come months of growing.

Howard Box, 1926—
Used by permission

THE SEASONS: SPRING

263 Earth Awakes Again

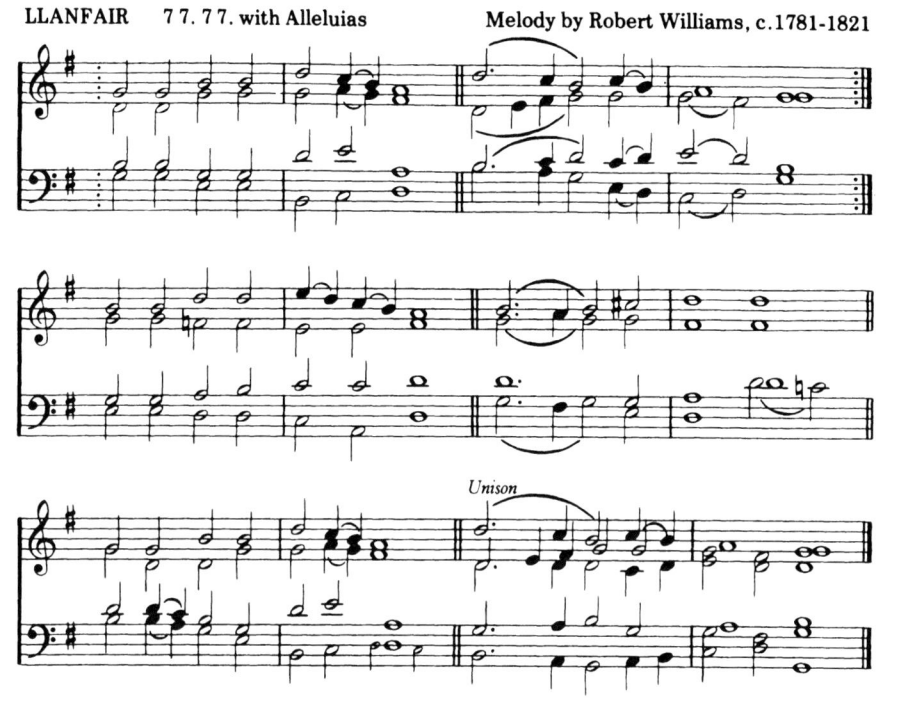

LLANFAIR 7 7. 7 7. with Alleluias

Melody by Robert Williams, c.1781-1821

Lo, the earth awakes again, *Alleluia!*
From the winter's bond and pain. *Alleluia!*
Bring we leaf and flower and spray, *Alleluia!*
To adorn this happy day. *Alleluia!*

Once again the word comes true, *Alleluia!*
All the earth shall be made new. *Alleluia!*
Now the dark, cold days are o'er, *Alleluia!*
Light and gladness are before. *Alleluia!*

Change, then, mourning into praise, *Alleluia!*
And, for dirges, anthems raise. *Alleluia!*
How our spirits soar and sing, *Alleluia!*
And our hearts leap with the spring. *Alleluia!*

From Samuel Longfellow, 1819-92

THE SEASONS: SPRING

264 Spring Buds of Hope

LUCERNA LAUDONIAE 7 7. 7 7. 7 7. David Evans, 1874-1948

From the Revised Church Hymnary, 1927, by permission of Oxford University Press

In moderate time

In the springtime of our year
Silver buds of hope appear.
Will they blossom? Will they grow?
We who plant the seed must know.
Will they blossom? Will they grow?
We who plant the seed must know.

Tender shoots thirst for the sun,
Surging with each day begun.
Banish darkness, hate and fear:
Golden fruit will soon appear.
Banish darkness, hate and fear:
Golden fruit will soon appear.

Welcome, children, welcome here,
Silver buds of our late year.
May our harvest still increase
Joys of fellowship and peace.
May our harvest still increase
Joys of fellowship and peace.

William Wolff
*Used by permission of Janet Wolff
and the Hodgin Press, Los Angeles*

THE SEASONS: SPRING

265   Life's Yearly Triumph

MORNING LIGHT   7 6. 7 6. D.   George James Webb, 1803-87

Come, sing with holy gladness,
   High Alleluias sing!
Lift up your hearts and voices
   With new-awakened spring.
The time of resurrection!
   Earth sings it all abroad,
And celebrates with gladness
   The joy of life restored.

Now let the heavens be joyful,
   The seas their bright waves swell;
The earth in new-born glory
   Life's yearly triumph tell.
Now let the seen and unseen
   In one glad anthem blend,
Let all our hearts be risen
   To life that has no end!

After John J. Daniell, 1819-98

THE SEASONS: SPRING

266 The Awakening Season

TEMPUS ADEST FLORIDUM 7 6. 7 6. D. Trochaic *Piae Cantiones*, 1582

Spring has now unwrapped the flowers,
  Day is fast reviving;
Life, in all her growing powers,
  Towards the light is striving:
Gone the iron touch of cold,
  Winter time and frost time;
Seedlings, working through the mould,
  Now make up for lost time.

Herb and plant that, winter long,
  Slumbered at their leisure,
Now bestirring, green and strong,
  Find in growth their pleasure:
All the world with beauty fills,
  Gold the green enhancing;
Flowers make glee among the hills —
  Set the meadows dancing.

Earth puts on her dress of glee;
  Flowers and grasses hide her;
We go forth in charity —
  Kindred all beside her;
For as we this glory see
  In the waking season,
Reason learns the heart's decree —
  Hearts are led by reason.

Piae Cantiones, 1582
from tr. Percy Dearmer, 1867-1936
By permission of Oxford University Press

THE SEASONS: SPRING

267 We Sing the Roses Waiting

EWING 7 6. 7 6. D.
Alexander Ewing, 1830-95

We sing of golden mornings,
 We sing of sparkling seas,
Of fenlands, valleys, mountains,
 And stately forest trees.
We sing of flashing sunshine
 And life-bestowing rain,
Of birds among the branches,
 And springtime come again.

We sing the heart courageous,
 The youthful, eager mind;
We sing of hopes undaunted,
 Of friendly ways and kind.
We sing the roses waiting
 Beneath the deep-piled snow;
We sing, when night is darkest,
 The day's returning glow.

from Ralph Waldo Emerson, 1803-82

THE SEASONS: SPRING

268 Moods of Summer

CALON LÂN   8 7. 8 7. D.   John Hughes (Glandŵr), 1872-1914

When the summer sun is shining
Over golden land and sea,
And the flowers in the hedgerow
Welcome butterfly and bee;
Then my open heart is glowing,
Full of warmth for everyone,
And I feel an inner beauty
Which reflects the summer sun.

THE SEASONS: SUMMER

When the light of summer sunshine
   Streams in through the open door,
Casting shadows of tree-branches,
   Living patterns on the floor;
Then my heart is full of gladness,
   And my soul is light and gay,
And my life is overflowing
   Like the happy summer day.

When the summer clouds of thunder
   Bring the long-awaited rain,
And the thirsty soil is moistened,
   And the grass is green again;
Then I long for summer sunshine,
   But I know that clouds and tears
Are a part of life's refreshment,
   Like the rainbow's hopes and fears.

When, beneath the trees of summer,
   Under leafy shade I lie,
Breathing in the scent of flowers,
   Sheltered from the sun-hot sky;
Then my heart is all contentment,
   And my soul is quiet and still,
Soothed by whispering, lazy breezes,
   Like the grasses on the hill.

In the cool of summer evening,
   When the dancing insects play,
And in garden, street and meadow
   Linger echoes of the day;
Then my heart is full of yearning,
   Hopes and memories flood the whole
Of my being, reaching inwards
   To the corners of my soul.

                              Sydney Henry Knight, 1923—
                                    Used by permission

                                 THE SEASONS: SUMMER

269 We Plough the Fields

WIR PFLÜGEN 7 6. 7 6. D. 6 6. 8 4. Johann Abraham Peter Schulz, 1747-1800

We plough the fields, and scatter
 The good seed on the land,
But it is fed and watered
 By God's almighty hand:
The snow is sent in winter,
 The warmth to swell the grain,
The breezes and the sunshine,
 And soft refreshing rain.
  All good gifts around us
   Are sent from heaven above;
  Then thank the Lord, O thank the Lord,
   For all his love.

THE SEASONS: HARVEST

God only is the maker
  Of all things near and far,
Who paints the wayside flower
  And lights the evening star;
The winds and waves are governed,
  And still the birds are fed;
Much more to us, earth's children,
  God gives our daily bread.
    All good gifts around us
      Are sent from heaven above;
    Then thank the Lord, O thank the Lord,
      For all his love.

We thank thee then, Creator,
  For all things bright and good,
The seed-time and the harvest,
  Our life, our health, our food.
Accept the gifts we offer
  For all thy love imparts,
And, what thou most desirest,
  Our humble, thankful hearts.
    All good gifts around us
      Are sent from heaven above;
    Then thank the Lord, O thank the Lord,
      For all his love.

                    Matthias Claudius, 1740-1815
              From tr. Jane Montgomery Campbell, 1817-78

THE SEASONS: HARVEST

270 Harvest Prayer

SHIPSTON 8 7. 8 7.

English Traditional Melody
Melody coll. Lucy Broadwood, 1858-1929
adpt. & arr. Ralph Vaughan Williams, 1872-1958
from the English Hymnal
by permission of the Oxford University Press

God, whose farm is all creation,
    Take the gratitude we give;
Take the finest of our harvest,
    Crops we grow that men may live.

Take our ploughing, seeding, reaping,
    Hopes and fears of sun and rain,
All our thinking, planning, waiting,
    Ripened in this fruit and grain.

All our labour, all our watching,
    All our calendar of care,
In these crops of your creation,
    Take, O God: they are our prayer.

John Arlott, 1914—
Used by permission

THE SEASONS: HARVEST

271 Give Thanks

STOWEY 11 11. 12 12. Anapaestic

English Traditional Melody
coll. Cecil James Sharp, 1859-1924
arr. & har. Ralph Vaughan Williams, 1872-1958
from Songs of Praise, by permission of Oxford University Press

Give thanks for the corn and the wheat that are reaped,
For labour well done and the barns that are heaped,
For the sun and the dew and the sweet honeycomb,
For the rose and the song and the harvest brought home.

Give thanks for the commerce and wealth of our land,
For cunning and strength of the hard-working hand,
For the beauty our artists and poets have wrought,
For the hope and affection our friendships have brought.

Give thanks for the homes that with kindness are blessed,
For seasons of plenty and well-deserved rest,
For our country extending from sea unto sea,
For the ways that have made it a land for the free.

Author Unknown

THE SEASONS: HARVEST

272 Harvest Home

ST. GEORGE, WINDSOR 7 7. 7 7. D. George Job Elvey, 1816-93

Come, ye thankful people, come,
Raise the song of harvest-home;
All is safely gathered in,
Ere the winter storms begin;
God, our maker, doth provide
For our wants to be supplied:
Come to God's own temple, come,
Raise the song of harvest-home!

All the world is God's own field,
Bearing fruit and richest yield;
Wheat and tares together sown,
Unto joy or sorrow grown:
First the blade, and then the ear,
Then the full corn shall appear;
God of harvest, grant that we
Wholesome grain, and pure may be.

From Henry Alford, 1810-71

THE SEASONS: HARVEST

273 Not By Bread Alone

GOTT WILL'S MACHEN   8 7. 8 7.   J. L. Steiner, 1688-1761

In the spring we ploughed our furrows,
  Planted well the fertile seeds;
Now we gather in at harvest
  Food to meet the body's needs.

Shining pebbles on the sea-shore,
  Sunsets in the western skies,
Autumn leaves and winter snowflakes
  Bring a harvest for the eyes.

Science widens our horizons
  Till we marvel at each find,
And the ripened fruits of knowledge
  Bring a harvest for the mind.

All the arts we strive to master
  With perfection as our goal,
And the times of prayer and worship
  Bring a harvest for the soul.

John Andrew Storey, 1935—
Used by permission

THE SEASONS: HARVEST

274   Seeds of Goodness

SHERINGHAM   8 7. 8 7.   Melody, John Andrew Storey, 1935—
har. David Dawson
Used by permission

        As we celebrate the harvest,
          Food provided for our need,
        See the natural law prevailing—
          Every fruit true to its seed.

        Does the pine grow from an acorn?
          Tulip bulb produce the rose?
        Does the farmer harvest barley
          From the rye seed which he sows?

        Can the selfish reap contentment?
          Or the self-indulgent, health?
        Can the indolent glean knowledge
          Or the idle gather wealth?

        As we sow, we reap the harvest,
          In our lives as in the field:
        Seeds of goodness freely scatter,
          From them reap a joyful yield.

                                        John Andrew Storey, 1935—
                                          Used by permission

THE SEASONS: HARVEST

275 Look at the Hillside

BUNESSAN 5 5. 5 4. D.

Old Gaelic Melody
arr. & har. Martin Fallas Shaw, 1875-1958

From Enlarged Songs of Praise, by permission of Oxford University Press

Look at the hillside,
Look at the mountain,
Look at the colours,
  Red, green and gold.
  Look at the maples,
  Look at the birches,
  Look at the oak trees,
Look and behold!

Think of the springtime,
Think of the summer,
Think of the winter,
  Soon to be here.
  But this is autumn,
  Glorious autumn,
  Beautiful autumn,
Best of the year.

Each tree is special,
Each leaf is lovely,
Each season needed,
  Each has a goal.
  So are you special,
  So are you lovely,
  So are you needed,
Part of the whole.

Marion Sheahan Whitcomb, 1924—
Used by permission

THE SEASONS: AUTUMN

276 Autumn Fields

LOWBURY 6 6. 6 6. D. Anapaestic

Melody, Sydney Henry Knight, 1923 —
arr. David Dawson
Used by permission

Unison. Plaintively.

In sweet fields of autumn
The gold grain is falling,
The white clouds drift lonely,
The wild swan is calling.
Alas for the daisies,
The tall fern and grasses,
When windsweep and rainfall
Fill lowland and passes.

The snows of December
Shall fill windy hollow,
The bleak rain trails after,
And March wind shall follow.
The deer through the valleys
Leave print of their going,
And diamonds of sleet mark
The ridges of snowing.

The stillness of death shall
Stoop over the water,
The plover sweep low where
The pale streamlets falter;
But deep in the earth clod
The black seed is living,
When spring sounds her bugles
For rousing and giving.

Elizabeth Madison

THE SEASONS: AUTUMN

By permission of the Hodgin Press, Los Angeles

277 Autumn Ways

CONSOLATION C.M.

From *Repository of Sacred Music, Part II*, 1813
of John Wyeth, 1770-1858
har. Henry Leland Clarke, 1907—
By permission of the Beacon Press, Boston, Mass.

I walk the unfrequented road
  With open eye and ear;
I watch afield the farmer load
  The bounty of the year.

I gather where I did not sow,
  And bind the mystic sheaf,
The amber air, the river's flow,
  The rustle of the leaf.

A beauty springtime never knew
  Haunts all the quiet ways,
And sweeter shines the landscape through
  Its veil of autumn haze.

I face the hills, the streams, the wood,
  And feel with all akin;
My heart expands: their fortitude
  And peace and joy flow in.

Frederick Lucian Hosmer, 1840-1929

THE SEASONS: AUTUMN

278 Midwinter

NOS GALAN 8 9. 8 9. D.

Welsh Traditional

Deck the halls with boughs of holly,
  Fa la la la la, La la la la,
'Tis the season to be jolly,
  Fa la la la la, La la la la,
Don we now our gay apparel,
  Fa la la, Fa la la, La la la,
Troll the ancient Yuletide carol;
  Fa la la la la, La la la la.

See the blazing yule before us,
  Fa la la la la, La la la la,
Strike the harp and join the chorus,
  Fa la la la la, La la la la,
Follow me in merry measure,
  Fa la la, Fa la la, La la la,
While I tell of Yuletide treasure,
  Fa la la la la, La la la la.

Fast away the old year passes,
  Fa la la la la, La la la la,
Hail the new, ye lads and lasses,
  Fa la la la la, La la la la,
Sing we joyous, all together,
  Fa la la, Fa la la, La la la,
Heedless of the wind and weather,
  Fa la la la la, La la la la.

Welsh Traditional

THE SEASONS: MIDWINTER

Morning and Evening

279 Chinese Morning Hymn

LE P'ING 5 5. 5 5. D.

Melody Hu Te-Ai, b.circa 1900
har. David Dawson

Golden breaks the dawn;
Comes the eastern sun
Over lake and lawn—
Set his course to run.
Birds above us fly,
Flowers bloom below,
Through the earth and sky
God's great mercies flow.

As the spinning globe
Rolls away the night,
Nature wears her robe
Spun of morning light.
Dawn break in me too,
As in skies above;
Teach me to be true,
Fill my heart with love.

First Verse from the Chinese of T.C.Chao, b.1888
tr. Frank W. Price and Daniel Niles.
second verse John Andrew Storey, 1935—

MORNING

280 Morning Has Broken

BUNESSAN 5 5. 5 4. D.
Old Gaelic Melody
arr. & har. Martin Fallas Shaw, 1875-1958
From Enlarged Songs of Praise, by permission of Oxford University Press

> Morning has broken
> Like the first morning,
> Blackbird has spoken
> Like the first bird.
> > Praise for the singing!
> > Praise for the morning!
> > Praise for them, springing
> > Fresh from the Word!

Sweet the rain's new fall
Sunlit from heaven,
Like the first dewfall
  On the first grass.
    Praise for the sweetness
    Of the wet garden,
    Sprung in completeness
Where his feet pass.

Mine is the sunlight!
Mine is the morning
Born of the one light
  Eden saw play!
    Praise with elation,
    Praise every morning,
    God's re-creation
Of the new day!

Eleanor Farjeon, 1881-1965
From The Children's Bells, published by Oxford University Press
by permission of David Higham Associates, Ltd.

MORNING

THORNBURY 7 6. 7 6. D.   Basil Harwood, 1859-1949
Used by permission of the Exors. of the late Dr. Basil Harwood

MORNING

281 Darkness Put to Flight

The morning hangs a signal
   Upon the mountain crest,
While all the sleeping valleys
   In silent darkness rest.
From peak to peak it flashes,
   It laughs along the sky,
Till glory of the sunlight
   On all the land doth lie.

Above the generations
   The lonely prophets rise,
While truth flings dawn and day-star
   Within their glowing eyes;
And other eyes, beholding,
   Are kindled from that light,
And dawn becomes the morning,
   The darkness put to flight.

The soul hath lifted moments,
   Above the drift of days,
With life's great meaning breaking
   In sunrise on our ways.
Behold the radiant token
   Of faith above all fear;
Night shall be lost in splendour
   And morning shall appear!

                William Channing Gannett, 1840-1923

MORNING

282 Sunrise is Born

WATCHMAN (DAWN)   6 4. 6 4. 6 6. 6 4.   Thomas Herbert Ingham, 1878-1948

From Enlarged Songs of Praise, by permission of Oxford University Press

High o'er the lonely hills
  Black turns to grey,
Birdsong the valley fills,
  Mists fold away;
Grey wakes to green again,
Beauty is seen again —
Gold and serene again
  Dawneth the day.

So, o'er the hills of life,
  Stormy, forlorn,
Out of the cloud and strife
  Sunrise is born;
Swift grows the light for us;
Ended is night for us;
Soundless and bright for us
  Breaketh God's morn.

Hear we no beat of drums,
  Fanfare nor cry,
When Christ the herald comes
  Quietly nigh;
Splendour he makes on earth;
Colour awakes on earth;
Suddenly breaks on earth
  Light from the sky.

Bid then farewell to sleep:
  Rise up and run!
What though the hill be steep?
  Strength's in the sun.
Now shall you find at last
Night's left behind at last,
For humankind at last
  Day has begun!

Jan Struther (Mrs. Joyce Anstruther Placzek), 1901-53
From Enlarged Songs of Praise
by permission of Oxford University Press

MORNING

283 Awake, my Soul

MORNING HYMN L.M. François Hippolyte Barthélemon, 1741-1808

Awake, my soul, and with the sun
Thy daily stage of duty run:
Shake off dull sloth, and joyful rise
To pay thy morning sacrifice.

My vows, O God, I now renew:
Scatter my sins as morning dew;
Guard my first springs of thought and will,
And with thyself my spirit fill.

Direct, control, suggest this day
All I design, or do, or say,
That all my powers, with all their might,
In thy sole glory may unite.

Praise God, from whom all blessings flow;
Praise God, all creatures here below;
Praise God, ye heavenly hosts above;
Praise God, my soul, for all this love!

From Thomas Ken, 1637-1711

284 Goodnight Hymn

DIX 7 7. 7 7. 7 7.

Abridged from a Chorale
by Conrad Kocher, 1786-1872

To you each, my friends, tonight
I give thanks for company;
We have shared the inner light:
May that light go forth with thee.
May we give each other power—
Live with courage every hour.

As we face the coming week,
With its worries and its strife,
Strength and wisdom let us seek
In this hour's remembered life.
May we give each other power—
Live with courage every hour.

In our homes and in the street,
In a world with sadness rife,
May we show to all we meet
Glory that we find in life.
May we give each other power—
Live with courage every hour.

To you each, my friends, tonight
I give thanks for company;
We have shared the inner light:
May that light go forth with thee.
May we give each other power—
Live with courage every hour.

Peter Galbraith
Used by permission

EVENING

285 All Praise to Thee this Night

TALLIS' CANON   L.M.   Thomas Tallis, c.1505-85

All praise to thee, my God, this night,
For all the blessings of the light;
Keep me, O keep me, King of kings,
Beneath thine own almighty wings.

When in the night I sleepless lie,
My soul with heavenly thoughts supply;
Let no ill dreams disturb my rest,
No powers of darkness me molest.

Teach me to live, that I may dread
The grave as little as my bed;
That with the world, myself, and thee,
I, ere I sleep, at peace may be.

O may my soul on thee repose,
And may sweet sleep mine eyelids close,
Sleep that shall me more vigorous make
To serve my God when I awake.

From Thomas Ken, 1637-1711

EVENING

ABBOT'S LEIGH 87.87.D.   Cyril Vincent Taylor, 1907—
From the BBC Hymnbook, by permission of Oxford University Press

EVENING

286   Vesper Hymn

Now on land and sea descending,
   Brings the night its peace profound;
Let our vesper-hymn be blending
   With the holy calm around.
Soon as dies the sunset glory,
   Stars of heaven shine out above,
Telling still the ancient story—
   Their Creator's changeless love.

Now our wants and burdens leaving
   To that care, which cares for all,
Cease we fearing, cease we grieving,
   At God's touch our burdens fall.
As the darkness deepens o'er us,
   Lo! eternal stars arise;
Hope and faith and love rise glorious
   Shining in the spirit's skies.

                                From Samuel Longfellow, 1819-92

287 The Day Thou Gavest

ST. CLEMENT 9 8. 9 8. Clement Cotterill Scholefield, 1839-1904

The day thou gavest, Lord, is ended,
　The darkness falls at thy behest;
To thee our morning hymns ascended,
　Thy praise shall sanctify our rest.

We thank thee that thy church unsleeping,
　While earth rolls onward into light,
Through all the world her watch is keeping,
　And rests not now by day or night.

EVENING

As o'er each continent and island
    The dawn leads on another day,
The voice of prayer is never silent,
    Nor dies the strain of praise away.

The sun, that bids us rest, is waking
    Our kindred 'neath the western sky,
And hour by hour fresh lips are making
    Thy wondrous doings heard on high.

So be it, Lord; thy throne shall never,
    Like earth's proud empires, pass away;
Thy kingdom stands and grows for ever,
    Till all thy creatures own thy sway.

                          From John Ellerton, 1826-93

EVENING

288 Guard us Night and Day

AR HYD Y NOS   8 4. 8 4. 8 8 8. 4.   Welsh Traditional Melody

        God that madest earth and heaven,
           Darkness and light;
        Who the day for toil hast given,
           For rest the night;
        May thine angel-guard defend us,
        Slumber sweet thy mercy send us,
        Holy dreams and hopes attend us
           This livelong night.

When we in the morn awaken,   Guard us waking, guard us sleeping,
   Guide us thy way;   And, when we die,
Keep our love and truth unshaken   May we in thy mighty keeping
   In work and play;   All peaceful lie;
In our daily task be near us,   Thou wilt not in death forsake us,
In temptation keep and hear us,   But to fuller life wilt wake us,
And with holy counsel cheer us   And to nobler service take us
   The livelong day.   With thee on high.

                                            Reginald Heber, 1783-1826, and others

EVENING

Seasons
of Human Life

TURN AROUND   P.M.   Malvina Reynolds and Alan Greene

SEASONS OF HUMAN LIFE

Turn Around

Where are you going, my little one, little one,
Where are you going, my baby, my own?
Turn around and you're two,
Turn around and you're four,
Turn around and you're a young girl
Going out of my door.
Turn around, turn around,
Turn around and you're a young girl
Going out of my door.

Where are you going, my little one, little one,
Dirndls and petticoats, where have you gone?
Turn around and you're tiny,
Turn around and you're grown,
Turn around and you're a young wife
With babes of your own.
Turn around, turn around,
Turn around and you're a young wife
With babes of your own.

Malvina Reynolds, Harry Belafonte and Alan Greene
Copyright (c) 1958; Renewed 1986 Alan Greene Songs (ASCAP) and Clara Music Publishing Corp. (ASCAP), Julie Music Corp, Shari Music Publishing Corp. Worldwide rights for Alan Greene Songs administered by Cherry Lane Music Publishing Company Inc, USA. Worldwide rights for Clara Music Publishing Corp. administered by Next Decade Entertainment, Inc. International copyright secured. All rights reserved. (60%) Emi Songs Ltd, London, WC2H 0QY. Reproduced by permission of International Music Publications Ltd. All rights reserved.

SEASONS OF HUMAN LIFE

SARIE MARAIS   C.M.D.   Traditional South African

Steady Rhythm

SEASONS OF HUMAN LIFE

Unfolding Life

When I was a child I spoke as a child,
   I sang my childlike themes;
I understood as children do
   And dreamed my children's dreams.
But when in all good time I grew
   And called myself mature,
I put away my childish ways,
   For they could not endure.

As life unfolds from stage to stage,
   I play in many roles.
The object is to find myself
   Amid these tight controls.
O, have you ever been a son,
   A parent, daughter, wife?
O, have you ever wondered when
   You might live your own life?

I'll try to make some time each day
   For liberating me.
I'll build a bridge or write a song,
   And that will set me free.
For when I've made some goal my own,
   I'll take the rest in stride,
Adjusting and adapting to
   The changes that abide.

Marion Sheahan Whitcomb, 1924—
Used by permission

291 Early in Life's Morning

RUTH   6 5. 6 5. D.   Samuel Smith, 1821-1917

Early in life's morning,
Lord, we come to thee:
Raise our song of gladness,
Lowly bend the knee;
While the dew still sparkles
In the woodland ways,
While the freshness lingers,
Hear our hymn of praise.

For the spring we thank thee,
For the flowers that bloom;
For the new life rising
From dark winter's tomb;
Birds are singing round us;
We would also praise,
Hearts and voices blending
In the song we raise.

Early in life's morning
May we hear thy call;
While the brightness lingers,
Ere the shadows fall;
May we yield thee gladly
All our future days,
So shall our whole lifetime
Be a song of praise.

SEASONS OF HUMAN LIFE   Helen Summers, b.1857

292 Undying Echoes

ROCKINGHAM L.M. Adpt. Edward Miller, 1731-1807

The lives which touch our own each day
Are influenced unconsciously
By views we hold, the things we say,
Our simple acts of charity.

On earth we still receive the light
Of stars burnt out in aeons past,
The lives of those who served the right
Shine with a lustre that will last.

This life of ours can never end,
Its influence still perseveres;
For by our deeds we ever send
Undying echoes down the years.

John Andrew Storey, 1935—
Used by permission

SEASONS OF HUMAN LIFE

293 Here and Now

MENDIP C.M. — English Traditional Melody

No longer forward nor behind
  I look in hope or fear;
But, grateful, take the good I find,
  The best of now and here.

I break my pilgrim staff, I lay
  Aside the toiling oar;
The angel sought so far away
  I welcome at my door.

For all the jarring notes of life
  Seem blending in a psalm,
And all the angles of its strife
  Slow rounding into calm.

And so the shadows fall apart,
  And so the west winds play;
And all the windows of my heart
  I open to the day.

John Greenleaf Whittier, 1807-92

SEASONS OF HUMAN LIFE

294 No More Alone

MARTYRDOM C.M.

Hugh Wilson, 1766-1824
arr. Robert Archibald Smith, 1780-1829

When lonely shadows steal the light,
   Like summer swallows flown,
And in the silence of the night
   I know that I'm alone....

When life has claimed my family,
   And all the friends I've known
Are but repeated memory,
   And I am left alone....

When silent rooms, each empty hour,
   Would turn my lips to stone,
How can I feel in me the power
   To face life all alone?

Yet other humans ache apart
   For human touch or tone:
United here in voice and heart,
   Need any feel alone?

Our church shall be a family
   When all in love have grown
To be companions neighbourly
   Each day to those alone.

God plants in each an inner need
   Compassion to enthrone:
We make of God a friend indeed,
   When we befriend the lone.

Sydney Henry Knight, 1923—
Used by permission

SEASONS OF HUMAN LIFE

295 Transcience

O PERFECT LOVE 11 10. 11 10.

Joseph Barnby, 1838-96

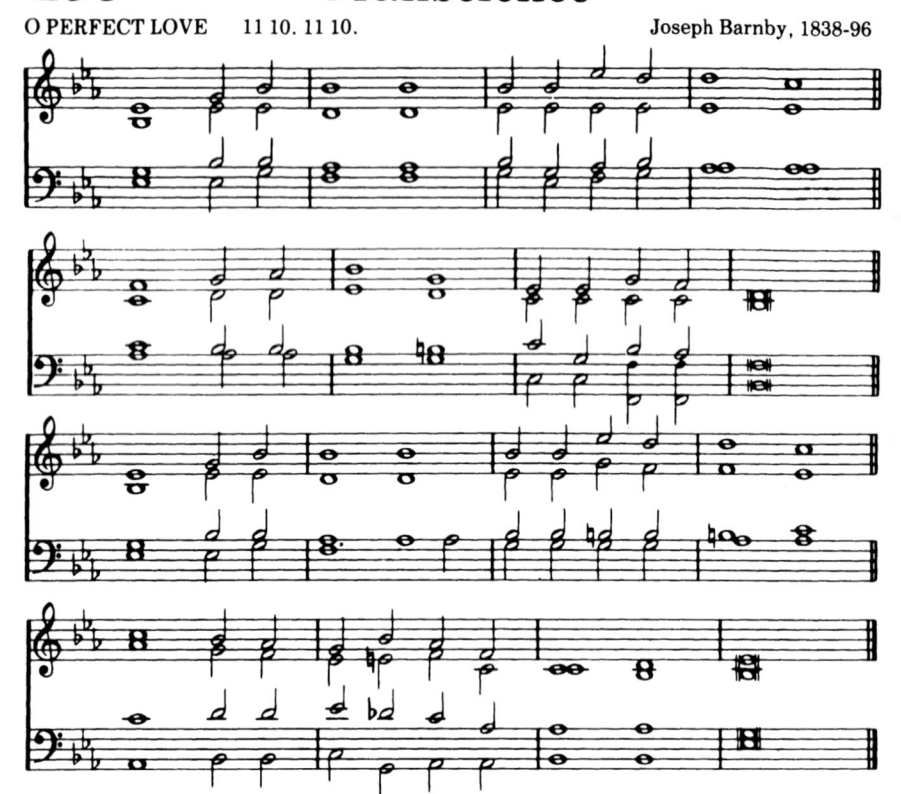

Nay, do not grieve, though life be full of sadness,
  Dawn will not veil her splendour for your grief,
Nor spring deny their bright, appointed beauty
  To lotus blossom and ashoka leaf.

Nay, do not pine, though life be dark with trouble,
  Time will not pause or tarry on its way;
Today, that seems so long, so strange, so bitter,
  Will soon be some forgotten yesterday.

Nay, do not weep; new hopes, new dreams, new faces,
  Joy yet unspent of all the unborn years,
Will prove your heart a traitor to its sorrow,
  And make your eyes unfaithful to their tears.

from Sarojini Naidu, 1879-1949
from *The Bird of Time*
By permission of William Heinemann, Ltd.

SEASONS OF HUMAN LIFE

Heroes

Fair is their fame who stand in earth's high places,
   Rulers of armies, strong to break and bind.
Fairer the light which shines from comrade faces,
   Those we have loved, and lost, and kept in mind.

These be our heroes, hearts unnamed in story,
   Foot-firm that stood, and swerved not from the right;
Though in the world's eyes they attained no glory,
   Girt to their goal they gained the wished-for height.

They are the race—they are the race immortal,
   Whose beams make broad the common light of day.
Though time may dim, though death hath barred their portal,
   These we salute, which nameless passed away.

Laurence Housman, 1865-1959
From *The Collected Poems of Laurence Housman*
*by permission of the Executors of the Laurence Housman Estate
and Jonathan Cape, Ltd.*

SURREY 88.88.88.   Henry Carey, 1692?-1743

SEASONS OF HUMAN LIFE

297 Facing Death

The wise one should, with spirit calm,
Reflect that death can bring no harm:
For there may be, as poets tell,
A place where after death we dwell,
And there in glory meet at last
The noble heroes of the past.

And if I wholly cease to be
When death at last shall come to me,
Then I for one will count it gain
To be beyond the reach of pain:
For nothing then can cause me fright
If death be but a single night.

The wise and good should never dread
Whichever fate awaits the dead:
To live again, or rest in sleep,
Gives no one any cause to weep:
So may one tread with footsteps brave
The path that leads one to the grave.

Socrates, before 469-399 B.C.
Recast by John Andrew Storey, 1935—
Used by permission

298 Living and Dying

CORINTH (TANTUM ERGO) 8 7. 8 7. D.

Melody from *Antiphons* (1792)
of Samuel Webbe, 1740-1816

Sing of living, sing of dying,
   Let them both be joined in one,
Parts of an eternal process
   Like the ever-circling sun.
From the freshness of each infant
   Giving hope in what is new,
To the wisdom of the aged
   Deepened by a longer view.

Open to a deeper loving,
   Open to the gift of care,
Searching for a higher justice,
   Helping others in despair.
Through the tender bonds of living
   In a more inclusive way
We are opened more to suffering
   From the losses of each day.

When a special life has ended,
   If our lives were interlaced,
We are carried into darkness
   By that presence unreplaced.
Standing at the edge of meaning
   Struggling to be free from pain,
Wondering if our hearts will ever
   Dare to fill with love again.

Even when our grief o'erwhelms us
   And our aching hearts seem lost,
Life is dancing all around us,
   Even while it counts the cost.
Slowly in our inner darkness,
   Love may light the saddened will,
Giving us a way to see that
   Life has meaning for us still.

Thomas Jarl Mikelson, 1936—
Used by permission

SEASONS OF HUMAN LIFE

299 Now I Recall my Childhood

LIMPSFIELD   10 10. 10 10.

Andrew Freeman

Now I recall my childhood when the sun
Burst to my bedside with the day's surprise:
Faith in the marvellous bloomed anew each dawn,
Flowers bursting fresh within my heart each day.

Looking upon the world with simple joy,
On insects, birds, and beasts, and common weeds,
The grass and clouds had fullest wealth of awe;
My mother's voice gave meaning to the stars.

Now when I turn to think of coming death,
I find life's song in star-songs of the night,
In rise of curtains and new morning light,
In life re-born in fresh surprise of love.

Recast from Rabindranath Tagore, 1861-1941
From The Collected Poems and Plays of Rabindranath Tagore

Used by permission of Macmillan,
London and Basingstoke

SEASONS OF HUMAN LIFE

FRESHWATER   P.M.   Charles Hubert Hastings Parry, 1848-1918

SEASONS OF HUMAN LIFE

300 Crossing the Bar

Sunset and evening star,
   And one clear call for me!
And may there be no moaning of the bar,
   When I put out to sea;
But such a tide as moving seems asleep,
   Too full for sound and foam,
When that which drew from out the boundless deep
   Turns again home.

Twilight and evening bell,
   And after that the dark!
And may there be no sadness of farewell,
   When I embark;
For though from out our bourne of time and place
   The flood may bear me far,
I hope to see my Pilot face to face
   When I have crost the bar.

Alfred Tennyson, 1809-92

301 Abide With Me

EVENTIDE 10 10. 10 10. William Henry Monk, 1823-89

Abide with me! fast falls the eventide;
The darkness deepens; Lord, with me abide:
When other helpers fail and comforts flee,
Help of the helpless, O abide with me!

Swift to its close ebbs out life's little day;
Earth's joys grow dim, its glories pass away;
Change and decay in all around I see;
O thou who changest not, abide with me!

I need thy presence every passing hour:
What but thy grace can foil the tempter's power?
Who like thyself my guide and stay can be?
Through cloud and sunshine, O abide with me!

I fear no foe, with thee at hand to bless;
Ills have no weight, and tears no bitterness.
Where is death's sting? where, grave, thy victory?
I triumph still, if thou abide with me.

Come then in light before my closing eyes;
Shine through the gloom, and point me to the skies.
Heaven's morning breaks, and earth's vain shadows flee:
In life, in death, O Lord, abide with me!

Henry Francis Lyte, 1793-1847

SEASONS OF HUMAN LIFE

Close of Worship

ST. MATTHEW   C.M.D.   Probably by William Croft, 1678-1727

CLOSE OF WORSHIP

302   As Each Day Ends

As each day ends, may I have lived
  That I may truly say:
I did no harm to humankind,
  From truth I did not stray;
I did no wrong with knowing mind,
  From evil I did keep;
I turned no hungry soul away,
  I caused no one to weep.

Ancient Egyptian, c.4500 B.C.
from The Book of the Dead.
Version by John Andrew Storey, 1935—
Used by permission

303   Through all the Coming Week

Not on this day, O God, alone
  Would we thy presence seek,
But fain its hallowing power would own
  Through all the coming week.
If calm and bright its moments prove,
  Untouched by pain or woe,
May they reflect a thankful love
  To thee, from whom they flow.

Or should they bring us griefs severe,
  Still may we lean on thee,
And, though our eyes let fall the tear,
  At peace our spirits be.
In every scene, or dark, or bright,
  Thy favour may we seek;
And O, do thou direct us right
  Through all the coming week!

William Gaskell, 1805-84

CLOSE OF WORSHIP

ELLERS   10 10. 10 10.   Edward John Hopkins, 1818-1901

CLOSE OF WORSHIP

304   Our Parting Hymn of Praise

Now, once again, to thy dear name we raise
With one accord our parting hymn of praise;
We stand to bless thee ere our worship cease,
Then, lowly kneeling, wait thy word of peace.

Grant us thy peace upon our homeward way;
With thee began, with thee shall end the day:
Guard thou the lips from sin, the hearts from shame,
That in this house have called upon thy name.

Grant us thy peace throughout the coming night,
Turn thou for us its darkness into light:
From harm and danger keep thy people free,
For dark and light are both alike to thee.

Grant us thy peace throughout our earthly life,
Our balm in sorrow, and our stay in strife;
Then, when thy voice shall bid our conflict cease,
Call us, O God, to thine eternal peace.

From John Ellerton, 1826-93

305   Go With Us, God

Now as we part and go our several ways,
Touch every lip, may every voice be praise:
Go with us hence, O God; we only ask
That thou be sharer in our daily task.

From William Vaughan Jenkins, 1868-1920

306   Lord, as We Part

Lord, as we part and take our homeward way,
May faith sustain and guide us, we would pray;
That, in our hearts, a greater love shall be
A bond of fellowship and joy in thee.

Herbert Pickles, 1903—
Used by permission

CLOSE OF WORSHIP

GOD BE IN MY HEAD Irregular Henry Walford Davies, 1869-1941
By permission of Oxford University Press

God be in my head: and in my un-der-stand-ing;
God be in mine eyes; and in my look-ing; God be in my mouth: and in my speak-ing; God be in my heart: and in my think-ing; God be at mine end, and at my de-part-ing.

CLOSE OF WORSHIP

307 God Be in My Head

God be in my head,
    And in my understanding;
God be in mine eyes,
    And in my looking;
God be in my mouth,
    And in my speaking;
God be in my heart,
    And in my thinking;
God be at mine end,
    And at my departing.

Book of Hours, 1514

CLOSE OF WORSHIP

Closing Verses

OLD HUNDREDTH   L.M.   Louis Bourgeois, c.1523-1600

308

Let people living in all lands
Declare that fear and war are done,
Joined by the labours of their hands,
In love and understanding, one.

*Kenneth L. Patton, 1911—
Used by permission*

309

Lift up your voices, rise and sing!
Let every faltering heart take wing!
Let freedom come, in word and deed
To meet the human spirit's need.

*Walter Royal Jones, Jr., 1920—
Used by permission*

CLOSE OF WORSHIP

Closing Verses

WINCHESTER NEW L.M. from *Musikalisches Handbuch*, Hamburg, 1690

310

From all that dwell below the skies
Let faith and hope with love arise,
Let beauty, truth and good be sung
Through every land, by every tongue.

Adapted from Isaac Watts, 1674-1748

311

With joy we claim the growing light,
Advancing thought, and widening view,
The larger freedom, clearer sight,
Which from the old unfold the new.

With wider view, comes loftier goal;
With fuller light, more good to see;
With freedom, truer self-control;
With knowledge, deeper reverence be.

from Samuel Longfellow, 1819-92

312

O never harm the dreaming world,
The world of green, the world of leaves,
But let its million palms unfold
The adoration of the trees.

Kathleen Raine, 1908—
From 'Vegetation' in Collected Poems.
Used by permission of
George Allen & Unwin [Publishers] Ltd.

CLOSE OF WORSHIP

Closing Verses

TALLIS' CANON   L.M.   Thomas Tallis, 1505-85

313   Praise God, the love we all may share:
Praise God, the beauty everywhere:
Praise God, the hope of good to be:
Praise God, the truth that makes us free.

Charles H. Lyttle, 1884-1980
By permission of Bradford Lyttle

314   Let peace encircle all the world,
Let all on earth join hand in hand,
A living bond of fellowship,
A voice of love in every land.

Author unknown

315   Rejoice in love we know and share,
In law and beauty everywhere;
Rejoice in truth that makes us free,
And in the good that yet shall be.

Charles H. Lyttle, 1884-1980
By permission of Bradford Lyttle

CLOSE OF WORSHIP

316 Closing Verses

PEN-LAN 7 6. 7 6. D.

David Jenkins, 1848-1915

O star of truth, down shining
  Through clouds of doubt and fear,
I ask but 'neath thy guidance
  My pathway may appear:
However long the journey,
  However hard it be,
Though I be lone and weary,
  Lead on, I'll follow thee.

Minot Judson Savage, 1841-1918

CLOSE OF WORSHIP

317 Shalom Havayreem

SHALOM HAVAYREEM   P.M.
Accompanied, unison
Traditional Jewish

Shalom havayreem, shalom havayreem,
Shalom, shalom;
Shalom havayreem, shalom havayreem,
Shalom, shalom.

Glad tidings we bring of peace on earth,
Goodwill to all;
Of peace on earth, of peace on earth,
Goodwill to all.

Shalom havayreem, shalom havayreem,
Shalom, shalom;
Shalom havayreem, shalom havayreem,
Shalom, shalom.

Traditional Jewish

Unaccompanied, four-part round

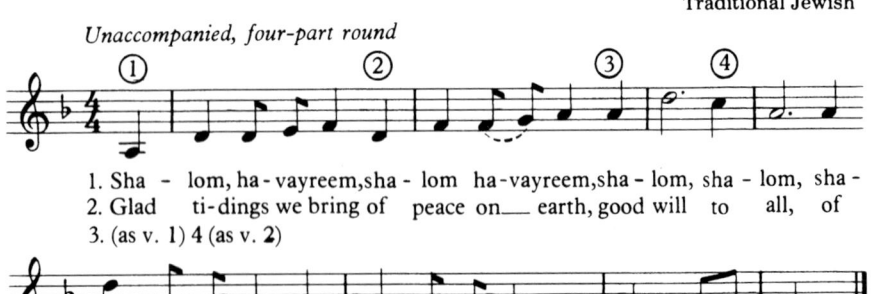

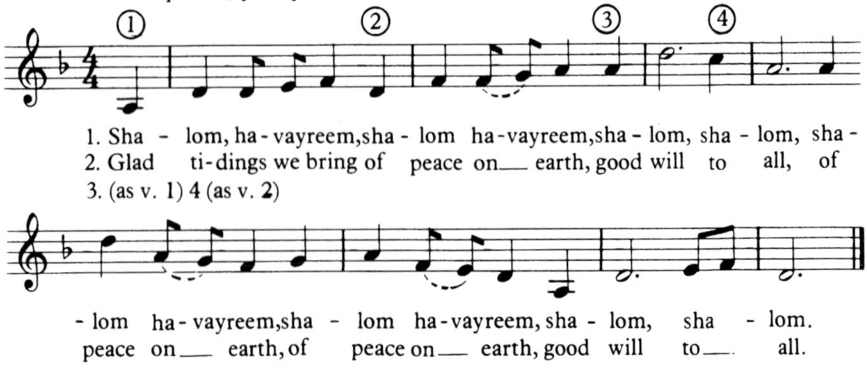

1. Shalom, ha-vayreem, shalom ha-vayreem, shalom, shalom, shalom ha-vayreem, shalom ha-vayreem, shalom, shalom.
2. Glad tidings we bring of peace on earth, good will to all, of peace on earth, of peace on earth, good will to all.
3. (as v. 1)
4. (as v. 2)

CLOSE OF WORSHIP